War and Society
in Medieval and Early Modern Britain

War and Society
in Medieval and Early Modern Britain

edited by Diana Dunn

LIVERPOOL UNIVERSITY PRESS

First published 2000 by
Liverpool University Press
4 Cambridge Street
Liverpool
L69 7ZU

Copyright © Liverpool University Press 2000

British Library Cataloguing-in-Publication Data
A British Library CIP record is available

ISBN 0 85323 875 8 *hardback*
    0 85323 885 5 *paperback*

Typeset by Northern Phototypesetting Co. Ltd, Bolton, UK
Printed and bound in the European Union by Bell & Bain Ltd, Glasgow

Contents

vi   **Contents**

Illustrations

Cover Illustration:
An army on the move, from *The Three Kings' Sons*, an English Romance, *c*.1480 (British Library, Harley MS 326, f. 90, reproduced by permission of the British Library). The editor acknowledges with gratitude the help of Pamela Porter of the Department of Manuscripts, British Library, in the selection of the cover illustration.

Contributors

Christopher Allmand is Emeritus Professor of Medieval History, University of Liverpool.

Matthew Bennett is a Senior Lecturer at the Royal Military Academy Sandhurst.

Hugh Collins is an independent scholar.

Paul Dalton is Reader in History, Liverpool Hope University College.

Diana Dunn is Senior Lecturer in History, Chester College of Higher Education.

Peter Gaunt is Reader in History, Chester College of Higher Education.

Philip Morgan is Senior Lecturer in History, University of Keele.

Mark Stoyle is Lecturer in History, University of Southampton.

Graeme White is Head of History, Chester College of Higher Education.

Abbreviations

BIHR	*Bulletin of the Institute of Historical Research*
BL	British Library, London
CCR	*Calendar of Close Rolls*
CPR	*Calendar of Patent Rolls*
DNB	*Dictionary of National Biography*, eds L. Stephens and S. Lee, 22 vols (1908–9)
EHR	*English Historical Review*
Gesta Stephani	*Gesta Stephani*, edited and translated by K.R. Potter, with a new Introduction by R.H.C. Davis (Oxford, 1976)
PRO	Public Record Office, London
TRHS	*Transactions of the Royal Historical Society*
VCH	*Victoria County History*

Unless otherwise stated, the place of publication is London.

Introduction

Diana Dunn

The nine papers in this volume were delivered at a colloquium held at Chester College in April 1999, in association with the University of Liverpool.[1] The aim of the colloquium was to draw together historians working within the broad area of the impact of war on government and society in the medieval and the early modern periods. This coincides with the research interests of a number of members of the history department at Chester College who contribute to the teaching of a recently established MA course in Military Studies. It was decided to focus on three English civil wars: the civil war of King Stephen's reign, the Wars of the Roses, and the civil war of the seventeenth century, setting them into the wider context of political, military and social developments. Each of these civil wars has a broader geographical dimension which requires the historian to consider the relationship between England and her neighbours, whether close like Wales and Scotland or overseas, especially France. Civil war in England cannot be studied in isolation from events in Europe, and characteristics of civil war must be studied alongside developments in European warfare.

That the study of military history is as popular today as it has ever been is borne out by the proliferation of publications addressing not only the subject of war itself but the economic, social and political consequences of war throughout history.[2] These papers are mainly concerned with the general theme of the interaction of war and society rather than details of individual campaigns and battles. Nevertheless all the papers inform us about the nature of war and the way it was conducted in the medieval and early modern periods, as well as the way it is recorded and interpreted by contemporaries and later commentators. These issues are central to Christopher Allmand's paper 'The Reporting of War in the Middle Ages' and Philip Morgan's paper

'The Naming of Battlefields in the Middle Ages'. Taken together the papers invite us to consider whether the civil wars of the twelfth, fifteenth and seventeenth centuries have characteristics in common and whether such characteristics are shared with other conflicts of the period, such as the border wars against the Scots and the Welsh or the Hundred Years War.

It has been stated recently that medieval commanders sought to avoid battle whenever possible, seeking instead to wear down their opponents by waging wars of devastation.[3] 'Battle was a last resort, to be avoided unless victory seemed assured, in the knowledge that chance would always be a factor in what Orderic Vitalis called "the uncertain verdict of battle"'.[4] In his paper, Philip Morgan notes the routine absence of battle names in medieval contemporary narrative accounts and the use by historians of a range of labels such as 'skirmish' or 'preliminary engagement' to describe a variety of violent conflicts not accorded the status of battles. The evolution of the nomenclature and landscape of battlefields is complex and intriguing, involving the desire or need to control the memory of the event. But sometimes even the precise site of a battle is uncertain, the most obvious example being that of Bosworth Field, its exact location still generating fierce debate. However, battles could be decisive and might be sought to bring a particular phase of a conflict to a conclusion, or to confirm the military reputation of a particular commander or ruler.

Jim Bradbury has noted the close, almost inseparable, relationship between sieges and battles in Norman warfare.[5] Whereas the number of battles in the civil war of Stephen's reign was limited, sieges were common, the aim being to establish and maintain control over territory by the capture of key fortresses.[6] Sieges could be protracted affairs and might involve considerable suffering for both besieged and besiegers as well as high financial costs. Within the first few pages of the *Gesta Stephani*, one of the key sources for Stephen's reign, we find a graphic description of the country in a state of civil war, a theme re-emphasised at the end of the work when the author reflects on the waste caused by the conflict. He especially deprecates attacks on churches and religious houses and reminds his readers that such acts will be punished by God, as demonstrated by the fate of the earl of Gloucester and his supporters, who savagely plundered Wilton nunnery in 1143.[7] The response of the Church to war in Stephen's reign is the subject of Paul Dalton's wide-ranging paper. He discusses the numerous ways in which the Church responded to war, especially its role in mediation and peace-making, and the significance of religious houses as safe havens and refuges from war.

Graeme White's paper 'Earls and Earldoms during King Stephen's Reign' examines in detail the reasons for the creation of new earldoms by both Stephen and his rival, the Empress Matilda. He questions the assumption made by some historians that they were the result of a deliberate policy of decentralising government. White argues for a more 'ad hoc' attitude to the creation of earldoms by Stephen whose motives changed in response to his particular military and administrative needs in time of civil war. There was considerable variation in the powers devolved by the king to his earls in their shires, but once civil war had begun, there was greater emphasis on ensuring that they were sufficiently powerful in their localities to maintain control and resist attack. After 1141 the role of the earls in the localities diminished as both Stephen and Matilda sought to administer the shires without them. This policy was continued by Henry II, who tried to ensure that sheriffs and other local officials answered not to the earls as intermediaries but directly to him.

Border warfare against the Welsh for much of the medieval period and against the Scots, intermittently until the end of the sixteenth century, had its particular characteristics – raids and the burning of estates and property as well as attacks on individuals. It is sometimes described as guerilla warfare, 'unsophisticated' and 'lacking formal action between rival armies'. Clearly its impact upon the local economy and society could be devastating.[8] Christopher Allmand compares this kind of warfare with the chevauchées or swift raids of the English into parts of French territory during the Hundred Years War. The aim was not to capture land or castles but rather to ravage the countryside and instill fear into the enemy population, thereby undermining the authority of the French king.[9] This method of warfare inevitably involved the whole of French society, including civilians. French chroniclers of the late fourteenth and early fifteenth centuries comment on the undisciplined behaviour of soldiers guilty of taking the law into their own hands, and show a growing awareness of the suffering caused by war.[10] Despite the prominence accorded them in narrative accounts of the Hundred Years War, like Froissart's *Chroniques*, there were, in fact, few battles. The aim of the war was to avoid direct confrontation with the enemy for as long as possible. Allmand notes a change in attitude to the place accorded to battle in the war – it was no longer regarded as the great opportunity for individual acts of courage but more as the culmination of a military process.[11]

However, evidence to the contrary is provided in Hugh Collins's paper. He examines the behaviour of two prominent individuals at the battle of Patay in 1429, which resulted in a disastrous defeat for the English and charges of cowardice being levelled against one of them. In John Talbot, earl of Shrewsbury, and Sir John Fastolf, we have representatives of two types of courageous soldier, both regarded by contemporaries as heroes of the Hundred Years War. Central to an understanding of their actions is the question of honour, which even today may be rewarded by the bestowal of an outward symbol of nobility such as the award of the Order of the Garter. Within the broad context of long-standing Anglo-French hostilities, Collins explores 'the value system of the English chivalric classes in the fifteenth century'. The motives which lay behind Fastolf's decision to flee the battlefield, thereby evading capture by the French, are examined in detail through a close analysis of primary source material. He concludes that 'Fastolf behaved with nothing other than tactical good sense'. But this was not how Fastolf's actions were regarded at the time especially by his rival Talbot, who was captured in the battle, imprisoned for four years and ransomed. He accused Fastolf of cowardice and unknightly behaviour on the field of battle and bore him a grudge long after. Collins's paper reminds us that a sense of honour and adherence to a chivalric code of conduct were still very important to the aristocracy in the fifteenth century, a period traditionally associated with a decline of chivalry.[12] Collins suggests that the ways in which Talbot and Fastolf viewed their world may have been very different from each other, Talbot sticking steadfastly to a belief in a chivalric code of conduct on the battlefield whilst Fastolf responded to the situation with pragmatism and common sense, demonstrating the characteristics of a professional soldier (in the modern sense), concerned for his own personal survival as well as that of his fellow soldiers. Both Christopher Allmand and Matthew Bennett engage in the debate raised here over the impact of the rise of the professional soldier on the nature of warfare at the end of the medieval period.

Anthony Goodman has argued that English fighting methods in the Wars of the Roses were heavily influenced by experience gained during the Hundred Years War in the raising and commanding of armies, and the use of artillery and hand-guns.[13] However, the nature of these wars was very different. K.B. McFarlane described them as 'short sharp engagements in the field with intervals of inactivity as well as longer periods of peace', and some historians have even questioned the appropriateness of the usual vocabulary of war to the period at all.[14] We know very little about the organisation of armies and tactics employed on the battlefield during the Wars of the Roses. Frequently armies were raised speedily and for very short periods of time. Many of the so-called battles of the Wars of the Roses were small in scale, famously the first battle of St Albans, which was described by Charles Oman as 'little more than a short scuffle in the street'.[15] Yet other battles, notably Towton, Tewkesbury and Bosworth, seem much more significant both in terms of scale and outcome. Unlike the civil war of Stephen's reign and the Hundred Years War, the Wars of the Roses are not remembered for long sieges, apart from attacks on some key fortresses in the north-east between 1460 and 1464 and on Harlech castle in north Wales in the 1460s, and the siege of London in 1471.[16] The impact of the civil wars on society is difficult to gauge because of the limitations of the source material, but the idea of later fifteenth-century England as particularly lawless and violent is no longer accepted by historians. The revisionist view of the Wars of the Roses regards them as small in scale when compared with conflicts in other parts of Europe, especially the Hundred Years War, and causing minimal disruption to civilian life. But recently some historians have argued that their impact was perhaps greater than the scale of the military activity might lead one to expect, pointing to the indirect effects of civil war on the economy and society.[17]

The nature of the mid seventeenth-century civil war and the correct title for it have long been debated. Peter Gaunt argues that the conflict might be seen not as 'one civil war but numerous regional conflicts, often with little cooperation or communication between the various theatres, and sometimes producing very different results'.[18] Major battles involving the principal or combined armies were rare, and from spring 1643 the war in England and Wales became a series of regional conflicts, each involving a fraction of the total royalist or parliamentary strength. It became 'a rather dour and protracted conflict', in which territory was controlled or conquered through garrisoning, raiding and limited engagements. But some set-piece battles were an important part of the war. Charles Carlton, for example, has described battles as 'decisive events because they are intended to render a decision. Usually they are deliberate occasions in which both sides agree to stand and fight'. However, Carlton agrees that raids, and more especially sieges, played a crucial role in the course and impact of the civil war: 'the casualties, exactions and horror inflicted by garrison-based raids were nothing when compared to sieges – the most brutal and prolonged experience of the British civil wars'. Of some 645 military actions identified by Carlton in England and Wales during the three civil wars, 198 (31 per cent) of them were sieges.[19] Siege fighting could indeed be extremely intense and brutal, affecting civilians as well as soldiers and sometimes involving high concentrations of each.

As indicated earlier, assessing the impact of war on society in the medieval and early modern periods is difficult because of the limitations of the source material. Christopher Allmand emphasises the need to consider the interests and aims of writers in their recording and interpretation of events: all sources were written for a purpose, from a particular point of view, and with a particular audience in mind. Often the source is of as much interest for what it reveals of the attitude towards war expressed by the writer as for its account of the events themselves, details of individual battles often being particularly difficult to establish. At least until the fourteenth century, most sources were written by churchmen. They reflect the concern of the Church with the moral justification of war and they increasingly comment on the impact of war on non-combatants. To such writers, war is an invitation for divine intervention carried out through God's instrument, the soldier. Between the fourteenth and seventeenth centuries, the focus of interest in the reporting of war changes. In his *Chroniques*, Jean Froissart, reflecting the outlook and interests of late fourteenth-century chivalric society, describes many individual acts of bravery and heroism on the battlefield. By the end of the fifteenth century the focus of narrative accounts has shifted away from notable personal deeds to the actions of the army as a national force, reflecting changes in its organisation and financing. These changes were to revolutionise the relationship between war and society in the early modern period.[20]

The sources for the three periods of civil war under discussion are quite different in character and clearly shape our understanding and interpretation of events in distinctive ways. Documentary evidence on the civil war of Stephen's reign is of three types: royal and private charters (surviving mostly as cartulary copies) sometimes relate to the repair of war-damage or seek to delimit the conflict;[21] others refer to an incident for dating purposes.[22] However, such is the consistency of use of standard formulae that it would be possible to read the vast majority of charters of Stephen's reign without realising that a war was going on at all. The Pipe Roll evidence from the beginning of Henry II's reign (there are no Pipe Rolls extant from Stephen's reign) might be interpreted as an indicator of serious physical damage especially in some Midlands shires.[23] The third type of evidence, crucial to an understanding of the war, is the testimony of the chroniclers.[24] Though all writers of narrative accounts were ecclesiastics, it would be wrong to see them all as presenting a view from the cloister. Several seem to have had access to eye-witness accounts of the war. Henry of Huntingdon, for example, gives a very full description of two major engagements, the battles of the Standard in 1138 and Lincoln in 1141; although much space is devoted to speeches delivered to the combatants before the commencement of fighting, there is also a fair amount of detail on the course of each conflict.[25]

The warfare these twelfth-century chroniclers describe consists mostly of sieges and assorted acts of plunder and brigandage. The essentially localised nature of their outlook is often apparent. The *Gesta Stephani*, for example, supposedly written in or near Bath, focuses on campaigns in Gloucestershire, Somerset, Dorset and Wiltshire, with coverage of the capture of such castles as Cerney, Corfe, Devizes and Winchcomb. Just as the Hexham chroniclers stress the impact of the Scots, so John of Worcester dwells on the incursions of the Welsh. The best-known account of the miseries of Stephen's reign, the annal for 1137 in the Peterborough Chronicle, was probably heavily influenced by the reign of terror of Geoffrey de Mandeville, ten miles away at Ramsey abbey.[26] That said, the inclusion of a lament bewailing the sufferings of the time is common to several writers from different parts of the country: there are comparable passages in a number of chronicles. While some of the language is borrowed from biblical or classical sources and may also have been influenced by the provisions for the Peace of God,[27] it is difficult to escape the conclusion that the civil war of Stephen's reign was a prolonged war of attrition during which royal authority was in abeyance over large parts of the country and that it caused widespread distress.

Historians have repeatedly pointed to the shortcomings of the contemporary source material for the study of military aspects of the Wars of the Roses. Despite the growth of literacy and the spread of the vernacular in fifteenth-century England, the main narrative sources, the chronicles, remain primitive in style and approach, lacking any critical reflection or analysis of the events they describe. It is difficult to find even basic information about the numbers and identities of those present on the battlefield or details of military engagements.[28] The southern origin of most of the writers of accounts of the political and military events of the period had a significant effect upon perceptions of the wars. This is particularly evident in the way in which the march of the Lancastrian army, allegedly led by Queen Margaret of Anjou from Yorkshire towards London in 1461, is reported.[29] An important development in the period is the use of history as a propaganda weapon by both the Lancastrians and the Yorkists. Some of the earliest official histories, such as the *Historie of the Arrivall of Edward IV in England* and the *Chronicle of the Rebellion in Lincolnshire*, were commissioned by Edward IV partly with the intention of circulating copies abroad to keep foreign observers informed of the current political situation.[30] The only source which presents the wars in a chivalric way is John Hardyng's English verse *Chronicle*, which survives in several versions presented to different patrons. Hardyng's writing was influenced by his military background: he served in France in the retinue of Henry Percy (Harry Hotspur) in 1415 and participated in wars on the Scottish borders. His theme is the importance of strong government and unity as a means of preventing attack from external enemies such as the Scots or French.[31]

In contrast to the rather limited evidence for the fifteenth century, there is a wealth of material for the study of the civil war of the seventeenth century. With the collapse of censorship in 1641–42, the civil war period was the first time a free press operated in England. Printing presses were not expensive or complicated and the new freedom of the civil war years, linked with the desire of both sides to present their cases and to report events to their advantage, led to a mushrooming of typeset material. Printed works from the civil war years range from broadsheets and weekly newspapers to pamphlets, tracts and longer works.[32] Many published works seek to advance the royalist or parliamentarian case and to condemn their opponents' cause and inevitably contain a large propaganda element. This is the focus of Mark Stoyle's paper, which discusses the anti-Welsh pamphlets produced by the parliamentarian presses in London between 1642 and 1646. Even the more straightforward accounts of battles and campaigns contained in newspapers and in the many pamphlets of the 1640s should be treated with caution as they are inevitably biased. However, by running together a range of published accounts it is often possible to reconstruct the essential story of the civil war.

Although the traditional elements of central and local government often broke down during the war years, both sides maintained an element of central administration generating official, if incomplete, governmental records.[33] At the local level, the principal records are financial and are much stronger on the parliamentarian side than the royalist. They record the money and goods collected and expended in waging an intensive four-year war.[34] In addition to official records, a wide range of the letters, journals and memoirs of soldiers and civilians caught up in civil war, both royalist and parliamentarian, has come down to us. Some were printed within the lifetime of their authors; many survived in manuscript to be published in the nineteenth and twentieth centuries.[35] These written records can be supplemented by a limited range of illustrative material, most notably contemporary battle plans, engravings of the protagonists, often with battle scenes in the background, and various satirical and allegorical images. Mark Stoyle emphasises the strong visual element in the propaganda campaign waged against the Welsh, found in woodcuts which illustrated printed pamphlets of the period (see Figure 1, p. 169, *The Welch Man's Inventory*, 1641–42).

Together these sources can supply a fairly full story of the wars, the overall course of events and important engagements. Less thoroughly documented is the low-level, small-scale raiding and counter-raiding and we do not always get a full picture of the impact of war at the local level. Despite the lack of some substantial pieces of evidence such as a battle plan and an account of events by the principal royalist commander, Peter Gaunt has made an assessment of a battle and, more broadly, the social and economic impact of the war on one locality, Montgomery, which he believes may be typical of many smallish towns in England and Wales in the seventeenth century. He argues that, although at first sight Montgomery 'does not seem to have been drawn deeply into the conflicts of the mid-seventeenth century nor to have suffered heavily during the civil war', there were nevertheless serious social and economic consequences for the townspeople. The war also had an impact on the townscape, resulting in the destruction of the medieval castle and some houses. He suggests that this experience may have marked a turning-point in the physical and mental landscape of the local community.

Although historians have recently tried to reconstruct the experience of common people in the civil war, the sources for such attempts are very limited and the resulting accounts are inevitably incomplete and in places suspect. Conversely, the sources tell us a lot about the costs and materials of war. Drawing upon this multiplicity of source material, historians have produced differing images of the ferocity of the civil war and of the degree to which it directly impacted upon the civilan population. However, most historians now stress its destructive effects, arguing that a large proportion of the adult male population was in arms at some stage in the war, and that the death toll of the civil war seen as a percentage of the national population was perhaps comparable with that of the First World War. The civil war imposed a very heavy, indeed unprecedented, financial burden on the population and, for many communities, even those away from the main theatres of combat, it was a burdensome and traumatic experience.[36]

Some common themes emerge from the papers, one being the identification of scapegoats in time of war: either 'foreigners' or women. Consistently singled out for criticism and accused of stirring up discord and rebellion are the Welsh. Prejudice against the Welsh is evident from the author of the *Gesta Stephani*, who describes them as a rebellious and lawless nation. They are 'savages' who laid ambushes for the English and ravaged land under their control, plundering, burning and slaughtering.[37] This is not an uncommon view of the Welsh held in the medieval period. In his description of Wales of 1188, Gerald of Wales, himself a descendant of Welsh princes, reveals an ambivalent attitude to the Welsh people, describing them as 'so agile and fierce that they often win battles fought against such odds', 'being unarmed against those bearing weapons' and 'on foot against mounted cavalry'. There are many qualities in the Welsh that he admires: their hospitality and cleanliness; their sharp minds, intelligence and wit; their musicality and their distinguished ancestry; their piety and devotion to the Christian faith. However, a consideration of their 'good points' is offset by their 'less good points' which include an analysis of 'their weakness in battle'. Although at first the Welsh are fierce and throw themselves into battle courageously, they quickly take fright and retreat in a cowardly manner, so that they are easily conquered.[38] Matthew Bennett points out that underlying such prejudices of English writers is a sense of fear, the product of the Welsh Revolt of 1136–38. These attitudes prevailed into the seventeenth century, when we are told by Mark Stoyle that the Welsh were attacked vociferously by the London press, resurrecting earlier medieval prejudices.

The Welsh were not the only group of 'foreigners' to be regarded with hostility in the twelfth century: the Scots also fell victim to

English prejudice and victimisation. This is hardly surprising at a time when there was an almost permanent state of war between the two countries across the northern borders. The author of the *Gesta Stephani* describes the Scots as 'barbarous and filthy'.[39] Another twelfth-century writer, William of Newburgh, expresses deep admiration for King David I of Scotland in his *History of English Affairs* (comparing him with the civilised and virtuous psalmist, King David), but criticises him for unleashing savage attacks upon the English. The Scots were an 'uncivilised race' whose 'uncontrolled savagery made them thirst for blood and unwilling to spare age and sex'.[40] Richard of Hexham describes King David's army as 'barbarian'.[41] Bennett's explanation for the reputation of the Scots as ravagers lies in the nature of the border territories and the style of warfare characteristic of the region.

The 'greedy' Flemings also fare badly. Regularly employed as mercenaries by the twelfth century, they seem to have been regarded with universal contempt, being stereotyped as treacherous and deceitful, ready to commit any crime and sacrilege.[42] In the *Gesta Stephani* they are described as 'utterly steeped in craft and treachery, very ready to set pillage and strife on foot everywhere, most eager to commit crime and sacrilege. For, after gaining castles sometimes by stealth and sometimes by valour and force of arms, they were oppressing all their neighbours in many ways and especially the possessions of the churches'.[43] Bennett discusses the attitude of chroniclers to William of Ypres, the most prominent captain of Flemish mercenaries used by Stephen, who was accused of burning the nunnery of Wherwell and who apparently defected at the battle of Lincoln in 1141, thus attracting opprobrium. However, Bennett has found evidence of another 'type' of Fleming, who performed loyal service to Stephen and transferred smoothly into the service of Henry II. He concludes that generally the behaviour of Flemish mercenaries was not dissimilar to the English or French fighting men. Allmand also presents us with a positive view of the Flemings in the *Annales Gandenses* which records the war against the French culminating in the Flemish victory at Courtrai in 1302. It is perhaps worth noting that foreign observers of the English held equally prejudiced views of the behaviour of the English in time of war.[44]

Another group in medieval society frequently used as scapegoats for inexplicable events were women. The causes of civil wars are always complex and subject to a variety of interpretations and explanations. In an age when it was impolitic, not to say foolhardy, to criticise the king, the Lord's anointed, blame tended to be placed else-where.[45] Women were convenient targets for many reasons, and in the context of civil war a foreign-born queen might readily be condemned for her malign influence over her husband, even though she might also be regarded as useful as a peace-maker and mediator. Diana Dunn points out that one of the most obvious explanations for expressions of hostility voiced by both contemporaries and later commentators against Margaret of Anjou is that she happened to be married to one of the most incompetent medieval kings, whose reign was dominated by political unrest, faction and ultimately civil war. From today's perspective it seems clear that the root cause of the civil wars of the second half of the fifteenth century was the weakness of a king who failed to provide effective leadership either at home or abroad and who lacked the political acumen necessary to control rival factions amongst the nobility. Henry VI's wife was a convenient scapegoat for his inadequacies: both her French nationality and the fact that she failed to conform to contemporary expectations of queenly behaviour by involving herself in politics contributed to her unpopularity. As a result of this attitude it is likely that Margaret's role in the military and political developments that we now call the Wars of the Roses has been exaggerated, at least for the period up to the mid-1450s. After *c.* 1456 the queen does indeed appear to have been politically active, rallying support behind her husband and her son against her rival for power, Richard, duke of York. Although prevented by her sex from taking any direct part in the fighting, she was physically close to the site of battle on a number of occasions: Blore Heath in 1459, St Albans in 1461 and Tewkesbury in 1471, ready to respond to the outcome. There is no doubt that she played a crucial part in the Wars of the Roses but the eventual victory of the Yorkists had a detrimental effect on the way in which her role has been interpreted from the later fifteenth century onwards, especially at the hands of the most influential presenter of English medieval history, Shakespeare.

It is interesting to compare the treatment of Margaret of Anjou by contemporary commentators with attitudes to Stephen's queen Matilda in the twelfth century. In the *Gesta Stephani*, Queen Matilda is praised for her efforts to defend the kingdom by raising an army and leading it against the enemy: she 'brought a magnificent body of troops across in front of London from the other side of the river and gave orders that they should rage most furiously around the city with plunder and arson, violence and the sword, in sight of the countess and her men'. Admiration for her unconventional behaviour is expressed: 'forgetting the weakness of her sex and a woman's softness she bore herself with the valour of a man'. This is in direct contrast to the way in which her rival the Empress Matilda is described – arrogant and haughty, seeking to make herself a queen. She is condemned for being arbitrary and headstrong, greedy and grasping for power, whereas the real queen is 'a woman of subtlety and a man's resolution'.[46] The explanation for this inconsistency of attitude towards women in positions of power can to a great extent be provided by the political circumstances of the times in which they lived. Margaret of Anjou's reputation clearly suffered as a result of being on the losing side and thereby becoming the victim of highly effective political propaganda. The use of propaganda to blacken the reputation of one's opponents is an enduring theme in the context of war, and central to Mark Stoyle's paper on attacks on the Welsh in the London press in the seventeenth century: the Welsh are depicted as alien and barbaric, speaking a different language and living a primitive lifestyle.

Although the colloquium led to the identification of some common themes, it is certainly not the primary purpose of this collection of papers to suggest that the civil wars of the medieval and early modern periods were the same either in scale, style or impact. They each had their own particular causes, characteristics and outcomes. It is unhelpful to generalise about the nature of such conflicts in terms of military activity and conduct. However, historians seeking to reconstruct the events of individual civil wars and their impact upon government and society face similar problems with the nature of the source material and the way in which past events have been recorded and interpreted by contemporary chroniclers, war reporters and later commentators. Their motives and concerns changed between the early medieval and early modern periods, and a comparison of their methodologies and approaches to the events they describe is as illuminating and valuable as the study of the wars themselves.

NOTES

1 My thanks are due to my colleagues in the history department and to Dr Glyn Turton, Dean of Arts and Humanities at Chester College, for their help and support

in the organisation of the colloquium. I am also grateful to all the contributors to the volume for their enthusiastic response to the original idea of the colloquium and for delivering the final versions of their papers so promptly.

2 See, for example, the journal *War in History*, launched in 1994. Its premise states: 'Recognising that the study of war is more than simply the study of conflict, the journal embraces war in all its aspects: economic, social and political as well as purely military.'

3 J. Gillingham, 'Richard I and the Science of War in the Middle Ages', in *War and Government in the Middle Ages*, eds J. Gillingham and J.C. Holt (Woodbridge, 1984), p. 81; J. Bradbury, *Stephen and Matilda: The Civil War of 1139–53* (Stroud, 1996), pp. 64, 83. This view has been described as 'the new orthodoxy' by Michael Prestwich in *Armies and Warfare in the Middle Ages: The English Experience* (1996), p. 11.

4 J. Bradbury, 'Battles in England and Normandy, 1066–1154', in *Anglo-Norman Warfare*, ed. M. Strickland (Woodbridge, 1993), p. 184.

5 Ibid., p. 183.

6 Prestwich, *Armies and Warfare*, p. 281; Bradbury, *Stephen and Matilda*, pp. 64–66, 83–88.

7 *Gesta Stephani*, ed. K.R. Potter (Oxford, 1976), pp. 1–5, 146–49.

8 See T. Thornton, ' "The Enemy or Stranger, That Shall Invade their Countrey": Identity and Community in the English North', in *War: Identities in Conflict 1300–2000*, eds B. Taithe and T. Thornton (Stroud, 1998), pp. 57-72.

9 C.T. Allmand, *The Hundred Years War: England and France at war c. 1300– c. 1450* (Cambridge, 1988), p. 55.

10 C.T. Allmand, 'War and the Non-Combatant in the Middle Ages', in *Medieval Warfare: A History*, ed. M. Keen (Oxford, 1999), pp. 261–67.

11 Allmand, *The Hundred Years War*, p. 54.

12 Michael Jones also emphasises the importance of the concept of chivalry to an understanding of the motives underlying the actions of the two main protagonists in the early stages of the Wars of the Roses: see M.K. Jones, 'Somerset, York and the Wars of the Roses', *English Historical Review*, vol. 104 (1989), pp. 285–307. See also S. Walker, 'Janico Dartasso: Chivalry, Nationality and the Man-at-Arms', *History*, vol. 84 (1999), pp. 31–51.

13 A. Goodman, *The Wars of the Roses: Military Activity and English Society, 1452–97* (1981), pp. 165–69, 170–74.

14 K.B. McFarlane, 'The Wars of the Roses', in *England in the Fifteenth Century: Collected Essays*, ed. G.L. Harriss (1981), p. 242; J.R. Lander, *The Wars of the Roses* (1965), pp. 20–21; C.D. Ross, *The Wars of the Roses* (1976), ch. 4.

15 C. Oman, *The Political History of England, 1377–1485* (1920), p. 367.

16 Goodman, *The Wars of the Roses*, pp. 181–88.

17 See Lander, *The Wars of the Roses*, pp. 23–24; Ross, *The Wars of the Roses*, ch. 5, esp. pp. 163–76; J. Gillingham, *The Wars of the Roses* (1981), pp. 1–15. An alternative view can be found in Goodman, *The Wars of the Roses*, ch. 9, esp. pp. 213–26, and A.J. Pollard, *The Wars of the Roses* (1988), ch. 4.

18 P. Gaunt, *The Cromwellian Gazetteer* (Stroud, 1987), p. x.

19 C. Carlton, *Going to the Wars: The Experience of the British Civil Wars, 1638–50* (1992), pp. 114, 154–55.

20 The so-called 'military revolution' debate is not specifically addressed in these

papers. It has been the subject of numerous articles and books published over the past 20 years or so, usefully summarised in the 'Introduction' to *The Medieval Military Revolution: State, Society and Military Change in Medieval and Early Modern Europe*, eds A. Ayton and J.L. Price (1995), pp. 1–22. See also the 'Conclusion' of M. Prestwich, *Armies and Warfare*, pp. 334–46, which presents the arguments for a military revolution in the late medieval period.

21 For example, *Regesta Regum Anglo-Normannorum*, vol. III, eds H.A. Cronne and R.H.C. Davis (Oxford, 1968), nos 81, 285, 491; *Earldom of Gloucester Charters*, ed. R.B. Patterson (Oxford, 1973), nos. 95–96.

22 For example, *Early Scottish Charters*, ed. A.C. Lawrie (Glasgow, 1905), nos 141–42.

23 H.W.C. Davis, 'The anarchy of Stephen's reign', *EHR*, vol. 18 (1903), pp. 630–41; E.M. Amt, 'The Meaning of Waste in the early Pipe Rolls of Henry II', *Economic History Review*, vol. 44 (1991), pp. 240–48; E.M. Amt, *The Accession of Henry II in England: Royal Government Restored, 1149–1159* (Woodbridge, 1993), pp. 133–43. But for recent comment on this interpretation, see G.J. White, *Restoration and Reform, 1153–1165: Recovery from Civil War in England* (Cambridge, 2000), pp. 154–57.

24 The chronicle sources are discussed in R.H.C. Davis, *King Stephen 1135–1154* (1990), pp. 144–48, and A. Gransden, *Historical Writing in England c. 550–c. 1307* (1974), chs 10 and 13.

25 Henry, archdeacon of Huntingdon, *Historia Anglorum*, ed. D. Greenway (Oxford, 1996), pp. 712–19, 724–39.

26 *The Anglo-Saxon Chronicle*, ed. D. Whitelock et al. (1961), pp. 199–200.

27 C. Clark, *The Peterborough Chronicle* (Oxford, 1970), pp. xxxvi–xxxvii; William of Malmesbury, *Historia Novella*, ed. E.J. King (Oxford, 1998), pp. xcv–xcvi, 71 note 173.

28 A useful overview of the sources for the Wars of the Roses is provided by M.A. Hicks in *The Wars of the Roses*, ed. A.J. Pollard (1995), pp. 20–40. The English and foreign chronicle accounts are discussed in detail in A. Gransden, *Historical Writing in England II, c. 1307 to the early Sixteenth Century* (1982), pp. 249–307.

29 Pollard, *The Wars of the Roses*, pp. 88–89; B.M. Cron, 'Margaret of Anjou and the Lancastrian March on London, 1461', *The Ricardian*, vol. 11, no. 147 (Dec. 1999), pp. 590–615.

30 Gransden, *Historical Writing in England II*, pp. 251–52; C. Richmond, 'Propaganda in the Wars of the Roses', *History Today*, vol. 42 (July 1992), pp. 12–18.

31 Gransden, *Historical Writing in England II*, pp. 274–87.

32 See especially the *Catalogue of the Pamphlets, Books, Newspapers and Manuscripts Relating to the Civil War, the Commonwealth and Restoration Collected by George Thomason* (2 vols, 1908), a catalogue of the collection of printed works amassed by a London bookseller during the 1640s and 1650s, totalling well over 20,000 individual items.

33 See PRO, *Calendar of the Proceedings of the Committee for Compounding, 1643–60* (5 vols, 1889–93); *Calendar of the Proceedings of the Committee for Advance of Money, 1642–56* (3 vols, 1888); *Calendar of State Papers Domestic of the Reign of Charles I* (23 vols, 1858–97); *Privy Council Registers, 1637–45, Preserved in the Public Record Office, Reproduced in Facsimile* (12 vols, 1967–68); *The Royalist Ordnance Papers*, ed. I. Roy, Oxfordshire Record Society, vol. 43 (1964), and I. Roy, 'The Royalist Council of War, 1642–6', *BIHR*, vol. 35 (1962). Important manuscript sources are to be found at:

Bodleian Library, Tanner MSS. 59–63; PRO, SP 16–28; PRO, WO 55/423, 457–9, 1661; BL, Harleian MSS. 6802, 6804, 6851–2; BL, Add. MS. 34325.

34 PRO, SP 28.

35 See *The Impact of the English Civil War*, ed. J. Morrill (1991), p. 144.

36 Carlton, *Going to the Wars*; M. Bennett, *The Civil Wars in Britain and Ireland 1638–1651* (Oxford, 1997); M. Bennett, *The Civil Wars Experienced: Britain and Ireland 1638–51* (2000); P. Tennant, *Edgehill and Beyond: The People's War in the South Midlands 1642–45* (Stroud, 1992); D. Underdown, *Revel, Riot and Rebellion: Popular Politics and Culture in England 1603–1660* (Oxford, 1985); M. Stoyle, *Loyalty and Locality: Popular Allegiance in Devon during the English Civil War* (Exeter, 1994).

37 *Gesta Stephani*, pp. 14–15, 172–73, 194–95.

38 Gerald of Wales, *The Journey through Wales and The Description of Wales* (Harmondsworth, 1978), pp. 233–70; see also R. Bartlett, *Gerald of Wales* (Oxford, 1982), ch. 6.

39 *Gesta Stephani*, pp. 54–55; see also the interesting discussion of English attitudes to the 'Celtic barbarian' by John Gillingham in 'Conquering the Barbarians: War and Chivalry in Twelfth-Century Britain', *Haskins Society Journal*, vol. 4 (1992), pp. 67–84.

40 William of Newburgh, *The History of English Affairs, Book I*, eds P.G. Walsh and M.J. Kennedy (Warminster, 1988), p. 103.

41 Richard of Hexham, *Historia* in *Chronicles of the Reigns of Stephen, Henry II and Richard I*, ed. R. Howlett, Rolls Series, (1884–89), vol. 3, pp. 139–78.

42 For a general discussion of the use of mercenaries in medieval warfare, see Prestwich, *Armies and Warfare*, ch. 6, and *Medieval Warfare*, ed. Keen, ch. 10.

43 *Gesta Stephani*, pp. 188–89.

44 Gillingham, 'Conquering the Barbarians', pp. 82–83.

45 See M. Strickland, 'Against the Lord's Anointed: Aspects of Warfare and Baronial Rebellion in England and Normandy, 1075–1265' in *Law and Government in Medieval England and Normandy*, eds G. Garnett and J. Hudson (Cambridge, 1994), pp. 56–79.

46 *Gesta Stephani*, pp. 118–19, 122–23, 126–27.

The Reporting of War in the Middle Ages

Christopher Allmand

As a theme, war was central to the written culture of the middle ages. The Bible, in particular the Old Testament, as well as the romances of the period, reflected the moral conflict between good and evil, encouraged the acceptance of the hero and the heroic, and underlined the commonly held belief that God intervened actively in human affairs. This chapter is concerned with the reporting of war found in the chronicles, mainly from the twelfth century onwards. Such chronicles developed from the earlier, briefer annals, which often recorded military events such as the outcome of battles and wars, but left the bare record unencumbered by detail or commentary explaining the reasons for the victory of one side over the other. Here is an example, chosen at random from the *Anglo-Saxon Chronicle*:

> 943. In this year, Anlaf stormed Tamworth and there was great slaughter on both sides: the Danes had the victory and carried great booty away with them. On this raid Wulfrun was taken prisoner ...
> 944. In this year king Edmund brought all Northumbria under his sway, and drove out two kings, Anlaf Sihtricson and Raegnald Guthfrithson.
> 945. In this year king Edmund ravaged all Strathclyde, and ceded it to Malcolm, king of Scots, on condition that he would be his fellow worker both by sea and land.[1]

What can we learn from the 'In this year ...' approach? Certainly that this was a society which made war by raiding and ravaging enemy territory, leaving many dying on the field, but by that means securing land and booty, including prisoners. This is important information for those seeking to describe the nature of war in tenth-century Britain; yet if we are hoping for more, we are likely to be disappointed. A century later, however, the same *Chronicle* is able to serve us better: the results of the battle of Hastings, upon both winners and losers, are described with a sense that battles do have effects. We are moving in the right direction.

In subsequent centuries the nature of war reporting would be profoundly influenced by a number of factors, not least the personalities of the writers themselves, their upbringing and education and the position which they occupied in society. Almost without exception, at least until the mid-fourteenth century (a significant date in other respects, too) writers of chronicles were men of religion: some (seculars) living in the world; others (regulars) separated to some extent from the world by the walls of the cloister; and the friars constituting that curious mixture, regulars who lived in the world. It may not be unfair to say that the monastic chronicler was not necessarily the best guide to the complexities of war reporting, although the account of the Norman Conquest written by William of Poitiers, who had seen military service before entering the monastery, reflects something of his early upbringing and training.

Experience of the world, and of the soldier's world in particular, was clearly an asset to be taken advantage of. Secular clerks were often men of the court, who had either witnessed at least some of the events which they described, spoken to those who had played a role in them, or been given access to documentation – in royal records, for instance – which enabled them to chronicle wars more effectively. William of Poitiers, as we have seen, had military experience upon which to draw. The Franciscan friar who, centuries later, compiled the *Chronicle of Lanercost* (1272–1346) may have had similar experience, for he showed a practical knowledge of the realities of war and was particularly good at describing sieges.[2] In the same way Geoffrey le Baker would demonstrate a knowledge of military tactics,[3] while the anonymous author of the *Gesta Henrici Quinti*, who cited documents kept among the royal records, wrote from the vantage point of having also accompanied Henry V's army through the triumphal campaign of 1415.[4] It would be mainly regarding the prolonged Anglo-French conflict that the chroniclers from Hainault, Jean le Bel and Jean Froissart, would write. Both were secular clerks who mixed easily in court circles. It was this link which in 1327 enabled le Bel to accompany an English army into Scotland, an experience which gave him the material to write a highly realistic account of the campaign and of the hardships endured by the soldiers.[5] Froissart was to glean much of his material from listening to the tales of personal exploits which many were only too anxious to tell him. Inevitably, many of these were coloured, yet they tended to reflect the military and social values of the time, so that, frequently based on the evidence of the participants themselves, his *Chroniques* enjoy the benefit of greater liveliness in the way that they report the events of the past.[6]

With the question who wrote must surely go two further related questions: who would read these writers, and was the prospective readership likely to influence the choice of material entered into a chronicle, and how it would be arranged and presented? We know that chronicles were read by many different kinds of people: medieval book lists reveal that Latin histories were fequently found in monastic libraries, as well as in the collections of members of the military caste, who preferred works in the vernacular. As the anonymous Franciscan author of the *Annales Gandenses* set out in his prologue, history was something which an intelligent man might be interested in, particularly in the events concerning the *communis utilitas* or well-being of the community to which he belonged. Let us listen to our friar, writing early in 1308:

> One day when I was not very busy, it occurred to me that as I enjoy reading and hearing stories and true facts about old times, and write quickly ... I might set forth ... in chronological order ... those manifold battles and perils ... of various kinds, expeditions, sieges, and attacks both passive and active, which had befallen our land of Flanders, and the diverse happenings of my times – at all of which I was either present and an eye-witness, or else ascertained the facts with certainty from the relation of those who were present – and leave it to posterity, if interested in reading and hearing such things, to register them in a subtler and finer fashion ... My motive was to please and entertain some of the brothers who at times enjoyed hearing and reading such things. Moreover, I had in mind the common welfare, for, so it seems to me, when any events are sinking [into oblivion], it is most useful to know about them.[7]

Here was a man of awareness, proud of being a Fleming, who saw history as a form which satisfied many demands. Not only did it entertain (since it could be read silently or aloud), it could also be regarded as part of the national heritage which people should know about. No doubt he was right, for his *Annales*, seemingly recorded with care and accuracy, were concerned with a particularly glorious period of Flemish history which was expressed, above all, in the victory won by its burgher army over the chivalric might of France at Courtrai in July 1302.

Another famous justification, or mission statement, this time the one with which Jean Froissart began his *Chroniques* more than half a century later, gives us a different approach.

> In order that the honourable enterprises, noble adventures and deeds of arms which took place during the wars waged by France and England should be

fittingly related and preserved for posterity, so that brave men should be inspired thereby to follow such examples, I wish to place on record these matters of great renown.[8]

The historian is presented here as a memorialist, who uses history to preserve important and significant actions for the public memory (*ad perpetuam rei memoriam*, as the well-known diplomatic formula had it). Like the herald of a chivalric order, whose task it was to record the outstanding actions of its members, the chronicler was anxious to recall notable personal deeds which might serve to inspire or give example to those who came later. The didactic significance of his choice was thus important, for actions were recorded both in an attempt to recall truth and as *exempla* of values to be emulated in attempts to reach even greater heights.[9]

Writers of chronicles had different motives in mind when selecting material for inclusion in their texts. Robert of Avesbury, for instance, wrote what was 'virtually a military history of Edward III's reign', his aim being to record 'the wonderful deeds of the magnificent king of England, the Lord Edward the third after the Conquest, and of his nobles', in particular the courage of the king himself.[10] The cynical may think that this was to curry favour; yet we should recognise that Avesbury's motive may have been a genuine wish to honour the king by placing him at the forefront of his narrative. In any event, he left his readers in no doubt about the importance of the individual's role in war. Other works had other purposes: to encourage enterprise; to justify and glorify actions, and, in particular, successes; to commemorate the achievements of the past,[11] thus making of history the instrument of public memory; and to teach, through example, how war could bring fame to the individual and glory to the country which he served.

We would say today that a proper understanding of war requires the reporter to explain, at least in some measure, the causes lying behind a conflict. Not all writers were successful in achieving this appreciation of the reasons why wars broke out. The 'national' chronicles, some with ties with London, normally tried to explain or justify wars in terms such as those used by the author of the *Anonimalle Chronicle*, who wrote that Edward III sent an army to France in 1370 'pur mayntiner le droit del roy Dengleterre devers soun adversary de Frauns'. An invasion of France, carried out with help from the public purse and still a relatively unusual event, required some word of explanation or justification, however formal and inadequate.

Likewise, when English kings led expeditions to Scotland, these were trumpeted in the chronicles, and the ambitions of the English explained. Not all wars, however, had 'causes': some just 'happened'. For instance, the state of permanent hostility which separated the English from the Scots in the Border country hardly needed explaining. Nor was the kind of war fought there one in which great feats, of the traditional 'chivalric' kind, took place. It was with a tinge of regret that the author of the *Anonimalle Chronicle* wrote, of the year 1355, that an English army, having advanced as far as Edinburgh and burned it, soon returned south 'sauuz ascune notable exploite' being performed.[13] It is the local *Lanercost Chronicle*, essentially the history of a region, which provides a more accurate and realistic picture of the kind of war which characterised those parts, with its descriptions of almost constant conflict, the nature of which is reflected to this very day in the form of the bastels, or rural defensive dwellings, found scattered over the Border country. This was essentially an unsophisticated war not unlike that characteristic of the tenth century cited above, lacking formal action between the armies of the rival peoples, characterised more by the raid, the burning of farms and settlements, and the driving away of cattle; in brief, a kind of war which cost little or nothing to undertake, but which, since it was aimed at the enemy's economy and civilian population, could bring advantage to those who took part in it. The regular appearance in the pages of the *Lanercost Chronicle* of raids, of tribute being paid to secure peace, of the redemption of both persons and property for ransoms, underlines the fact that in these relatively poor areas war had its place not merely as a military activity, but as an economic and social one as well.[14] Pity the chronicler as he struggled to make a story out of this material! Unless he chose to write in the romance style, as John Barbour did when he wrote *The Bruce* in lowland Scots dialect in the 1370s, there was little that he could do with such unpromising material.

The importance of the reporter – the 'presenter' as he might be called today on the media – is underlined by the very different emphasis placed on the war of raids and opportunism by a reporter such as John Barbour. His *Bruce* is a celebration of success, occasionally given to exaggeration but containing many fine descriptions of encounters and combats. These successfully bring together the realism of the historian and the romance of chivalry as he unfolds the story of Robert Bruce, the man who led the Scots nation in its war of independence against the English. What is significant in the present discussion is how Barbour raises some of the methods characteristic of the border war, just discussed, to new heights which enable him to make a great deal out of what might otherwise be regarded as banal action. His success lies in his ability to describe not merely guerrilla war of the kind seen on the Borders and in the Highlands, but a conflict in which Bruce and his followers, like Maccabeus and his people, are fighting for the highest stakes; their freedom, which may be achieved by defeating the English largely through the clever use of fabian tactics and the unexpected attack, and the political advantage to be derived from such wearying methods. It needed an author skilled in writing to transform the raid, the oldest known way of doing harm to an enemy, into an important method of advancing a war, indeed a way of advancing to victory itself.[15]

In the difficult task of recreating battles, one of the main problems faced by the reporter of war was how to give focus to his story. This might be done by introducing a strong narrative element into the text. The reporter of one particular form of modern conflict, the international football match, has an altogether easier task. From his vantage point in the centre of the stadium, or high up above it, he can see almost everything, in addition to keeping his eye on what really counts, the action around the ball. The medieval chronicler, on the other hand, faced with a battlefield probably many acres in dimension, could not be everywhere at once (supposing, indeed, that he was there at all!). How to surmount the problem of simultaneity?[16] A possible response was to generalise, to emphasise those things probably going on everywhere on the battlefield. That was the solution adopted by Thomas Walsingham in his brief and unsatisfying account of the battle of Agincourt. Walsingham was not present on this famous occasion, so his report of what occurred would be, at best, 'impressionistic', the emphasis being on the noise caused by the men, the clash of weapons and the deadliness of the falling English arrows (in this last respect he got it right); it is a curious description of a decisive battle, consisting of general statements sewn together with a thread of classical quotations, which prove how difficult it is to write descriptive pieces which are accurate as well.[17] Alternatively, the writer might decide to concentrate on the actions of an individual or group, chosen for this purpose to symbolise the achievements of the entire army, the action being described with particular emphasis to underline the sense of honour, skill and bravery: at Agincourt, the focus was on the skill of the English archers and the bravery of the English knighthood, the latter being contrasted with the pride and conceit of the French nobility who, imagining the outcome to be a foregone conclusion, celebrated their anticipated victory the night before the battle. In such a way both the victory of one side and the defeat of the other are explained both implicitly and explicitly, and a clear moral lesson is drawn for the reader's enlightenment.

In terms of resolving the problems of narration, the attraction of telling a story through the actions of a notable individual or representative group was considerable, for the method provided no more than a limited number of focal points on which to concentrate the reader's attention. There were further advantages which should not be ignored. The method emphasised the role of inspired leadership in achieving success, a leadership normally provided by the military caste and, in particular, by the elite among that caste. It had the further advantage that it fulfilled the hopes of such men that their military exploits and moments of glory might be recorded for posterity. Furthermore, by placing emphasis on the virtues of prowess, courage and skill in the performance of notable deeds (what the *Anonimalle Chronicle* had termed 'exploite') Froissart and others were providing the new, lay reading public with the kind of material which appealed to it. Not surprisingly, therefore, there emerged, mainly in the fourteenth century (although we see it before: in the life of William the Marshal, for example) an anthropocentric literature of war which placed great emphasis upon the acts of chosen persons and upon their influence on the wars in which they took part. In an English context, we think of the *Life of the Black Prince* by the Chandos Herald,[18] followed not so many years later by the host of lives and chronicles written about Henry V and his successes against the French.[19]

Both the manner in which general military activity was presented and the description of the notable acts of named individuals were intended to reflect chivalric values. By stressing the danger of the fight, the length of the encounter, the hard blows exchanged between courageous and determined protagonists, the chronicler was able to convey to the reader something of the thrill of action and the elation and sense of honour achieved in the hour of victory. From the writer's point of view, associating an outcome largely with the efforts of an individual or a group had the further advantage of attributing huge importance to their fate, in particular to their success. In this way, the aspirations of a whole nation could be linked with the decisive actions of a small group of named individuals – the national team of today –

which would be representative of what was being done, perhaps unseen and unrecorded, elsewhere on the battlefield. Where one knight was acting nobly and bravely, it was assumed that others were doing the same elsewhere, the approach through a particular focus conveying something of the whole action, a single incident conveying the essence of the whole.

Although the emphasis placed upon individual action, particularly in battle, made for good stories, it does not not always satisfy the modern way of seeing things. Above all, it fails to explain the relationship between cause and effect in accounting for the outcome of battles in general and wars in particular. All too often the answer to the question of why one side emerged victorious would be explained in a fatalistic acceptance of an outcome as the expression of divine favour (for the victor) or divine punishment (of the defeated party): God stood behind those with a just cause, while he used war to punish those who had offended him.[20] The much-quoted Book of Maccabees made the point: 'victory in war does not depend on the size of the fighting force; it is from heaven that strength comes',[21] or, as another version put it, 'victory does not come from numbers alone.' The idea, established early, had a long innings. It occurs repeatedly, in one form or another, in the twelfth-century *Gesta Stephani*;[22] in the fourteenth-century *Anonimalle Chronicle*, the English were victorious at the battle of Neville's Cross in 1346 'come Dieu voloit', a divine judgement made in response to the prayers of the Virgin and St Cuthbert; while the success achieved by the Black Prince at Poitiers ten years later was achieved 'par devyne grace et nyent par force de homm', a statement which thus legitimised all that the Prince had done.[23] The tradition still had a long way to travel: it was the so-called 'Protestant Wind' which helped to defeat the Spanish Armada in 1588.

In the age of faith and piety it was not unnatural to see divine judgements, to which Dame Fortune and her wheel provided a rather less Christian parallel, deciding the outcome of war or battle. King John II of France was taken prisoner at Poitiers 'by the will of God and the opposition of Fortune who makes the outcome of wars uncertain'.[24] Such a fatalistic approach to events was well in keeping with medieval attitudes. What could men do if God (or Fortune) had 'awarded' the victory to one side? Of one thing we can be certain: it discouraged a spirit of enquiry into the causes of victory or, more significantly, defeat, which might otherwise have been explained in very different, more rational terms. And yet we would be wrong to see all those who described war in their chronicles as reluctant to interpose a rational explanation of events; wrong, too, to think of them as incapable or unwilling of making intelligent observations about them.

For purposes of illustration of some of these points, let us consider the *Gesta Stephani* as a piece of war reporting. What sort of war does the author, perhaps Robert, bishop of Bath, place before his reader? From the work's opening line the guiding theme is division in a country rent by the self-advancing actions of barons and others who will not recognise the authority of Stephen to act for the common good. In this way of presenting things, war is immediately seen as a physical response to a moral and practical problem. The death of Henry I, 'pax patriae gentisque suae pater', 'the peace of the country and father of his people',[25] sets off a conflict in which the bonds which keep the nation together (by strong implication the personality of the late king and the power of the office which he exercised) are broken, and men now act in the name of self-interest. In the following pages we are told of a spirit of vengeance which encouraged men to turn upon one another, a loosening of the restraints of justice, a society sick in soul, upon which violence, the 'noise of war and the fury of Mars', is unleashed.[26] A skilful and deliberate choice of words (inspired, perhaps, by the author's desire to emulate Roman models) creates the atmosphere into which steps Stephen, a man of piety and courage, to provide the effective rule which the country needs. Although elected by the elders of London, Stephen is seen by the author as having been sent by Providence. His aim is to make peace among a people which has turned to plunder and pillage, but it is a peace which depends upon order being restored, and this can only be done if the succession is settled.

It is worth drawing attention to a number of factors in this account of a civil war. First, the obvious one, that war provides the dominant theme for the entire work, a fact which makes it into much more than a chronicle, more like a work intended, through its step-by-step approach, to provide at least a justification for, at best an explanation of, what happened. The initial 'scene-setting' is used to give the reader the causes of the conflict which Henry I's death has set off. Many will not accept the choice of king made by the Londoners, nor their right to act in the name of the people. The rebels are determined to use force as they resist the king's authority, so that Stephen is obliged to arm himself in order to make peace, a move which brings to mind the saying of the fourth-century Roman writer Vegetius, 'let him who desires peace prepare for war.'[27] All the while the king's opponents encourage conflict, much of it directed against the poor, for their own advantage; even the late king's doorkeeper is ready to 'do harm and most eager to offer violence to the poor' in this effort to undermine the king's authority.[28] It follows quite naturally that the war which Stephen is fighting is both morally right and legitimate: both as the guarantor of the peace of society and as a defender of royal authority, he has a duty to protect the weak and the oppresssed against those who break that peace. The repeated reminder that the civil war is causing great harm to the king's less fortunate subjects recalls and underlines his obligation to them. Stephen is not fighting only for his right to be king; he is fighting for the right of all his subjects to live without the threat of violence hanging over their heads.[29]

Before long Stephen has succeeded in restoring a measure of peace (*consueta pax*) and tranquillity (*solitas quietas*) against *discordia* and *rebellum*, the forces of disorder. But his labours, like those of Hercules, are never-ending: when one of the Hydra's heads is cut off, another appears.[30] Yet God intervenes in favour of Stephen, who has chosen to restore the powers of the Church, which Henry I had oppressed. Called to deal with rebels (*proditores*) at Exeter, the king besieges the castle and is eventually successful when the besieged run out of water. A discussion as to why this should have happened ensues. Some say that it was the sun which dried up the source, while others claim that the water was diverted back into the earth. The author will have none of this. In his view, an unexpected or extraordinary event such as this could be attributed only to divine power, the same power which led directly to the king's success.[31] The story had a message: God approved of what Stephen had done. Sadly for us the author, having invoked the blanket explanation of divine intervention, did not feel it necessary to explain matters any more. Yet his relative even-handedness is shown in his description of the eventual capture of Stephen, also explained as divine punishment 'for his sin' which, once atoned for, allows him to be restored 'wondrously and gloriously by God's favour'. This process duly occurs and, principally after the capture of Faringdon, more and more of the king's enemies become disheartened, less keen than previously to take up arms against him, while some agree to make peace (*pax, concordia*).[32]

The way that the author has arranged his narrative shows that his theme is to justify war as a preliminary to peace. The military action by the barons and others is regarded as detrimental to the general good of the kingdom, whereas the actions instigated by the king ultimately lead to joy and quiet, tranquillity and peace. In this text war represents the means of bringing peace to a divided society; the king is shown as one who is not afraid to use force in the service of the common good. We are in a world in which kingship is asserting itself against the forces of disruption, represented by elements among the baronage. In France only a few years earlier Louis VI had taken similar action against his barons, assuming to himself the sole right to make war within his kingdom. The themes and aims of the writers at the royal abbey of Saint-Denis, who recorded the French king's actions, and the author of the *Gesta Stephani* were not so different: to use war as a means of praising individual kings and to show how it was used to extend the power of the monarchy over the country. In brief, war was an instrument used to achieve a particular social and political end, a strong crown ruling over a peaceful people.

The *Annales Gandenses* were given their unity by a different theme. In this case war is reported in such a way as to suggest the impetus which it can give to – and the manner in which it expresses through action – a developing patriotic consciousness, which achieves its own glory on the field of Courtrai in July 1302. The first encounters between the Flemings and the invading French occur in May in Bruges, where a number of French are killed. Acccording to the chronicler, the French claim that these early losses are the result of treachery. This does not satisfy him: 'so far as I was able to find out by diligent investigation', he writes, this was not the case, as he 'found no sure proof of this'. Rather, he argued, the French have brought defeat upon themselves by not taking sufficient account of the fact that around Bruges there are many 'strong, well-armed and almost desperate' men ready to attack them. There is therefore no purpose in blaming the set-back thus suffered upon anyone but themselves. On the other hand, the account of the battle of Courtrai is disappointing; it is too short, and does not make enough of the remarkable victory won by relatively poorly armed burghers, albeit united together by a strong bond, against the sophisticated might of France. It is not sufficient to say that the Flemings were 'manly, well-armed, courageous and under expert leaders'; one could hope for better than that. None the less, over the years which he purports to cover, the Franciscan author, whose weakness lies not in gathering information but rather in his reluctance to engage in narrative, offers an intelligent account of an unusually important decade in Flemish history, in which the role played by war

in creating and encouraging a local patriotism and a sense of unity is
well brought out.

By the fourteenth century, however, we may perceive a greater will-
ingness to question why events turned out in the way they did. Jean le
Bel, for instance, not only described but analysed, too. His account of
the battle of Crécy attempts to take account of factors, such as the rain,
which may have had an effect upon a French army which, already
weary, arrived on the battlefield late in the day. Mistakes were then
made by the French leadership, which was influenced by the nobility's
desire to fight in spite of advice expressed to the contrary.[33] Nor were
the French willing to contemplate a retreat which might have saved
them. Roman military writings had allowed for the need to retreat in
order to fight another day. In the language of chivalry, however, retreat
spelt desertion and disgrace; it was better to suffer defeat than either
of these.

By the fifteenth century change was definitely in the air. The
chronicle whose story was founded on chivalric values, great deeds
and 'feats of arms', sometimes those of the leader, was beginning to
take on a secondary role. This significant change of emphasis lay in a
move away from the importance hitherto attached to the individual
towards an evolving view of the army as a whole and a growing appreciation of its role in war. By the second half of the fifteenth century
military history in Europe as a whole is coming to be written less in
terms of individual contributions to a particular outcome, more in
terms of what was being achieved by armies, namely by men, often
using different weapons, fighting together. This was the result of a
number of factors. One was the greater role being given to their armies
by nascent nation states and the care and money being accorded to
their development. Another was the growing importance of the part
played by archers who, forming the collective arm, fought in numbers
and killed anonymously from a distance. Yet another was the growing
appreciation of a central message of the classical military tradition,
conveyed in the works of such writers as Frontinus, Vegetius and others, whose doctrines were propagated in manuscript form right across
Europe and whose works would be among the first to be printed in the
'new age' to come. This tradition placed far greater emphasis on the
role to be played by armies, whose successes resulted from preparation, discipline and team-work (all these at the heart of the
classical message), which served to draw attention to their role in
the wars involving the Swiss and the Burgundians in the 1470s, in the

completion of the Spanish *reconquista* in the 1480s and in the Italian wars of the 1490s and early 1500s.

We observe this same shift in emphasis in England, too. The *Gesta Henrici Quinti* reflects both the traditional and the new. It is traditional in that the entire work is based on the theme of the king's determined leadership when he is obliged to pursue his quarrel with the duplicitous French by making war upon them: the conflict is presented as a just war fought by a commander of remarkable talent, whose personal contribution to the successes won by his country was enormous. It is new in the way that the author also emphasises the role of the army in the achievement of those successes. This is done in two different ways. The accounts of the battle of Agincourt and other encounters with the French allow the author to present the army not only as the immediate instrument of victory, but also as one arm of the nation at war (the other being the many left at home praying for victory as the king and his soldiers prepare to do battle). The needs of England are to be met by an identifiable force of Englishmen, those very same men who are later rewarded with a 'ticker-tape' welcome on their triumphal return to London. We are told, too, that Henry modestly disclaimed all credit for the victory, which he attributed to God.[34] This may have been a subtle and indirect way of underlining the fact that the victory had been a triumph for the army, and thus a triumph for England as a nation, just as the French nation had suffered shame, ridicule and dishonour from the defeat of its army and the capture of its king at Poitiers in 1356.[35]

Another characteristic of this author is his concern for the moral and physical well-being of the soldiers who make up the army. His understanding of the growing mental strain experienced by a force marching through hostile territory to an unknown future is brilliantly recorded in the text.[36] The author had witnessed the capture of Harfleur and joined the 6,000-strong army which Henry V led off to Calais, thought to be eight days' march away. At the start, a feeling of confidence prevailed even though it was suspected that a French army, not far away, was pressing ahead to cut off its opponents. After nearly a week, with Calais still many miles away, it was learned from prisoners that the ford across the Somme towards which the English were marching was guarded by the French. This serious blow was to be made worse by a rumour which spread through the English force that a large French army was waiting for Henry's 'little band' of men. The author has the English soldiers discussing the future: they are divided in their opinion of whether the French will dare to attack, granted the political problems which they are experiencing, and, if they are to do so, when and where the attack will come. The discussion suggests that the men were frightened, and their weariness and lack of provisions did not improve their state of mind. Morale plumetted, and it required all the king's skills of leadership to urge his men on, up the river Somme (at the head of which, rumour again had it, a mighty enemy army was awaiting them) before they could find a place at which to cross. That achieved, and the worst behind them, confidence returned, only to be suddenly shattered by signs of recent heavy troop movements on the road just ahead. The awful reality of the situation now hit them: a battle could no longer be avoided. As this began on the morrow, after a night spent in extreme discomfort, the king addressed his soldiers with words of encouragement. Only if one has read the remarkable account of the march to Agincourt can one fully understand that this was not an ordinary 'pep talk', but an address upon which the outcome of the coming battle could depend. Victory, the texts of both Maccabees and Vegetius agreed, lay not in numbers alone. Where they differed was in deciding what did count. For Maccabees, it was God who judged the outcome of battles; for Vegetius, victory was more likely to lie in the physical and mental condition, as well as in the practical skills, of those who took part. Preparation and readiness (which included being adaptable to physical conditions, as urged by Frontinus) were the factors most likely to bring success, which was not 'God-given' but 'man-won'.[37]

By the fourteenth century, and increasingly in the fifteenth century, attitudes to war – and, consequently, to the reporting of war – were changing. Traditionally, the battle of Courtrai marked a watershed: the dominance of the nobility, feudalism's military caste, had been broken, and it would not be long before men recognised that things would never to be the same again. Crécy proved how right they were. War was coming to be regarded in terms of the advantages, such as the conquest of land, the settlement of a territorial claim or the defence of economic interest (this last seen in the famous tract *The Libelle of Englyshe Polycye*, written about 1436),[38] which could be won or defended by the force wielded by armies (or navies). That view reflected the classical vision of the army as the nation (or state) in arms. It was influenced by the teaching of Vegetius, who had underlined the importance of having an army drawn from suitable persons: the army with which Edward IV regained his kingdom in 1471 was said to comprise 'well chosen' men.[39] It had to do with a growing awareness that war was an activity which increasingly involved whole communities, whole nations, which could be asked to contribute both money and service. In terms of the personnel of armies, the nobility as the shock troops were now being overtaken in effectiveness by such forces as the archers of England or, a little later, the squares of the Swiss Confederation. Nor should we ignore the influence which the development of cannon was to have on the conduct of war. Furthermore, as modern studies of societies at war have shown, war was coming to mean the active involvement of others than those who fought. The work of H.J. Hewitt on the organisation of fourteenth-century war proved that armies could do their work successfully only if they had proper logistical support.[40] The development of taxation, raised specifically for war with greater and greater regularity, was to give the population an interest in how its money was spent, so that we find, by the fourteenth century, a conscious effort on the part of government to keep the population of England informed about how war was going and, in particular, if any successes had been won. The voting and raising of subsidies, so vital for the pursuit of a successful military policy, was now clearly understood by the chroniclers to be an activity closely associated with war. Diplomacy, a further important development of the fourteenth century, was increasingly seen as part of waging war, as the chronicler Adam Murimuth, who had a particular interest in it, makes clear.[41] The wider use made of training in arms was actively encouraged by some European princes; in England, too, archery practice was also encouraged by royal order. In brief, the need to achieve victory, both on the field and around the diplomatic table, was becoming increasingly important. War was no longer (if, indeed, it had ever been) primarily a show, an opportunity to win glory and reputation. It was now coming to be fought by whole societies which experienced, and often suffered from, its activities. The changes in the perception and practice of war brought about as time advanced led to developments in its reporting: as war changed, so did the way men wrote about it. The fact that this happened should come as no surprise to us.

NOTES

1 *The Anglo-Saxon Chronicle*, trans. G.N. Garmonsway (1953), p. 111.

2 A. Gransden, *Historical Writing in England II: c. 1307 to the Early Sixteenth Century* (1982), pp. 14–15.

3 Ibid., p. 79.

4 *Gesta Henrici Quinti: The Deeds of Henry the Fifth*, trans. F. Taylor and J.S. Roskell (Oxford, 1975).

5 Gransden, *Historical Writing II*, pp. 84–85.

6 P.F. Ainsworth, *Jean Froissart and the Fabric of History: Truth, Myth, and Fiction in the 'Chroniques'* (Oxford, 1990), ch. 4. Chroniclers also made use of letters and reports sent home by those on campaign: see K.A. Fowler, 'News from the Front: Letters and Despatches of the Fourteenth Century' in *Guerre et Société en France, en Angleterre et en Bourgogne, XIVe–XVe siècle*, eds P. Contamine, C. Giry-Deloison and M.H. Keen (Lille, 1991), p. 77.

7 *Annales Gandenses: Annals of Ghent*, ed. and trans. H. Johnstone (Oxford, 1985), p. 1.

8 Froissart, *Chronicles*, ed. and trans. G. Brereton (Harmondsworth, 1968), p. 37. The reader is also referred to another statement of intent contained in *The Unconquered Knight: A Chronicle of the Deeds of Don Pero Niño, Count of Buelna, by his Standard-Bearer, Gutierre Díaz de Gamez (1431–1449)*, trans. J. Evans (1928), pp. 1–15.

9 Ainsworth, *Jean Froissart*, pp. 77–78, 124, 142, and references there to other works.

10 Gransden, *Historical Writing II*, p. 68.

11 Ibid., p. 60.

12 *The Anonimalle Chronicle 1333 to 1381*, ed. V.H. Galbraith (Manchester, 1970), p. 63.

13 Ibid., p. 34.

14 *The Chronicle of Lanercost 1272–1346*, trans. H. Maxwell (Glasgow, 1913), pp. 194–95, 198, 200, 205, 210, 216–17 etc.

15 Gransden, *Historical Writing II*, pp. 80–83.

16 N. Chareyron, *Jean le Bel: Le Maître de Froissart, Grand Imagier de la Guerre de Cent Ans*, Bibliothèque du Moyen Age, vol. 7 (Brussels, 1996), p. 105. The difficulty was well expressed by the duke of Wellington in a letter written from Paris on 8 August 1815: 'The history of a battle is not unlike the history of a ball. Some individuals may recollect all the little events of which the great result is the battle won or lost; but no individual can recollect the order in which, or the exact moment at which, they occurred, which makes all the difference as to their value or importance.' See *The Dispatches of Field Marshal the Duke of Wellington during his Various Campaigns in India, Denmark, Portugal, Spain, the Low Countries, and France*, ed. Colonel [J.] Gurwood (1852), vol. 8, p. 231. I owe this reference to Michael Johnstone.

17 *The St Albans Chronicle 1406–1420*, ed. V.H. Galbraith (Oxford, 1937), pp. 94–96. The author cites quotations from the works of Virgil, Lucan, Persius and Statius.

18 *'La Vie du Prince Noir' by Chandos Herald*, ed. D.B. Dyson (Tübingen, 1975).

19 Gransden, *Historical Writing II*, ch. 7, 'The Biographies of Henry V'.

20 The idea was accepted throughout the middle ages. An example 'The French

had possession of the place of slaughter, as God granted them because of the nation's sins' comes from the *Anglo-Saxon Chronicle* for 1066 (see note 1), p. 199.

21 Macc. 3.19, cited, for example, in *Chronicle of Lanercost*, p. 140.

22 *Gesta Stephani*, index *sub* 'God'.

23 *Anonimalle Chronicle*, pp. 27, 38.

24 'Volente Domino et adversante fortuna quae bellorum ambiguos dat eventus'. See *The Chronicle of Jean de Venette*, trans. J. Birdsall, ed. R.A. Newhall (New York, 1953), p. 64.

25 *Gesta Stephani*, pp. 2–3.

26 Idem.

27 Ibid., pp. 6–7. Vegetius' teaching, 'Qui desirat pacem, praeparet bellum', is in his *De re militari*, III, prologue.

28 *Gesta Stephani*, pp. 8–9.

29 Ibid., pp. 33, 91, 109, 147–49.

30 Ibid., p. 69.

31 Ibid., p. 39.

32 Ibid., pp. 184–85.

33 Chareyron, *Jean le Bel*, pp. 108–10.

34 *Gesta Henrici Quinti*, pp. 112–13.

35 F. Autrand, 'La déconfiture. La bataille de Poitiers (1356) à travers quelques textes français des XIVe et XVe siècles', in *Guerre et société en France*, p. 97.

36 *Gesta Henrici Quinti*, pp. 61–79.

37 Compare the text in Maccabees (cited note 21 and related text, above) with that in Vegetius, *De re militari*, I, i: 'In omni autem proelio non tam multitudo et virtus indocta quam ars et exercitium solent praestare victoriam.'

38 *The Libelle of Englyshe Polycye. A Poem on the Use of Sea-Power, 1436*, ed. G.F. Warner (Oxford, 1926).

39 *The Historie of the Arrivall of Edward IV in England and the Finall Recouerye of his Kingdomes from Henry VI. A. D. M.CCCC.LXXI*, ed. J. Bruce, Camden Society (1838), p. 1.

40 H.J. Hewitt, *The Organization of War under Edward III, 1338–62* (Manchester, 1966).

41 Gransden, *Historical Writing II*, p. 64.

The Naming of Battlefields in the Middle Ages[1]

Philip Morgan

> *King.* What is this castle call'd that stands hard by?
> *Herald.* They call it Agincourt.
> *King.* Then call we this the field of Agincourt.[2]

Why do battles receive the proper names by which they are known? The subject of this paper might seem to pose a question to which there is a self-evident answer, and one which Shakespeare had indeed provided in *Henry V.* According to the French chronicler Enguerrand de Monstrelet, the King had added that 'since all battles ought to bear the name of the fortress nearest to where they were fought, this battle shall, from henceforth, bear the ever-endurable name of Agincourt'.[3] Are battle names then mere locatives? Was it chance that Agincourt was not Maisoncelle, the village to which Henry retired after the battle, or Tramecourt, the village to the east, whose lords were responsible for the present-day memorial on the site and an earlier eighteenth-century chapel?[4] What weight, however, are we to place on Monstrelet's phrase 'ever-endurable name'? Why do some names endure and others pass away? Is there significance to be found in the matter of battlefield naming?[5]

The royal chaplain and author of the *Gesta Henrici Quinti*, who, as we know, was present at the rear during the battle of Agincourt, noted that the French had taken up a position 'in that field called the field of Agincourt'.[6] What is surely implicit here is that the battle site lay, either administratively or economically, within the territory of Agincourt. The 'allegiance' of the field before the event, rather than the royal fiat, determined the name; the battle, as it were, accommodated itself to the existing landscape of authority within which it was fought. Whether the battle derived its name in consequence of the lordship of the site or the extempore political will of the victor, we ought perhaps to recognise the possibility of some discourse, both in its creation and in its perpetuation. Names, as philologists and anthropologists have learned, are seldom accidental and rarely trivial; frequently the ritual encoded a historical meaning.[7] Battle names became self-sufficient and were parasitical on existing knowledge. In medieval sources lists of the names of battles, like those of kings, popes and emperors, from the twelve battles which Arthur fought against the English to those of the Wars of the Roses, needed no accompanying annal or narrative.

NAMES AND MEMORY

What exactly is a battle? Most medieval battlefields are what might be termed accidental landscapes. In cultural terms, they embody patterns of accepted ritual behaviour which culminate in particular places and in particular actions. For medieval chroniclers these ritual actions assumed the status of events to which proper names might be given largely because they so readily illustrated and explained the biblical model of divine authority and intervention and might do service as chronological markers.[8] Not all 'events' which comprised the characteristic range of ritual actions were accorded battle names, whilst others, as a consequence of their proximity, either in space or time, were assimilated by the larger name of an apparently more significant event. Thus, the battle and its name form part of a narrative discourse into which a series of facts and a particular landscape were subsumed. The events of the civil war in England in 1321–22 are a case in point. Whilst there were sieges in Kent and Shropshire, the movement of arms in half a dozen counties or more, and violent exchanges at Burton-on-Trent and Boroughbridge within days of each other, there was only one battle.[9] In the legal enquiries which followed actions at Burton-on-Trent the clerks talked of events 'after the defeat of the king's enemies', in the 'time of the conflict' or 'when the earl of Lancaster was able to flee'.[10] But it was Boroughbridge which became the battle name which, with the capture and execution of Thomas of Lancaster, encapsulated the prophetic and moral climax to the war. The process has left modern historians struggling with a range of labels such as 'skirmish' or 'preliminary engagement' to explain violent conflicts which were not accorded the status of events by medieval writers.

There is equally a persistent belief that the impact of battles on the physical landscape was a passing one. As George Bannatyne (1545–1608) observed:

We travelled in the print of olden wars;
  Yet all the land was green;
  And love we found, and peace,
  Where fire and war had been.

They pass and smile, the children of the sword –
  No more the sword they wield;
  And O, how deep the corn
  Along the battlefield!

What has been recognised anew, it is frequently suggested, is an indefinable aura. Dr Andrew Brown, the English Heritage inspector for the *Register of Battlefields* established in 1994, describes it thus: 'Battle fields may not be as obviously "presentable" as castles or abbeys, but they do create feelings of contemplation and empathy with visitors.' Of the site of the battle of Blore Heath, fought in 1459, the site whose proposed loss was the catalyst for the list, English Heritage observed, 'take away the corn and the cows, and a piece of history almost 550 years old stretches out before you.' A wider cultural landscape has become a site with definable limits.

The ambition to mark battlefields as special places or sites of memory is thus also assumed to be a peculiarly modern one.[11] However, whilst the literature on medieval war memorials is meagre, it is evident that memorialisation, including battlefield war memorials, was common.[12] Of the fate of the field at Agincourt Monstrelet reports that Philippe, comte de Charolois, commissioned the construction and consecration of a 25-yard-square hedged enclosure to accommodate the burial of the French dead whose corpses had not been recovered from the field.[13] Of an uncleared and perhaps unadopted battlefield, Orderic Vitalis records what may be an early example of battlefield tourism. Of the battle of Stamford bridge in 1066, in an account written half a century later, he wrote, 'Travellers cannot fail to recognize the field, for a great mountain of dead men's bones still lies there and bears witness to the terrible slaughter on both sides'.[14]

The name of the battle encapsulates the meaning of the event, but remains one element, alongside the fate of the landscape of the battle and the developing narrative of the battle as it appears in the written record, in the construction of the historical memory of that event. Historians have, on the whole, left the study of battle narratives to military historians, whose interests centre on the reconstruction of the battle as an event, have underestimated the degree to which medieval battle landscapes continued to be significant places, and have paid little or no attention to the process of naming.[15]

It is the contention of this paper that the appearance of battlefield names followed a process of negotiation, a discourse which ultimately represents the will to control the memory of an event.[16] The existence of alternative, perhaps even competing, names could be evidence of that discourse. Indeed, it could be argued that all three elements – the name of the battle; its physical and cultural landscape; and the ensuing narrative discourse – were each constructed to convey a memory of the act of conquest. Often, inevitably, the ambition was articulated by the state or its predecessor authorities, or on its behalf by its agents. The vocabulary of battle names is more often than not an official one for the historical landscapes of war are, as Petri Raivo has noted, a fundamental part of the national iconography. Battle sites and battle names remain visible because they embody a system of symbols and codes which evoke meaning. Contrariwise, of course, battles whose names have become invisible (and I shall return to the question of lost battles) have ceased to play a significant part in the dominant iconography.

Let me extrapolate from two modern cases in which the official impulse was explicit. During the Great War Max Hoffmann reportedly advised General Luddendorff, shortly after the Russian army on the Eastern front had been smashed in 1914, to address his victory dispatch not from his headquarters at Frögenau but from the nearby village of Tannenberg. The decision was to provide an emblematic reversal for the defeat of the Teutonic knights at Tannenberg at the hands of the Slavs in 1410.[17]

At the same moment in England the process was, of course, undertaken by resort to a committee, a War Office Battlefield Nomenclature Committee, whose deliberations speak of a profound continuity in the concerns which informed the naming of battlefields.[18] The committee rejected double-barrelled names, which, whilst there were 'advantages of the moment' (in 1920), were inconsistent with the tradition of 'practice of English historians or among the battle honours of British regiments' and, significantly, would be 'the only course likely to ensure the general adoption of the *official* name' [my emphasis]. The committee also considered calendar names, for example 1 July or 21 March, but rejected these too, on the grounds that 'historical precedent … proves that dates, although frequently used in contemporary writings, have not persisted in practice, but have always been replaced eventually by "*local*" names' [my emphasis again]. The committee recognised that official attempts to control nomenclature might be frustrated and regarded 'official adoption' of names 'which have become familiar to the British public, as well as the troops' as essential. 'The nomenclature adopted by the enemy', it was added frostily, 'has also been noted'.

It is evident that the committee (which early in its deliberations rejected the prospect of collecting individual officers' testimony) did not see itself as a novelty, but merely as a formalisation of past practice. It was important to situate this pattern of nomenclature 'in a longer historical context', for the armies in Flanders, as the footnote to the 1918 campaign put it, had fought in an honourable tradition:

> 'Compare Chaucer:
>
>> With him ther was his sonne, a yonge sqyer ...
>> Of twenty year he was of age, I gesse ...
>> And he had been some tyme in chivalrye [*sic*]
>> In Flandres in Artoys and in Picardie'

The concepts of 'official' and 'local' names remain useful.

THE TYPOLOGY OF BATTLEFIELD NAMES

Whilst battlefield names are recognised as part of a discourse of memory, they are also capable of bearing a more routine empirical analysis. They can be classified and organised. What follows is a preliminary attempt at a typology and a chronology of names. Battlefield names may be topographic, toponymic or iconic. For example, the earliest name for the battle of Bannockburn in 1314, *y polles*, 'the pows' or 'the burns', is a reference to the topography of the battlefield, a landscape crossed by streams or burns; whilst that for the battle of Tewkesbury in 1471 refers to the adjacent place or toponym. The third category is, of course, the broadest and might include, as an exemplar, the battle of 'palme sonday felde', a variant for the battle of Towton in 1461 derived from the timing of the battle rather than a local field-name.[19]

An iconic name may be descriptive but is also used to convey an added meaning, often from a cultural, religious or political echo. For example, the battle of Rouvray on 12 February 1429, in which Sir John Fastolf repelled a French force attempting to disrupt a convoy of salt fish en route to the English army at Orleans, is usually known as the battle of the Herrings. As Jean de Waurin noted, 'the said conflict from that day forward was commonly named the battle of the Herrings … because a great part of the waggons of the said English were loaded with herrings and other victuals for Lent'.[20] In this category it is evident that some topographic or toponymic names were used because of their iconic significance. The battle of Mortimer's Cross, fought within the parish of Kingsland near East Hereford in 1461, may have been so named from its proximity to a cross which coincidentally bore the name of the victorious Yorkist leader Edward Mortimer, earl of March. Similarly, the battle of Durham (1346), originally named from the adjacent toponym, may early have become Neville's Cross from a topographical feature at the centre of the English army, in allusion to two of the English knights, Sir Ralph Neville and Sir John Neville.[21]

Iconic names, especially those which did not embody a toponym, might prove susceptible to decay, and had either to be firmly embedded in the national iconography, or else adopted by a vigorous patron. The evidence for the battle of the Standard in 1138, named from an improvised Christian structure erected at the centre of the battlefield, illustrates both the perils and the possibilities. The principal early chronicle source is that of Richard of Hexham, a homiletic account of the campaign which paid particular attention to the emergence of the battle name.[22] Hexham's prophetic tone is rendered explicit in his characterisation of the two armies. David, king of Scots' army was revealed as heathen; two of his soldiers had plundered an oratory of Hexham priory but were driven mad. By contrast, King Stephen's northern English army declined to fight during Lent and accepted from Archbishop Thurstan of York an offer of the service of the 'priests of his diocese, bearing crosses … to march with them to battle', together with his archiepiscopal cross and the standard of St Peter. Two miles from Northallerton 'some of them soon erected, in the centre of a frame which they brought, the mast of a ship, to which they gave the name of the Standard … On the top of this pole they hung a silver pyx containing the host, and the banner of St Peter the Apostle, and John of Beverley and Wilfrid of Ripon'. Hexham also suggested that the ground of the battle had been divinely selected, observing that 'only the ground on which the battle was fought was the possession of St. Cuthbert, the whole surrounding district being owned by others: and this occurred not by design of the combatants, but by the dispensation of Providence.' That the battle was never known as the battle of Northallerton is perhaps one of the most successful examples of the effective creation of historical memory.

The continuing success of the battle name was ensured by the role which the narrative played in framing the matter of the North and the Border in the middle ages, but also by continuing recourse to the saintly banners which had been employed at the battle of the Standard. The church at Beverley may have played a significant role. In the *miracula* of St John of Beverley, compiled *c.* 1180, the use of the banner was perhaps retrospectively identified with Aethelstan's conquest of the Forth region.[23] By 1266 it had been accepted that when the Yorkshire levies were summoned to the royal army one man from the church at Beverley would muster carrying the saint's banner; the custom is known to have been followed in 1296, 1300 and 1310, 1312 and 1314 (though presumably without success in the year of Bannockburn), and later under Edward III and Henry IV. Agincourt was fought and won on 25 October, the feast of the saint's translation, a fact no doubt uppermost in Henry V's mind when he visited the shrine in 1420.[24]

Of course not all such enterprises were deliberate, and many were unsuccessful. The early name of Towton in 1461, 'palme sonday felde', was not widely adopted. Direct divine intervention was attributed to all battles; the bloody interruption of the Christian calendar was rarer, although a decade later Barnet was fought on Easter Sunday itself. The success of the name for the battle of the Standard was therefore more securely founded in concepts of regional identity and monastic lordship.

Behind most battle names a range of alternative and in some cases contested names are to be observed. Towton is, as well as 'Palme Sonday felde called York felde', also the 'bataill at Shirbourne beside Yorke'.[25] The battle of Edgecote in 1469 was also Banbury Field.[26] The examples are legion and in most cases might be suspected as documenting the pattern of actions before the emergence of the event and its site. In some cases, however, alternative names are to be seen as idiosyncratic scholarship. In the late fifteenth century William Worcester was calling the battle of St Albans in 1455, 'le jorney de wenlyngg', perhaps intending *waetlingceaster*, an anachronistic name for St Albans, rather as a few modern historians, to tease their peers and bemuse their readers, prefer the battle of Dadlington to Bosworth.[27] In other cases later antiquarian and historical energies have foisted erroneous names on readers, subtly contributing to the continuing discourse on the site.

The engagement at Empingham on 12 May 1470 seems to have received no name from contemporaries other than the topographical description applied to the attainder of Richard, Lord Welles, which recorded his treason as having taken place 'in a field called Hornefeld in Empyngham'.[28] Another field or parcel called 'Losecoat' field, from Old English *hlose-cot*, 'pigsty cottage', seems to have been the source for a local tradition, unrecorded before the early nineteenth century, that the name referred to the fact that the defeated Lancastrians had cast their liveries aside to escape detection after the battle.[29] It remains the battle of Losecoat field or Empingham, complete with explanations of the contemptuous appellation as contemporary, in most modern scholarship. Likewise, the naval battle off Winchelsea in 1350 is frequently reported as the battle of Espagnols sur Mer, possibly a précis of Froissart's description 'Ceste bataille sus mer des Espagnolz et des Engles'; but I can find no contemporary chronicler who uses this battle name.[30]

Historians have generally been interested in these contested or competing names as evidence for the precise location of a battle, rather than as part of the discourse of memory. Geoffrey Barrow has, for instance, followed the emergence of names for the battle of Bannockburn in 1314.[31] He argues convincingly that the name Bannockburn referred to a locality of dispersed settlement from which a local stream or burn took its name, and that the name was applied to the battle fought across its ground. Aside from sources which give the battle no name at all (a characteristic to which I shall shortly turn), and which included the *Vita Edwardi Secundi*, or those which are topographic, including *y polles*, 'the pows' or 'the burns', of the Welsh *Brut y Tywysogion*, there are two distinct traditions. The early English sources almost invariably call the engagement the battle of Stirling. These include both London chronicles, the *Annales Paulini* and the *Annales Londonienses*; the verse of the captive English poet, Robert Baston; and provincial authors like the Cistercian monk at Croxden in Staffordshire.[32] By contrast, the Scottish sources tend to call it the battle of Bannok or Bannockburn. The battle name is thus the name imposed by the victors. The discourse, like that of the battle of the Standard, may be more complex. A considerable part of the debate concerning the site of Bannockburn has arisen as a result of confusion about the meaning of the topographical names, including Bannockburn, with much debate on the inhospitable nature of the terrain. Is it conceivable that the adoption of the Scottish name was eased by a discourse which emphasised the difficult landscape to which the English army had been drawn?

THE PROCESS OF NAMING

Is it possible to suggest a chronology of naming and thus to provide a general explanation for the variety of battle names applied even to a single event? I would suggest a threefold process. In the first phase the battle is not perceived as a historical event and thus receives no name at all. Almost by definition, some actions are not accorded the status of an event in the subsequent historical discourse and remain unnamed. In the second phase there is commonly a process of competition or negotiation in which alternative names, including local topographic and toponymic names coined by participants and close observers, exist simultaneously, often in administrative records but also in narrative accounts. In the final phase the official or historical name comes to dominate the memory of the event. Implicitly there is occasionally a fourth phase in which the names, official or not, become lost or redundant.

Early records of battle names include contemporary narrative accounts, but also a plethora of administrative instruments of a private and public nature. The routine absence of battle names in both types of record is instructive. Although the author of the *Vita Edwardi Secundi*, writing his account of Bannockburn within a year or so of the battle, clearly regards the engagement as a significant event he gives it no name.[33] Two letters written to Francesco di Marco Datini's company in Florence, on 28 July and 9 August 1403, give no name to the battle of Shrewsbury, which had been fought on 21 July, nor any indication as to where it had been fought; with the urgency of foreign correspondents Domenico Caccini and Piero Cambini simply announced, 'have you heard the big news in this country'.[34] Although these and other battles are commonly unnamed, the character of the event as encompassing a specific site is often communicated by use of words like 'field' or by toponymic directions.

A signet letter of Edward IV in favour of the widow of a Dartford hosier shortly after the battle of Towton in 1461 spoke of him as having been 'slayn in our last feld in the northe parties'.[35] The earlier of the Datini letters on the battle of Shrewsbury likewise describes the Percies as having risen 'in the field' and their defeat having left 'their field broken', *rotto lor champo*. In these contexts the word 'field' would appear to encompass a range of meanings appropriate to the nature of a battle site, deriving in part from the *antebellum* and *postbellum* rituals routinely enacted, and in part from the necessity of securing possession of the field as evidence of victory.[36] Even unnamed battles may have become sites. The sense of the field as a specific site is also conveyed in the earliest narratives. The *Anglo-Saxon Chronicle* uses the word *wælstowe*, 'the place of slain', to denote battlefields: of the battle of Fulford, which it does not name, it is noted that 'the Norwegians had possession of the place of the slain'. The same phrase is used to conclude its discussion of Hastings.[37]

Naval battles were, it seems, particularly susceptible to remaining unnamed or, rather, failing to achieve the status of historical events. During the Hundred Years War only Sluys in 1340, Winchelsea in 1350, La Rochelle in 1372 and Harfleur in 1416 seem to have acquired status as battle names.[38] They may, however, have shared other features of the naming process, notably in the use of local names. The Leicester chronicler Henry Knighton called Sluys 'bellum apud Grongne', probably in reference to the long sea-bank on the west side of the estuary.[39] A well-known fifteenth-century polemical verse on the wisdom of effective control of the sea reflected on the example of 'the bataylle of Sluce the may rede every day', but most engagements remained anonymous or else were described in such stock phrases as *bellum navale in mari*.[40] As a result, incidents such as the destruction of a Franco-Castilian fleet off Margate on 24 March 1387 or the Earl of Warwick's three anonymous naval engagements in 1458, described by John Jerningham to Margaret Paston, although not accorded a name, as 'so gret a batayle upon the se this xl wyntyr', did not resonate in historical discourse, and the importance of naval warfare remained underestimated.[41]

Where battles were not named it was routine to include some toponymic pointers to location. Thus, the household expenses of Sir Henry Stafford on the day of the battle of Barnet, 14 April 1471, recorded the purchase of beer *apud la feld iuxta Barnet*.[42] The naval battle of Winchelsea in 1350 was *in mari iuxta Wynchelse*, whilst the earlier battle of Sluys in 1340 was described as *lieu de l'Escluse*; *devant l'Escluze*; *in conflictu enim stantes in ripa maris Flandrenses*; and *bellum navale apud Sluzam in aqua de Swyn*.[43] It is a moot point whether prepositions such as *apud*, *prope* and *juxta*, which seem to predominate in the earliest records and seem to be directional rather than nominal, and their final replacement by *bellum de* ... can be seen as significant clues in the chronology of the emergence of official battle names.[44] They are, however, most common in that phase when battles were known by a variety of names, many of which are topographically precise but redundant for orientation beyond the immediate locality. These, one suspects, are the names in common parlance amongst participants and observers of the battle and were used in its immediate aftermath.

Peter Foss has examined the variety of such names as they were applied to the battle of Bosworth in 1485.[45] The earliest, a York council report, records the battle on 'the feld of Redemore', duly enrolled in the York City House Book as *apud Redemore Juxta Leicestre.* 'Brownehethe', *bellum Miravallenses,* 'Sandeford' and 'Dadlyngton field' appear in other records. The official name, Bosworth, he adduces, 'did not emerge until twenty-five years after the event'. Foss suggests that premeditated encounters were often drawn to the waste margins of settlements, where there were fewer significant or recognisable locations, and that this allowed the emergence of Bosworth as the battle name.[46] However, the modest and ultimately unsuccessful investment of funds in a battlefield chantry at Dadlington church and the rise of a narrative discourse, exemplified inter alia by the tradition of Stanley versification in the Ballad of Bosworth Field, must equally have been important in the rise of the official name.[47]

This general hypothesis is confirmed by consideration of other battles, although the relationship between official and local names could vary. At Bosworth a novel official name had overwhelmed a range of weakly recognised local names. For Shrewsbury (21 July 1403) a number of local names seem to have existed alongside the official name for at least a century, whilst at Hastings (14 October 1066), as perhaps also at Bosworth, an official name had divorced the event from its site, although the site continued to be of great significance.

The battle of Shrewsbury was fought across the fields of the townships of Harlescott, Albright Hussey and Albright Lee to the north of the town on 21 July 1403. As we have seen, the earliest letters do not name the battle, but a variety of local names appear in early administrative records and those chronicles which seem to incorporate oral testimony. A royal wardrobe clerk noted that a servant had lost a horse *in campis de hynsifeld prope salopiam die belli,* the Dieulacres chronicler that Percy's army was deployed *in campo de Harlescote vocato vulgariter le Oldfelde;* whilst grants to the battlefield chantry college established on the site *c.* 1406 describe a two-acre field in the lordship of Albright Hussey called Hateleyfield.[48] A somewhat later chancery inquisition in 1415 adds *bellum de Bolefield,* 'the battle of Bull Field', in the township of Harlescott.[49]

Despite competition from four local variants, the official name was established fairly quickly. The king had written to his confessor, Philip Repingdon, on the day of the battle, speaking of his delivery *magno bello in campo Salopie*.[50] The Duchy of Lancaster clerks who entered the details of grants for good and loyal service to maimed and robbed soldiers at first glossed the event as *la bataille qe ceo fuist iatarde ioust nostre ville de salop*, but by the close of the year were calling it *la bataill de Salop*.[51] Given the proximity of the town, its recent history as a parliamentary venue and its importance as a base in operations against Owain Glyn Dŵr, this was perhaps unsurprising. More significant is the degree to which the local names continued to be refined in the ensuing historical discourse.

Adam Usk, writing his account of Shrewsbury in 1414, implicitly renamed the battle, calling it 'a fearsome assault ... at a place called Berwick, where the king later founded a hospital for the souls of those who had fallen there'.[52] Usk's 'battle of Berwick' did in fact draw upon a story current amongst contemporaries, and reported first by Thomas Walsingham, that Sir Henry Percy had called for his favourite sword at the outset of the battle and, on being told that it had been left in the nearby township of Berwick, recalled, ashen-faced, a prophecy that he would die at Berwick.[53] Many chronicle accounts of the battle also introduced the event by reference to the comet which had strikingly appeared in the skies in March 1402; for those, especially in Wales and the March, drawn to such prophetic discourse, Berwick continued to be important. To it was also added the reference to Bull Field, a name which could be accommodated to the Galfridian tradition of prophetic writing, in which people appeared under animal names.[54] Unusually, the dating of the battle by reference to the calendar of saints, in Welsh and Marcher sources the feast of St Praxedes and in others the eve of St Mary Magdalene, also remained a crucial element in battle narratives and annalistic entries. As a result Bull Field and Berwick, with their stellar and liturgical markers, continued to provide prophetic and iconic nuances to narrative writing on the battle alongside the official name throughout the century. For the author of Laud MS Miscellaneous 748, collecting annals with numerological and astrological significance, Shrewsbury was 'Bellum Salopie [*interlined* in Schrobbisbury] in campo vocato Haitlefeld alias Berwykfeld [*interlined* prope Salopiam].'[55] The account was preceded by that other battle fought under the influence of a comet, and whose changing nomenclature is also significant, Hastings.

Like Shrewsbury, Hastings generated a number of local names, 'at the old apple tree' of the *Anglo-Saxon Chronicle* and 'a place whose early name was Senlac' in Orderic Vitalis' history among them.[56] Others were collected during the twelfth century in the chronicle of Battle abbey, the memorial church founded by William on the site and for which the name *La Batailge* was first coined.[57] These included the site where William's cavalry mustered, *ad locum collis qui Hechelande dicitur, a parte Hastingarum situm* ('the hill called Hedgland which lies towards Hastings'), an 'enormous untilled field', and the *postbellum* name for a deep pit in which many of the Norman army perished at the close of the battle, *quod quidem baratrum sortito ex accidenti vocabulo Malfossed* ('This deep pit has been named for the accident, and today it is called Malfosse').[58] So central were the battle and its site to the iconography of the abbey that the original five monks clearly studied the topography with particular care, perhaps even attempting some battlefield archaeology.[59] Nowhere in the chronicle is it called the battle of Hastings. However, although some of the early sources gave no name to the battle, it is evident that the official name was coined soon after the event and quickly gained dominance. On the Bayeux Tapestry William's army left Hastings *et venerunt ad prelium contra haroldum rege*; but in Domesday Book it is already *bellum de hastinges*.[60]

No other battle site and name have generated so much interest; few can have had so continuous a history of pilgrimage. The bitter debate between Edward Freeman, who declared, 'I restore its true ancient name of Senlac' (and who, to be fair, contributed none of the bitterness), and J.H. Round, who countered, 'I make an earnest appeal to all who may write or teach history to adhere to the "true ancient name" of the battle of Hastings, and to reject henceforward an innovation which was uncalled for, misleading, and wrong,' confirms, if nothing else, the continuing iconic significance of battle names.[61] Both men recognised that the site of the battle was a relatively unexploited territory, and each cited the *Carmen de Hastingae Proelio*; 'there was a hill near the forest and a neighbouring valley and the ground was untilled because of its roughness'.[62] Within that landscape, bearing the name 'sand-stream' or 'sand-water-course' from Old English *sand, lacu*, there emerged Battle abbey, the largest and most successful of English battlefield chantries, its planned town and a surrounding dependent territory (*leuga*).[63] At the same time, as neither Freeman nor Round would recognise in their search for the 'right' name, a discourse had established both local and official battle names.

If the name of the battle acts as an encoded symbol then, as the name of the battle of Hastings demonstrates, it may act in part divorced from its site. The Arthurian battles of Badon Hill and Camlann also come to mind. However, where the site and the name become separated, the name is also vulnerable to the erosion of the discourse of the dominant ideology. I am thinking here of battles such as *Brunanburh*, fought in 937, or *Assandun*, fought in 1016, although there are many others. It is possible that the loss of the dominant ideology in 1066 encouraged the disappearance of the signs and symbols of Anglo-Saxon kingship; it is surely noteworthy that pre-conquest battles fared less well than early saints' cults, many of which were embellished and expanded. Yet battle names after 1066 were also prone to erosion and loss. The site of a 'skirmish' during the rising of 1075, placed by the Worcester chronicler near Cambridge and *in campo qui Fagaduna dicitur* in Orderic Vitalis' history, was quickly lost, although it has now been identified with the estate called 'Chaler's Maner' in Whaddon (Cambs.).[64]

In the case of *Brunanburh* the loss of the site occurred in spite of the panegyric poem on the battle, composed probably during the reign of Aethelstan's successor and younger brother, Edmund I, and added to the *Anglo-Saxon Chronicle* before 946.[65] A generation or so later Aethelweard noted that it was still called 'the great battle' by the common people, but knowledge of the battle site was already dimming. In the poem the defeated Norsemen fled across *Dingesmere*, possibly a poetic or figurative name for the Irish Sea ('the water which is named after the river Dee'); later sources preserved by the Durham chronicler Simeon called it *Weondune*; and the *Annals of Clonmacnoise* add 'the plaines of othlynn', perhaps meaning 'up to the Lyme', a regional name in Cheshire, cited as the county's eastern boundary in the charter of earl Ranulf III.[66] This mixture of topographical and iconic names will now be a familiar one. However, whilst the identification of the *Brunanburh* of the poem with the modern toponym Bromborough, represented uniquely by the Cheshire place of that name, is uncontested, the erosion of historical discourse in the middle ages allowed some 30 candidates to figure, first in antiquarian studies and later in scholarly debate.[67] Ignoring the toponym, Michael Wood argued for a site in the territory between Northumbria and Mercia south-west of Doncaster as being most likely; although the candidacy of Bromborough in the Wirral has recently been reasserted by Nick Higham.[68] Nevertheless, *Brunanburh* seems set to remain in that historical limbo of unlocated names and events which historians and others denote by italicisation.

In the case of *Assandun* the loss included the battlefield memorial church founded by Cnut in 1020, a 'cenotaph of national significance', although Warwick Rodwell has recently provided a compelling argument in favour of Ashdon, south-east of Cambridge.[69] Rodwell's review of antiquarian arguments in support of other sites raises some interesting questions about the nature of lost, or even unadopted, battle names and sites. It is as if lost or decaying battle sites and names return to that second phase of naming, the local arena. Much the greater volume of scholarship on battle sites and names is to be found amongst that which might be said to be motivated by place loyalty. This too may have its own history. The final great Welsh assault on Cheshire in 1146 was met close to the modern county boundary at Wych Brook and is described in the *Annales Cestrienses* as *apud Wichum*.[70] The decay of memory of the site and the name allowed a Cheshire witness at the Scrope–Grosvenor hearings in the 1380s to attribute the battle to Nantwich and identify one of his ancestors as a participant and beneficiary of comital gratitude.[71]

Did the local memory of events persist, the sites of local battles memorialised in the battle steads and fields, and the 'bloody meadows'? Many must refer to the sites of judicial combats or fields subject to such trials, and even to the colour of the soil, rather than to some lost battle. On occasion they do provide the fossil relics of local naming. The field name 'battle riggs' seems to me to be compelling in the sweepstake for the site of the battle of Otterburn in 1388.[72] But of the names of battles in general it might be said that they 'have makers, authors, readers and spectators, who both produce and re-produce the cultural and historic signifying processes attached to them'.[73]

NOTES

1 In memory of John McNeal Dodgson, who inspired.

2 *Henry V*, Act iv, scene vii.

3 *The Chronicles of Enguerrand de Monstrelet*, trans. Thomas Johnes, 2 vols (1867), vol. 1, p. 343.

4 R. Hawley Jarman, *Crispin's Day: The Glory of Agincourt* (1979), p. 180.

5 I am indebted to Petri Raivo of the University of Oulu for his discussions of

this subject, and to the audience at Chester for their valuable suggestions, several which I have tried to incorporate here.

6 *Gesta Henrici Quinti*, eds F. Taylor and J.S. Roskell (Oxford, 1975), pp. 80–81.

7 M. Gelling, *Place-Names in the Landscape* (1984), 'Introduction', pp. 1–9; S. Smith-Bannister, *Names and Naming Patterns in England 1538–1700* (Oxford, 1997).

8 N. Chareyron, *Jean le Bel: Le Maître de Froissart, Grand Imagier de la Guerre de Cent Ans*, Bibliothèque du Moyen Age, vol. 7 (Brussels, 1996), ch. 2, 'Batailles du siè-cle: spectacle ou explication?'

9 N.M. Fryde, *The Tyranny and Fall of Edward II* (1979), pp. 37–57.

10 PRO, Just 1/1389 mm. 1, 4v, 6v, *post discomfituram inimicorum regis*; *tempore con-flictionis*; *comes Lancastrie apud Burton brugge posuisset se in fugam*. Interestingly, Burton Bridge was a 'proposed unregistered candidate' for the English Heritage register of historic battlefields, but rejected as a 'skirmish' in which 'only a small proportion of armies [were] engaged'; *Battlefields: The Proposed Register of Historic Battlefields* (English Heritage, September 1994).

11 J. Carman, 'Bloody Meadows: The Places of Battle', in *The Familiar Past: Archaeologies of Later Historical Britain*, eds S. Tarlow and S. West (1999), pp. 233–45; M. Warnke, *Political Landscape: The Art History of Nature* (1994), p. 62.

12 A. Borg, 'Some Medieval War Memorials', in *Medieval Architecture and its Intel-lectual Context*, eds E. Fernie and P. Crossley (1990), pp. 1–7; E.M. Hallam, 'Monas-teries as "War Memorials": Battle Abbey and La Victoire', in *Studies in Church History*, vol. 20 (1985), pp. 47–57.

13 *Chronicles of Enguerrand de Monstrelet*, vol. 1, p. 347.

14 *The Ecclesiastical History of Orderic Vitalis*, vol. 2, ed. M. Chibnall (Oxford, 1969), p. 169.

15 The exception is the debate between Edward Freeman and J.H. Round on the 'true ancient name' of the battle of Hastings, for which see J.H. Round, 'Mr Freeman and the Battle of Hastings', in *Feudal England: Historical Studies of the Eleventh and Twelfth Centuries* (repr. 1964), pp. 259–63, but see below, pp. 45–47.

16 Petri Raivo, 'Politics of Memory: Historical Battlefields and Sense of Place', *Nordia Geographical Publications, NGP Yearbook*, eds J. Vuolteenaho and T. Antti Aikas (Oulu, 1998), pp. 59–66.

17 J. Wheeler-Bennett, *Hindenburg: The Wooden Titan* (1936), p. 28.

18 PRO, WO 161/102-3 (printed as Cmd 1138, 1922). I am grateful to John Bourne of the University of Birmingham for drawing the existence of this committee to my attention.

19 'A Short English Chronicle', in *Three Fifteenth-Century Chronicles*, ed. J. Gaird-ner, Camden Society, new series, vol. 28 (1880), p. 77.

20 Jehan de Waurin, *Recueil des Croniques et Anchiennes Istories de la Grant Bre-taigne*, eds W. Hardy and E.L.C.P. Hardy, Rolls Series, (1891), p. 164.

21 *The Anonimalle Chronicle*, ed. V.H. Galbraith (Manchester, 1927), pp. 25–28.

22 *Chronicles and Memorials of the reigns of Stephen, Henry II and Richard I*, ed. R. Howlett, Rolls Series (1886), vol. 3, pp. 151–54.

23 *Memorials of Beverley Minster: The Chapter Act Book*, Surtees Society, vol. 98 (1897), p. xxiv.

24 *VCH (Yorkshire East Riding)*, vol. 6 (1989), pp. 7–8.

25 *Three Fifteenth-Century Chronicles*, ed. Gairdner, p. 77; *The Politics of Fifteenth-Century England: John Vale's Book*, eds M.L. Kekewich, C. Richmond, A.F. Sutton, L. Visser-Fuchs and J. Watts (Stroud, 1995), p. 179. In this last account an engagement immediately prior to Towton is also characterised as 'battell at Feribrigge'.

26 William Worcestre, *Itineraries*, ed. J. H. Harvey (Oxford, 1969), p. 399.

27 Ibid., p. 344.

28 *Rotuli Parliamentorum*, vol. 6, 144b.

29 B. Cox, *The Place-Names of Rutland* (1994), pp. 140–41.

30 *Chroniques de Jean Froissart*, ed. S. Luce (Paris, 1873), vol. 4, p. 94; I. Friel, 'Winds of Change? Ships and the Hundred Years War', in *Arms, Armies and Fortifications in the Hundred Years War*, eds A. Curry and M. Hughes (Woodbridge, 1994), p. 187; K. Fowler, *The King's Lieutenant: Henry of Grosmont, First Duke of Lancaster, 1310–1361* (1969), pp. 93–95 and the references cited there.

31 G.W.S. Barrow, *Robert Bruce and the Community of the Realm of Scotland* (3rd edn, Edinburgh, 1988), pp. 215–16.

32 W. Bower, *Scotichronicon*, ed. D.E.R. Watt, vol. 6 (Aberdeen, 1991), p. 368; *Chronicles of the Reigns of Edward I and Edward II*, ed. W. Stubbs, Rolls Series, vol. 1 (1882), pp. 231, 276; BL, Cotton MS Faustina B vi, f. 79v.

33 *Vita Edwardi Secundi*, ed. N. Denholm-Young (1957), pp. 50–56.

34 Firenze, Archivio di Stato di Firenze a Prato, 664/509944; 664/308929. I owe these references and the English translation of the Italian text to the kindness of Helen Bradley.

35 *The Politics of Fifteenth-Century England*, ed. Kekewich et al., p. 160.

36 P. Contamine, *War in the Middle Ages* (1984), p. 261.

37 *Two of the Saxon Chronicles Parallel*, ed. J. Earle (Oxford, 1865), pp. 200–2.

38 C. Richmond, 'The War at Sea', in *The Hundred Years War*, ed. K. Fowler (1971), pp. 96–121.

39 G.H. Martin, *Knighton's Chronicle, 1337–96* (Oxford, 1995), p. 28.

40 *The Libelle of Englyshe Polycye*, ed. G.F. Warner (Oxford, 1926), line 1005.

41 *Westminster Chronicle, 1381–1394*, eds L.C. Hector and B.F. Harvey (1982), pp. 182–83; *The Paston Letters and Papers of the Fifteenth Century*, ed. N. Davis (Oxford, 1971–76), vol. 2, pp. 340–41; C. Richmond, 'The Earl of Warwick's Domination of the Channel and the Naval Dimension to the Wars of the Roses, 1456–1460', *Southern History*, vols. 20–21 (1998–99), p. 7.

42 London, Westminster Abbey, WAM 12183 f. 50.

43 *Duo rerum Anglicarum scriptores veteres viz Thomas Otterbourne et Johannes Whethamstede*, ed. T. Hearne, (Oxford, 1732), p. 134; *Istoire et Croniques de Flandres*, ed. K. de Lettenhove, vol. 1, Brussels (1879), p. 617; *Walteri Hemingford Canonici de Gisseburne Historia de Rebus Gestis Edwardi I, Edwardi II rt Edwardi III*, ed. T. Hearne, 2 vols (Oxford, 1731), vol. 2, p. 320; *Chronica monasterii de Melsa*, ed. E.A. Bond, Rolls Series, vol. 2 (1866), p. 45.

44 I owe the suggestion to Christopher Lewis.

45 P. J. Foss, *The Field of Redemore: The Battle of Bosworth, 1485* (Leeds, 1990), pp. 16–24.

46 Ibid., p. 19.

47 Charles Ross, *Richard III* (1981), pp. 235–37; C. Richmond, 'The Battle of Bosworth', *History Today*, vol. 35 (August 1985).

48 PRO, E101/404/21 f. 49; M.V. Clarke and V.H. Galbraith, 'The Deposition of Richard II', *Bulletin of the John Rylands Library*, vol. 14 (1930), p. 178; Oxford, Bodleian Library, Shropshire charters, 89.

49 *Calendar of Inquisitions Miscellaneous, 1399–1422*, vol. 7 (1968), p. 524.

50 BL, Cotton MS Vitellius F xvii, f. 42v.

51 PRO, DL42/15 f. 153 et seq.

52 *The Chronicle of Adam Usk 1377–1421*, ed. C. Given-Wilson (Oxford, 1997), p. 171.

53 'Annales Ricardi Secundi et Henrici Quarti', in *Johannis de Trokelowe et Anon Chronica et Annales*, ed. H.T. Riley, Rolls Series (1866), p. 365.

54 *A Guide to Welsh Literature, 1282–c. 1550*, eds A.O.H. Jarman and G. Rees Hughes (rev. edn, Cardiff, 1997), pp. 256–74.

55 Oxford, Bodleian Library, MS Laud Misc. 748, f. 83v.

56 *Two of the Saxon Chronicles Parallel*, ed. Earle, p. 202; *The Ecclesiastical History of Orderic Vitalis*, ed. Chibnall, pp. 172, 180, 186, 190, 266, 356.

57 Domesday Book, ff. 16a, 17d.

58 *The Chronicle of Battle Abbey*, ed. E. Searle (Oxford, 1980), pp. 37–39, 63.

59 Ibid., pp. 43, 64. The view of the chronicle's modern editor on contemporary appraisal of the site appears on pp. 16–17.

60 Domesday Book, f. 60c.

61 J.H. Round, 'Mr Freeman and the Battle of Hastings', pp. 261–63; see also R. Allen Brown, *The Normans and the Norman Conquest* (1969), p. 164 n. 114: 'Freeman's attempt to foist the name of Senlac … deservedly met with no lasting success.'

62 *The Carmen de Hastingae Proelio of Guy, Bishop of Amiens*, eds C. Morton and H. Muntz (Oxford, 1972), 24.5.

63 *The Place-Names of Sussex*, eds A. Mawer and F.M. Stenton (Cambridge, 1930), pp. 495–99.

64 B. Dickins, '*Fagaduna* in Orderic (AD 1075)', in *Otium et Negotium: Studies in Onomatology and Library Science presented to Olof von Feilitzen*, ed. F. Sandgren (Stockholm, 1973), pp. 44–45.

65 S. Walker, 'A Context for 'Brunanburh'?', in *Warriors and Churchmen in the High Middle Ages*, ed. T. Reuter (1992), pp. 21–39.

66 J.McN. Dodgson, *The Place-Names of Cheshire*, vol. 5, ii (Nottingham, 1997), pp. xxi, 249–61, 263; N. J. Higham, 'The Context of *Brunanburh*', in *Names, Places and People: An Onomastic Miscellany in Memory of John McNeal Dodgson*, eds A.R. Rumble and A.D. Mills (Stamford, 1997), p. 152 n. 66; *The Charters of the Anglo-Norman Earls of Chester* c. *1071–1237*, ed. G. Barraclough, Record Society of Lancashire and Cheshire, vol. 126 (1988), no. 394.

67 *The Battle of Brunanburh*, ed. A Campbell (1938), pp. 57–80.

68 M. Wood, '*Brunanburh* Revisited', *Saga Book of the Viking Society*, vol. 20 (1978–80), pp. 200–17; Higham, 'The Context of *Brunanburh*', pp. 144–56.

69 W. Rodwell, 'The Battle of *Assandun* and its Memorial Church: A Reappraisal', in *The Battle of Maldon: Fiction and Fact*, ed. J. Cooper (1993), pp. 127–58.

70 *Annales Cestrienses*, ed. R. Copley Christie, Record Society of Lancashire and Cheshire, vol. 14 (1886), pp. 20–21.

71 P. Morgan, 'Making the English Gentry', in *Thirteenth Century England*, eds P.R. Coss and S.D. Lloyd, vol. 5 (Woodbridge, 1995), p. 27.

72 C. Tyson, 'The Battle of Otterburn: When and where was it fought?', in *War and Border Societies in the Middle Ages*, eds A. Goodman and A. Tuck (1992), pp. 65–93.

73 Raivo, 'Politics of memory', p. 65.

Civil War and Ecclesiastical Peace in the Reign of King Stephen

Paul Dalton

It has long been recognised that leading churchmen involved them-selves in attempts to limit the damage caused by, and bring to an end, the civil war of Stephen's reign.[1] Study of their methods has focused partly on the legatine councils, which issued canons to uphold royal rights and protect churchmen against what they saw as unjust exac-tions, and the use and impact of excommunication in bringing perpe-trators of disorder to admit their wrongs and make reparations for them. It has also examined the guaranteeing of baronial peace treaties, the encouragement of both sides in the war to accept Stephen as king and Henry of Anjou as Stephen's lawful heir; the refusal to crown Stephen's son; the organisation of peace conferences; and the negoti-ation of the treaty of Winchester in 1153.[2] The value of this study is unquestionable, but the extent and variety of ecclesiastical peacemak-ing has still to be fully appreciated. This chapter aims to make a fur-ther contribution to this field.

Valuable light on this subject is cast, albeit indirectly, by the work of scholars who have examined the response of churchmen to violence and enemies of the Church in England and on the continent in earlier times, particularly those who have worked on hagiography and the cult of saints and on ecclesiastical reactions to the political and mili-tary troubles in France between *c.* 900 and *c.* 1200.[3] Some manifesta-tions of this response were the same as or similar to those identified in England in Stephen's reign. But the existence in England then of other features of it has received much less attention. These features include the invocation and demonstration of divine and saintly power; other practices that were part of the Peace of God movement; the provision of refuges; and the holding of courts and other assem-blies that sought to settle conflicts and bring men publicly to admit their wrongs. This chapter will show that all of these methods of protection and peacemaking were in widespread use by churchmen in England during Stephen's reign.

The invocation and demonstration of the power of God and the saints were manifest in the cult of saints (or relics) from early Christian times.[4] The cult had a complex series of functions, some of them related closely to the promotion of order and peace.[5] Peter Brown argued that in the late-antique period relics, relic translations (over distance) and saints' festivals expressed and promoted the solidarity, concord and unity of local Christian communities; and that relics spoke to the people about the triumph of power exercised as it should be over unjust power.[6] A major function of saintly power, which became a characteristic feature of the cult of saints, was the protection of the Church, its possessions and ministers, and other vulnerable elements within society, from harm or loss.[7]

The logic of this protective power has been associated by some historians with the sacred power employed by the early Peace of God movement in Frankia between c. 975 and c. 1050.[8] This movement was a response to the upheavals associated with the disintegration of Carolingian power and its aftermath. It was characterised by the holding of councils, presided over by bishops (sometimes with lay lords) and attended by monks (who often brought relics with them) and large numbers of nobles, knights and common people. At these councils decrees were issued to protect churches, churchmen and other non-combatants and their possessions from attack; sometimes threats of anathema were made against those who might contravene the decrees, laymen swore peace-oaths on relics and miracles occurred.[9]

Although there were similarities between these councils and the legatine councils held in Stephen's reign, there were also significant differences. The power of the saints and their relics had apparently little or no part to play in the legatine councils of the anarchy. But the churchmen of Stephen's reign made use of this power as a force for protection and peace in other ways. In a seminal and valuable study of war and peace in Stephen's reign, Christopher Holdsworth observed that men believed that God and the saints brought success to the righteous and the reverse to those who offended them, and that churchmen in this spirit recorded the tragic ends of some of those excommunicated for attacking Church property. He also observed that the idea of a just war, based partly upon the defence of country, Church and God, emerges in the speeches made before the battle of the Standard in 1138; that this battle was preceded by elaborate religious rituals, including the placing of relics and the consecrated host onto a cart around which the English army fought; and that a similar scene occurred in 1138 at the siege of Worcester, where the monks processed with St Oswald's relics to protect their city.[10] These observations provide important leads, for there are many more instances of churchmen invoking and demonstrating divine and saintly power to protect themselves (and sometimes others) and to promote peace during the anarchy; and some of them were similar in some respects to certain features of the Peace of God movement.

In 1140, according to Hugh Candidus, Martin abbot of Peterborough,

> completed the chancel of the church, and amid great rejoicing brought into the new church the holy relics and the monks on the day of the feast of St Peter. ... There were present on this occasion Alexander, bishop of Lincoln, the abbots of Ramsey, Thorney, and Crowland, many monks, barons, and knights, and a great concourse of people. The arm of St Oswald ... was then displayed to them and to all these people, and with him the bishop himself blessed them all. And all the relics were shown, and were washed by him in the presence of all the people. Even before that day the precious right hand ... had been shown to Abbot Martin for he desired to see it, either from curiosity, or because he doubted if it were authentic. So next day ... they very solemnly opened the chest, and produced it safe and sound, and with it blessed all the congregation, and washed it with great fear ... And many of the monks who were sick, were altogether healed, when they entered the church ...[11]

By 1140 relic translations, including examples similar to this one, had a long history in England and Europe; and in the twelfth century they were commonplace.[12] They were undertaken for a variety of purposes, often influenced by competition between religious houses, that might have little or no connection with protection or peacemaking.[13] The one at Peterborough probably had several of the traditional functions, including celebrating the completion of building work and encouraging pilgrimage to the abbey. But it may also have been intended to protect the abbey.

Almost immediately preceding his note of it, Hugh Candidus recorded that after Henry I's death the abbey suffered many troubles.[14] These are described in the Peterborough version (E) of the *Anglo-Saxon Chronicle*, the annal of which for 1137 contains what is perhaps the most graphic description of the violence and disturbances of the war.[15] This annal, like much of the *Chronicle*'s account of Stephen's reign, is chronologically flawed;[16] but here, at least, there may have been good reason. Immediately after its account of the troubles, which ends with the famous statement that 'they said openly that Christ and his saints were asleep', the annal for 1137 includes a note of the translation ceremony of 1140, even though the author knew its correct date.[17] Immediately after this the same annal records a description of a visit paid by Abbot Martin to Pope Eugenius III (which cannot have occurred before 1145) to obtain privileges, a statement that Martin had recovered lands that powerful men were holding by force, and the names of the men and the lands they had taken. The texts of the papal privileges, issued in December 1146, are supplied by Hugh Candidus. The provision of protection for the abbey and its possessions from outside ecclesiastical or lay interference, harm and encroachment are central to them.[18] Both chronologically and textually, the context of the Peterborough translation ceremony suggests that it was undertaken, partly at least, to protect the abbey and preserve its peace.[19]

Almost immediately after the *Anglo-Saxon Chronicle*'s description of Abbot Martin's recovery of lands, and the last thing recorded in the 1137 annal, is an account of the crucifixion and murder of a Christian boy named William, allegedly by the Jews of Norwich. The boy 'was a holy martyr, and the monks [of Norwich] took him and buried him with ceremony in the monastery, and through our Lord he works wonderful and varied miracles, and he is called St William.'[20] The chronology is again inaccurate, for William was killed in 1144; but the inaccuracy may well be the product of thematic coherence. The Peterborough translation ceremony, the securing of papal privileges of protection, the recovery of lands taken by barons, and the creation of a new saint at Norwich, it is possible to suggest, share a common theme: they were all (in part) responses of the Church to the circumstances that accompanied the war.

Further support for this suggestion is to be found in a book on the life and miracles of St William of Norwich written by Thomas of Monmouth, a monk of Norwich cathedral who lived through the war. This states that after William's death an accusation of murder was made against the Jews before a synod presided over by Everard bishop of Norwich, who was asked to do justice. Everard was prevented from doing so by John the sheriff of Norwich, who protected the Jews. William's body was subsequently buried in the monks' cemetery after processions and ceremonies attended by crowds, during which miracles occurred. But the development of the cult was opposed by a section of the Norwich convent, and it waned and nearly died out until, in 1150, Thomas of Monmouth revived it with the support of Bishop Everard's successor, Bishop William Turbe, and six of his fellow monks. This was done through visions, translation ceremonies and miracles.[21]

As with the promotion of any cult, several motives probably inspired the promotion of that of St William. Some of them were probably related to tensions which may have existed between the cathedral community, the sheriff of Norwich and the citizens of Norwich respecting their rights within the city and its suburbs.[22] With regard to the sheriff, the cult may have been partly defensive or protective in purpose. Sister Benedicta Ward noted that William was 'invoked to increase the glory of his own shrine and to defend his veneration, not to terrify temporal enemies of the shrine or reinforce the claims of his guardians';[23] but his power, or that of God Himself, is described by Thomas of Monmouth as protecting people and the cathedral from the sheriffs of Norwich. Thomas describes William helping to settle a conflict between one sheriff and two men whose property the sheriff had harmed; and he asserts that John the sheriff was punished by divine vengeance with internal bleeding for protecting William's murderers, and eventually with death for disturbing the peace of Norwich cathedral by interfering with Bishop William Turbe's election in 1146.[24] The threat John posed to this peace is also evident in the likelihood that he forced Bishop Everard to grant him church lands; this may have led to Everard's resignation in 1145 and retirement to the Cistercian abbey of Fontenay in France, where he died in 1146–47.[25] John repented for his (unspecified) sins on his death-bed by vowing to found a religious house, a vow fulfilled by his brother and successor, William. It is significant that William did so by founding a Cistercian abbey at Sibton in Suffolk, very shortly before the start of Thomas of Monmouth's campaign to promote the cult of St William of Norwich.[26]

The protective and pacificatory aspect of this cult is evident in other ways. Though most of St William's miracles were curative rather than punitive, they assisted captives suffering violence, familiar figures during the anarchy.[27] William's power also helped penitent foreign knights sentenced to exile by the Church for committing violent crimes.[28] Moreover, as Ward observed, William's miracles were similar in some respects to those of St Faith of Conques, and this was more than fortuitous since they were both martyrs and children, and a priory dedicated to St Faith was established at Horsham near Norwich by Robert fitz Walter, who visited Conques in 1100 and returned with two of its monks. It was probably more than coincidental that Robert was the father of John and William, sheriffs of Norwich, and that St Faith was a protective saint. As Ward noted, St Faith appears in the collection of her miracles (written 1013–60) as a force for order, a focus of knightly loyalties, a redresser of the balance of power between castles, a punisher of her detractors, a deliverer of captives, a protector of her own monks and people, and a lord as great as any other, in a countryside around Conques that – much like parts of England in Stephen's reign – was constantly at war.[29] St Faith was also associated with the Peace of God movement.[30]

The use of saintly power as a means of protection and peace promotion occurred elsewhere during Stephen's reign. When Geoffrey de Mandeville was marching on Ely during the winter of 1141–42, he was met by monks from Ely carrying crosses and reliquaries.[31] Abbot Martin of Peterborough may have been doing more than running away when, at some point between 1146 and 1154, the war troubled him so sorely that 'he could not endure it' and went abroad 'to visit the holy places of the saints there'.[32] The war may explain some of the relic acquisitions made during the anarchy; though such acquisitions were, of course, common and made for various purposes. At some point between 1137 and 24 June 1139, a period when northern England was troubled by Scottish aggression, Thurstan archbishop of York, who organised the defence against the Scots and the preparations for the battle of the Standard, told a council attended by many prelates and barons that relics had been discovered at Southwell Minster.[33] Probably in 1148, when Stephen had an opportunity to carry the war more forcefully to his opponents in the south-west, two bishops from this region, Robert of Hereford and Jocelin of Salisbury, wrote to Suger abbot of St-Denis to obtain relics.[34] Their requests are all the more significant in the light of Suger's career as a diplomat and peacemaker and the importance and role of his abbey and its patron saint.[35] Suger wrote *The Deeds of Louis the Fat* in the 1140s to reinforce and advertise the support of his abbey and St Denis for the French monarchy, which had a long history, and to present his king 'as the realisation of the highest ideals and goals of medieval kingship'.[36] Suger portrayed the king and St Denis as the special protectors of the kingdom (especially its Church, orphans, widows and poor) against the violence and injustices of the castellans of the Île-de-France and foreign powers which disturbed the peace.[37]

Miracles were an aspect of saintly power used by churchmen throughout Europe to deal with their enemies and to promote peace long before 1135.[38] They continued to be used in this way in England during Stephen's reign, as is shown by those recorded in the *Waltham Chronicle*, written shortly after 1177 by a canon who lived through the anarchy.[39] One of them occurred during a local war between Geoffrey de Mandeville and William earl of Arundel in 1143 or 1144. It was experienced by five of Geoffrey's Flemish soldiers when they invaded the secular college of Waltham in Essex, which possessed a sacred image of the crucified Christ known as the Holy Cross. They intended to steal bundles which had been taken there 'for peaceful protection and the preservation of property', but were prevented from doing so by the Holy Cross. According to the Waltham chronicler, the soldiers were

> not allowed to leave the church and remove the packages until everything had been restored to order, the antagonists had been removed from the district, and peace restored to the town. Our men, returning now from pursuing the foe, on entering the church to restore their packages to their proper owners, found these children of Belial still carrying them, for the church was full of boxes and chests because of this time of civil strife. When our men arrested them, being stirred to a fury they wanted to drive them out of that place of sanctuary, but the sacristan Warmund ... stopped them from doing this. He led these men, who had been deprived of their sight in both eyes ... straight to the altar, and pricked in their consciences ... they received a sound whipping. When their sight had been restored to them by God's mercy, Warmund led them through the vill, though many wanted to stop him, but showing reverence for the guide they let these sons of the devil go free.[40]

It is easy to see how this miracle story might have been manufactured. The Flemings may well have been surprised by the return of the men of Waltham and claimed sanctuary rights. The miracle looks like an ingenious attempt by Warmund to turn this situation to the advantage of his church. It gave him an opportunity to assert its sanctuary rights, and to arrange a public demonstration of the power of its sacred relic. By having the Flemings flogged he ensured that they were punished and tried to satisfy the men of Waltham. By releasing them he doubtless won their favour and that of their powerful master, Geoffrey de Mandeville, who was 'a good friend of the church [of Waltham] and devoted to it'.[41] In this way further violence was avoided and, in the best traditions of medieval compromise settlements, both sides involved in the conflict benefited in some way from its resolution.

The Waltham canons used their miracles in conjunction with other tried and tested methods of promoting peace. These included using or developing the social networks (formed by feudal, familial, friendship, neighbourhood and religious patronage ties) commonly employed in dispute settlement procedures in Western Europe.[42] When Humphrey of Barrington, a local forester, committed a violent offence against them during the war and was almost killed by divine vengeance, they permitted him to be carried into their church because he was their neighbour. There they prayed for him until he was restored to his right mind and gave them land in recompense.[43] The function of this miracle was not just punitive and protective; it also served to help the canons to restore harmonious social bonds, and to establish new ones, with their violent neighbour.[44]

The Waltham canons also used miracles in conjunction with a measure commonly employed by continental churchmen to protect themselves and their peace: the 'humiliation' of relics.[45] After Geoffrey de Mandeville burned some of their houses and refused a request for compensation, the canons 'decided, as a punishment for his sins, to take down the cross in the hope that that wealthy man would be pricked in his conscience by this action, and would be willing to reconsider'. Geoffrey was killed before he could do so, but not to be outdone the canons claimed that he received a mortal wound 'at the very hour the cross was taken down' and died within 40 days.[46]

Northern churchmen also relied on supernatural forces for protection and peace during Stephen's reign, as they had done for centuries.[47] During the first Scottish invasion of 1138, according to Richard of Hexham, Hexham priory offered tranquil security and safe refuge to its people because of the renown of its saints. Two Galwegian soldiers who robbed an oratory dedicated to St Michael belonging to the priory were horribly killed by divine vengeance.[48] This deterred some of the Scots from attacking the priory, which obtained from King David and his son Henry a guarantee of security from hostilities.[49] Further south, St Cuthbert was apparently no less busy in defending Durham.[50] There is no reason to doubt that these stories date from the anarchy: Antonia Gransden states that Richard of Hexham wrote about them fairly soon after 1139, and some of their elements appear in Ailred of Rievaulx's account of the battle of the Standard, which is usually dated to c. 1155 though it may have been written earlier.[51]

Ailred wrote this account to show that (discounting David's Scottish and Galwegian followers) the battle was a tragic and unnecessary confrontation between friends who had a great deal in common; and so to promote reconciliation and peace.[52] One of the devices Ailred used to do this was to emphasise that unjust causes would be opposed by heavenly authority. According to Ailred, Walter Espec told the English army that their cause had the support of St Michael, the angels, St Peter and the Apostles, whose churches the Scots had defiled, of the holy martyrs, whose shrines the Scots had burned, and of the holy virgins and Christ himself.[53] In 1154–55, a time when the relative stability which had characterised Anglo-Scottish relations between 1139 and 1153 looked as if it might soon come to an end, Ailred attended the translation of Hexham priory's relics and read a tract he had written on the miracles of its saints. One of his purposes was to show the ability of these saints to protect Hexham from Scottish attacks.[54] Here was a lesson for young Malcolm IV.

Defensive and punitive miracles were also said to have occurred at Ely and at Selby abbey during Stephen's reign.[55] Together with other miracles they throw light on other forms of ecclesiastical damage limitation and peacemaking, including the provision of refuges. The Selby miracles, like those at Waltham, show that when people felt threatened by warfare they sometimes took their possessions to the protection of churches and churchyards.[56] The provision of such refuges was vigorously promoted by some bishops, including Robert and Gilbert Foliot of Hereford; and it may also have been one of the services provided by hermits in their cells.[57]

Miracle stories also provide further evidence that some of those who harmed churches made reparations for their wrongs. Several baronial reparation charters issued during Stephen's reign have survived and, as Edmund King has argued, reflect the implementation of ecclesiastical measures for promoting peace which were an essential element in the process that brought the anarchy to an end.[58] One of the features of these charters that deserves fuller consideration is that they were often addressed to bishops and sometimes requested them to strengthen or protect the grant by their authority, justice or anathema; which suggests that bishops helped to generate such charters.[59] Another is that some of the charters notified grants made not only to religious houses but to their saintly patrons.[60]

A further aspect of reparation grants that deserves more attention is that they were sometimes made before large audiences, assemblies which indicate the continuation, even during some of the worst periods of the civil war, of major ecclesiastical courts or synods. At some point between 1144 and 20 February 1148 Robert fitz Vitalis issued a charter giving notification that Osbert, prior of St Augustine's priory, Daventry, had deraigned at Leicester, before Alexander bishop of

Lincoln, various churches of which Robert had unjustly disseised the priory. Robert stated that in the third year after this, moved by remorse, he went to Daventry and reseised St Augustine's of these churches which it had held (by his gift) until the ninth year of Stephen's reign 'when I occupied it'. Robert added that 'I have recognised my guilt and unjust action there publicly and before numerous clerics and laymen and asked God and St Augustine whom I had offended for forgiveness'.[61]

A few years later, in April 1153, Roger de Mowbray, a powerful lord in the North and the Midlands, issued a charter notifying a reparation grant of land to the cathedral of St Peter's, York, for losses caused by him and to obtain absolution.[62] The charter acknowledges the royal title of Stephen and the archiepiscopal title of Henry Murdac, the questioning of which had been the source of much violent conflict.[63] It states that the grant was made publicly at St Peter's by Roger's own hand, and that it was witnessed by Ralph bishop of Orkney, two of Roger's clerics, several of Roger's men and a copious multitude of the clerics and *proborum hominum* of the city of York. It also reveals that Roger made his reparation grant on Good Friday. The holding of peace negotiations and ceremonies on holy days was a well-established method employed by some continental churchmen to encourage disputants to come to terms.[64] Good Friday was a particularly appropriate day for a reparation grant. It was the anniversary of the day when Christ had atoned for the sins of mankind through his crucifixion, and an occasion when York Cathedral was probably crowded.[65] Roger de Mowbray's very public reparation grant bears all the signs of having been orchestrated by churchmen to place considerable pressure on Roger to come to terms, and to have the maximum possible impact on a large and important congregation of people. The message to these people was clear. Everyone who had exploited the Church during the war, no matter how great they were, should atone for their sins and make reparation for them; and everyone should recognise the rightful archbishop of York and the rightful king of England.

Some of the ecclesiastical assemblies concerned with peacemaking appear to have made use of ecclesiastical and lay specialists in this field. At some point between 1150 and 1153 the abbot and monks of Byland abbey in Yorkshire made an agreement before the chapter of St Peter's, York, and Archbishop Henry Murdac, with Richard Cruer, to settle a dispute over land.[66] The abbot was advised in this by several people, including Robert de Daiville and Robert de Alney. Robert de

Daiville may have been the same Robert de Daiville who was, or soon became, constable of the honour of Roger de Mowbray, the most powerful baron in the region where the disputed lands were located. Robert de Alney was a hermit who lived at Hood in North Yorkshire and eventually became a monk at Byland abbey.[67] Major honorial officials, as Edmund King has shown, were often the go-betweens in the settlement of disputes in this period; and hermits, as Peter Brown and others have revealed, had a well-established role as advisers and arbitrators.[68] At about the same time as his involvement in the Byland–Cruer settlement (c. 1150), Robert de Alney may well have taken part in another agreement made before an ecclesiastical assembly between Matthew of Tealby and the Gilbertine priory of Sixle, concerning lands in Lincolnshire. Matthew's charter notifying the event states that he and his sons pledged their faith in Robert de Alney's hand to hold and warrant the agreement. Matthew also noted that in order that 'this our agreement may remain firm and unshaken we have made and contracted it before ... Robert the second, bishop of Lincoln, in the chapter of the mother church, by our hands in his hand, and we have confirmed it with our seal and corroborated it with the pendent seal of the same chapter'.[69]

The bishop of Lincoln's court may have been busy with such affairs in the later years of Stephen's reign. In 1151 or 1152 it appears to have settled, or to have confirmed the settlement of, another dispute between a layman, Robert of Meppershall, and a religious house, the Cistercian abbey of Biddlesden in Buckinghamshire, over possession of Biddlesden and other land. Robert's renunciation of his claim and confirmation of this property to the abbey were obtained, after the abbey (with the help and counsel of the earl of Leicester, who held the overlordship of Biddlesden) gave Robert ten marks, and are recorded in a charter of the bishop of Lincoln issued at St Albans and witnessed by several archdeacons and canons of Lincoln cathedral. It was probably no coincidence that the charter was granted, as it states, on the feast day of St Remigius.[70]

Cases such as this were also dealt with by other ecclesiastical courts or synods during the anarchic 1140s and early 1150s;[71] and these assemblies also continued to try to settle disputes between churchmen. There are several examples, but two are particularly noteworthy.[72] One occurred in 1147 when a dispute over land between Nicholas the priest and Alexander bishop of Lincoln was settled before a remarkable assembly of ecclesiastical witnesses.[73] The other

occurred in the period 1150–54 and concerned a dispute over possession of a manor between the monks of Ely cathedral and a clerk named
Henry. The dispute resulted in litigation at the papal court (on several
occasions), at the court of the bishop of Ely, at courts held on papal
instructions on two separate occasions by the archbishop of Canterbury and the bishop of Chichester, and at a court presided over by the
bishop of Hereford at Northampton.[74]

Some churchmen also worked with powerful barons to settle disputes in the later years of Stephen's reign. Probably on 11 January
1150, a dispute over possessions in and around Stone (Staffordshire)
between Stone priory and Ernald de Walton (whose father held Stone
from Nicholas of Stafford) was settled at Stone in the presence of
Robert of Stafford (son of Nicholas and a lord who had close links with
the priory and may have been its founder). '[S]ince the possession concerned was ecclesiastical', the archdeacons of Chester, Stafford and
London, were present 'on behalf of the lord Walter [Durdent], bishop
of Chester', to determine the case 'by an ecclesiastical judgement in the
place of the bishop'.[75] Robert informed his men of the proceedings in a
charter which stated that the canons of Stone priory produced charters
and muniments showing their just and canonical possession of the
property claimed by Ernald, since Ernald and his father had sold it to
them and this had been confirmed by Robert, Robert's father and
Roger, bishop of Chester and Coventry. Robert's charter also records
that the evidence produced by the canons showed that there had been
litigation concerning the property between the canons and Hugh the
watchman, which had been settled in favour of the canons in the court
of King Henry I, and that this had been confirmed by royal charter. In
addition, Robert's charter notes that the canons produced a papal
privilege of protection obtained from Pope Eugenius III, confirming
their possessions and threatening assaulters and perturbers of their
church with anathema. 'Therefore, understanding their case', declared
Robert, 'and the fact that the canons' possession was supported by so
many muniments and confirmed by so many authorities and moreover
being mindful of the peace, we have terminated the aforesaid con-
troversy by the common counsel of clerics as well as laymen by the
following composition'. In this composition Ernald gave up his claims
in return for a grant of other property from the canons.[76]

The case has several significant features. Bishop Walter Durdent
was a protégé of Theobald archbishop of Canterbury, one of the principal architects of the peace arrangements that brought the anarchy to

an end.[77] The involvement in the proceedings of William archdeacon of London also adds a national dimension to local affairs. Whether the hearing of the case by this court instead of the king's court, which had dealt with a related matter during the previous reign, was symptomatic of anarchy is difficult to say, but there was nothing apparently anarchic about the proceedings in which Robert of Stafford took part. They were attended by representatives of the local bishop, whose authority was clearly respected; and these representatives appear to have played a full part in the court's deliberations. These deliberations were based, even in the midst of the civil war, upon documentary evidence (baronial, episcopal, royal and papal) and the judgement of a royal court, and reveal a respect for proper procedure and traditional and legitimate forms of authority, and a concern to promote peace. The papal charter put forward by the canons was similar to that obtained from Eugenius III by Martin abbot of Peterborough in 1146. In France, in earlier times, such privileges helped to mediate local controversies in periods of disturbance, and it would appear that this was so in England during Stephen's reign.[78] The case is also significant because the final composition that terminated it was made in the church of Stone: 'and there', according to Robert of Stafford, 'touching the holy altar, Ernald confirmed that he would keep the peace and his pledge to the said church. And I Robert as brother and patron of the same church have confirmed this also on the altar.' It is quite possible that the altar contained elements of the relics of the Mercian saints Wulflad and Rufinus, whose remains may well have rested at Stone priory.[79] But whether this was the case or not, the peace promised by Ernald and confirmed by his lord on that altar was still, in one sense, the peace of God.

In conclusion, the intention of this chapter has not been to argue that all the churchmen of Stephen's reign always cultivated peace, or that they always did so for altruistic purposes.[80] Its aim has been to explore and illuminate several measures employed by some of these churchmen to protect their interests and (occasionally) those of other non-combatants, and to settle disputes, some of which helped to promote order and peace during the civil war. These measures were diverse and widespread, and in uncovering and studying them there is much to learn from the methods employed, long before 1135, by continental ecclesiastics to deal with their enemies and disorder. Although there was nothing in England during Stephen's reign quite like the continental Peace of God movement, churchmen then

employed measures for promoting protection and peace that
(arguably) were the same as, or at least similar to, a number of the
Peace movement's most important elements, some of which were
already old when it began in the 970s. In addition to holding legatine
councils that issued decrees aiming to provide protection and generate peace, these churchmen used relic translations, processions and
humiliations, miracles and peace oaths, some of which took place
before assemblies of high-ranking clergymen, nobles, knights and
crowds of people. The promotion of saints' cults, and particularly the
protective powers associated with them, was widespread during
Stephen's reign.[81] Some churchmen even appealed to the power of
saints closely associated with the Peace of God movement, one of the
most prominent of whom was Martial.[82] In c. 1143 the first English
Premonstratensian house was founded at Newhouse in northern Lincolnshire by a knight named Peter of Goxhill (lord of a castle at Newhouse) and dedicated to St Martial. It is unlikely to be a coincidence
that the land on which the abbey was founded was probably in dispute
between Peter's lord, Ranulf de Bayeux, and the earls of Chester and
Lincoln; that Alexander bishop of Lincoln, who was present at the
Peterborough translation ceremony of 1140 and worked hard to promote peace during Stephen's reign (especially by undertaking and
encouraging religious patronage), was closely involved in the foundation process; and that the abbot of Newhouse was soon to be involved
in an agreement between Peter of Goxhill and one of the earl of Lincoln's men which was probably intended to settle a dispute between
them over possession of lands near Newhouse.[83]

In addition to the power of the saints, some churchmen used other
more practical means of protection and peace-promotion during
Stephen's reign. They provided more ecclesiastical refuges. They
orchestrated reparation grants or settlements, sometimes before
crowds of people in churches and occasionally on holy days especially
appropriate for peacemaking. They continued to hold, even in the
1140s and early 1150s, courts, synods and other assemblies which
heard and settled disputes between churches or – sometimes in conjunction with lay courts – between churches and laymen, some of
which, we may suspect, would normally have been dealt with by the
king's court or the courts of his sheriffs and justices. They also took
advantage of the closer connections between the English Church and
Rome facilitated by the civil war to appeal to the papacy for privileges
and protection, much more frequently than they had ever done before

1135.[84] The continuity or growth of these and other methods of protection, dispute settlement and peace promotion should be added to the factors (such as the strength of royal authority before 1135) which explain why no fully developed Peace of God movement emerged during the anarchy. The significance of this extends beyond our appreciation of the role of churchmen in peacemaking. It has important implications for our understanding of the politics of Stephen's reign, the response of the aristocracy to the civil war that dominated it, the impact of this war on government and society, and the degree to which developments within England then were similar to, and can be illuminated by, the experiences of other countries which endured similar troubles in earlier times.

NOTES

1 See, for example, J.H. Round, *Geoffrey de Mandeville* (1892), p. 380.

2 The literature on this subject is extensive. For examples, see A. Saltman, *Theobald, Archbishop of Canterbury* (1956), pp. 16–19, 33–36, 39–41; R.H.C. Davis, *King Stephen 1135–1154* (3rd edn, 1990), pp. 43, 81–82, 102–3, 105, 113–15, 118–19, 123; T. Callahan, Jr, 'Ecclesiastical Reparations and the Soldiers of "The Anarchy"', *Albion*, vol. 10 (1978), pp. 300–18; *Councils and Synods with Other Documents relating to the English Church; I; AD 871–1204*, ed. D. Whitelock et al., 2 vols. (Oxford, 1981), vol. 2, pp. 768–78, 794–804, 821–28; E. King, 'The Anarchy of King Stephen's Reign', *TRHS*, 5th Series, vol. 34 (1984), pp. 133–43, 153; C. Holdsworth, 'War and Peace in the Twelfth Century: The Reign of Stephen Reconsidered', in *War and Peace in the Middle Ages*, ed. B.P. McGuire (Copenhagen, 1987), pp. 67–93, esp. pp. 81–82, 85; G.J. White, 'The End of Stephen's Reign', *History*, vol. 75 (1990), pp. 9, 11–12; E. King, 'Dispute Settlement in Anglo-Norman England', *Anglo-Norman Studies*, vol. 14 (1992), pp. 115–30; E. King, 'Introduction', in *The Anarchy of King Stephen's Reign*, ed. E. King (Oxford, 1994), pp. 19–20, 23–24, 29–31, 34–35; William of Malmesbury, *Historia Novella: The Contemporary History*, ed. E. King, trans. K.R. Potter (Oxford, 1998), pp. lv–lvi.

3 The literature on these subjects is extensive. For examples on the cult of saints, see R.C. Finucane, *Miracles and Pilgrims: Popular Beliefs in Medieval England* (1977); P. Brown, *The Cult of the Saints: Its Rise and Function in Latin Christianity* (Chicago, 1981); B. Ward, *Miracles and the Medieval Mind: Theory, Record and Event 1000–1215* (Aldershot, 1987); S.J. Ridyard, *The Royal Saints of Anglo-Saxon England: A Study of Saxon and East Anglian Saints* (Cambridge, 1988); D. Rollason, *Saints and Relics in Anglo-Saxon England* (Oxford, 1989); P.J. Geary, *Furta Sacra: Thefts of Relics in the Central Middle Ages* (Princeton, 1990); T. Head, *Hagiography and the Cult of Saints: The Diocese of Orléans, 800–1200* (Cambridge, 1990); B. Abou-El-Haj, *The Medieval Cult of Saints:*

Formations and Transformations (Cambridge, 1997). For examples on ecclesiastical reactions to the troubles in France, see note 9 below and B.H. Rosenwein, *Rhinoceros Bound: Cluny in the Tenth Century* (Philadelphia, 1982), esp. pp. 57–83, 106–12; S.D. White, 'Feuding and Peace-Making in the Touraine around the Year 1100', *Traditio*, vol. 42 (1986), pp. 195–263; B.H. Rosenwein, *To be the Neighbor of Saint Peter: The Social Meaning of Cluny's Property, 909–1049* (Ithaca and London, 1989), esp. pp. xii–xiii, 4, 8, 48, 200–2; B.H. Rosenwein, T. Head and S. Farmer, 'Monks and their Enemies: A Comparative Approach', *Speculum*, vol. 66 (1991), pp. 764–96; P.J. Geary, *Living with the Dead in the Middle Ages* (Ithaca and London, 1994), pp. 95–160.

4 Brown, *The Cult of the Saints*, esp. pp. 37–38, 44, 52–53, 88, 98–113, 122; Finucane, *Miracles and Pilgrims*, pp. 17–18, 22, 24; Rollason, *Saints and Relics*, pp. 3–20; Geary, *Furta Sacra*, pp. 29–32; Abou-El-Haj, *The Medieval Cult of Saints*, pp. 7–13.

5 For examples of the various religious, social, proprietorial, jurisdictional, political, economic and didactic functions, see A. Gransden, *Historical Writing in England c. 550 to c. 1307* (1974), pp. 62, 67–69, 73, 77–78, 88–91, 106, 117–21, 125–26, 173, 181; Finucane, *Miracles and Pilgrims*; Brown, *The Cult of the Saints*; H. Mayr-Harting, 'Functions of a Twelfth-Century Shrine: The Miracles of St Frideswide', in *Studies in Medieval History Presented to R.H.C. Davis*, eds H. Mayr-Harting and R.I. Moore (1985), pp. 193–206; Ward, *Miracles and the Medieval Mind*; Ridyard, *The Royal Saints*, pp. 23–25, 34–36, 79–114, 149–71, 191–226, 230–52; Rollason, *Saints and Relics*, pp. 34–35, 84–89, 110–28, 144–59, 188–213; Geary, *Furta Sacra*, pp. 18–22, 56–57, 82–86, 130–31; Head, *Hagiography and the Cult of Saints*, pp. 15–19, 45–46, 69–70, 98–103, 118–21, 127–31, 140–43, 181–88, 222–26, 240–42, 274–79, 287–91; S. Farmer, *Communities of Saint Martin: Legend and Ritual in Medieval Tours* (Ithaca and London, 1991), pp. 1–8; B. Töpfer, 'The Cult of Relics and Pilgrimage in Burgundy and Aquitaine at the Time of the Monastic Reform', in *The Peace of God: Social Violence and Religious Responses in France around the Year 1000*, eds T. Head and R. Landes (Ithaca, 1992), pp. 41–57; W.M. Aird, 'The Making of a Medieval Miracle Collection: The *Liber de Translationibus et Miraculis Sancti Cuthberti*', *Northern History*, vol. 28 (1992), pp. 1–24.

6 Brown, *The Cult of the Saints*, pp. 93–105.

7 For examples, see D.W. Rollason, 'The Miracles of St Benedict: A Window on Early Medieval France', in *Studies in Medieval History*, eds Mayr-Harting and Moore, pp. 73–90; Ward, *Miracles and the Medieval Mind*, pp. 37–38, 42–50, 60–65; Ridyard, *The Royal Saints*, pp. 148–50, 201–7, 227–30; Rollason, *Saints and Relics*, pp. 111–12, 194–99, 207–8, 221–23, 234; Geary, *Furta Sacra*, pp. 18–21, 56–57, 142–43; Head, *Hagiography and the Cult of Saints*, pp. 47–53, 106–7, 145–48, 177–81, 220–21, 235–37, 240–42, 278–81, 290–92; Farmer, *Communities of Saint Martin*, pp. 1–7, 31–34; Abou-El-Haj, *The Medieval Cult of Saints*, pp. 45–46, 55–60, 98–105, 111–12, 116–19, 132–33.

8 Töpfer saw the relics at peace councils as serving the same dual purpose as relic processions undertaken to protect monastic possessions from intruders: 'to draw the greatest possible public and secure the widest publicity and supernatural sanction to the Peace regulations'; Töpfer, 'The Cult of Relics', p. 56. Callahan states that the saints were the principal enforcers of the peace oaths and served as defenders of the faith and the faithful; and that their relics were intended to remind warriors of their mortality and the dire consequences of breaking peace oaths: D.F. Callahan, 'The Peace of God and the Cult of the Saints in Aquitaine in the Tenth and Eleventh

Centuries', in *The Peace of God*, eds Head and Landes, pp. 165–83, esp. pp. 172, 174–78. See also Geary, *Furta Sacra*, p. 21; G. Koziol, 'Monks, Feuds, and the Making of Peace in Eleventh-Century Flanders', in *The Peace of God*, eds Head and Landes, pp. 239–58. However, Head argues that the logic of protective saintly patronage associated with the cult of saints was different from the sacred power employed by the Peace movement: Head, *Hagiography and the Cult of Saints*, p. 293; T. Head, 'The Judgment of God: Andrew of Fleury's Account of the Peace League of Bourges', in *The Peace of God*, eds Head and Landes, pp. 232–38.

    9 For examples of work on the movement, see H.E.J. Cowdrey, 'The Peace and the Truce of God in the Eleventh Century', *Past and Present*, vol. 46 (1970), pp. 42–67; *The Peace of God*, eds Head and Landes; R. Landes, *Relics, Apocalypse, and the Deceits of History: Ademar of Chabannes, 989–1034* (Cambridge, MA, 1995).

    10 Holdsworth, 'War and Peace in the Twelfth Century', pp. 67–93, esp. 80–82.

    11 *The Chronicle of Hugh Candidus, A Monk of Peterborough*, ed. W.T. Mellows (1949), pp. 105–6; *The Peterborough Chronicle of Hugh Candidus*, ed. W.T. Mellows (Peterborough, 1941), p. 55. For Hugh Candidus, see *The Peterborough Chronicle*, ed. Mellows, p. x; *The Chronicle of Hugh Candidus*, ed. Mellows, pp. xv–xvii.

    12 For pre-1066 examples, see Finucane, *Miracles and Pilgrims*, pp. 18, 22; Ridyard, *The Royal Saints*, pp. 40, 106, 108, 155–56, 179, 191, 233; Rollason, *Saints and Relics*, pp. 10, 34–38, 41, 44, 49, 105, 178; Geary, *Furta Sacra*, pp. xi, 11–13, 40–42, 110–11; Head, *Hagiography and the Cult of Saints*, p. 162. For several translations in the period between 1066 and 1135, see J. Armitage Robinson, *Gilbert Crispin Abbot of Westminster: A Study of the Abbey under Norman Rule* (Cambridge, 1911), pp. 24–25; Ward, *Miracles and the Medieval Mind*, pp. 57, 61–62; Ridyard, *The Royal Saints*, pp. 58, 69, 204, 232–33; Aird, 'The Making of a Medieval Miracle Collection', pp. 5, 19–21; E. Cownie, *Religious Patronage in Anglo-Norman England 1066–1135* (Woodbridge, 1998), pp. 52, 94, 102, 105, 121, 126.

    13 For example, they might serve to confirm the status of relics and demonstrate their power; to enhance the prestige and popularity of the saint and church; to promote pilgrimages and benefactions; to celebrate building work; to promote political objectives; to support claims or title to lands; to associate a cult with a new political or ecclesiastical order; and to confirm the connections of a religious community with a cult. See Ridyard, *The Royal Saints*, pp. 110–11, 191–92; Rollason, *Saints and Relics*, pp. 34–38, 41, 177–80, 182, 209–12; Geary, *Furta Sacra*, pp. 82, 130, 154; Head, *Hagiography and the Cult of Saints*, pp. 14–43, 162; Aird. 'The Making of a Medieval Miracle Collection', pp. 1–24; Töpfer, 'The Cult of Relics', pp. 45–47, 49. Geary, *Furta Sacra*, p. 13, advocates caution when dealing with translation accounts.

    14 *The Chronicle of Hugh Candidus*, ed. Mellows, pp. 104–5; *The Peterborough Chronicle*, ed. Mellows, pp. 54–55.

    15 *The Anglo-Saxon Chronicle*, ed. D. Whitelock et al. (1961), pp. 199–200. The abbey may have suffered further harm in 1139–40, when Stephen attacked the Isle of Ely: *Liber Eliensis*, ed. E.O. Blake, Camden Society, 3rd ser., vol. 92 (1962), pp. 314–15, 433–36; *Gesta Stephani*, pp. 64–66, 98; *The Ecclesiastical History of Orderic Vitalis*, ed. M. Chibnall, 6 vols (Oxford, 1969–80), vol. 6, pp. 532–34; *The Chronicle of John of Worcester*, Vol. III, ed. P. McGurk (Oxford, 1998), pp. 246, 266, 280.

    16 *The Anglo-Saxon Chronicle*, ed. Whitelock, pp. 200–2.

    17 Ibid., p. 200.

18 *The Chronicle of Hugh Candidus*, ed. Mellows, pp. 108–19; *The Peterborough Chronicle*, ed. Mellows, pp. 57–63. For the relationship of Hugh's work to the *Anglo-Saxon Chronicle*, see Gransden, *Historical Writing*, p. 274.

19 As well as demonstrating the saint's power, the ceremony may have had other functions intended to promote peace. For a suggestion that translations and other public rituals in tenth- and eleventh-century Frankia were intended to communicate a 'vision of a society restored to peace by a new spirit of co-operation among its leaders', see G. Koziol, *Begging Pardon and Favor: Ritual and Political Order in Early Medieval France* (Ithaca and London, 1992), p. 7.

20 *The Anglo-Saxon Chronicle*, ed. Whitelock, p. 200. William was not officially canonised.

21 *The Life and Miracles of St William of Norwich by Thomas of Monmouth*, eds A. Jessopp and M.R. James (Cambridge, 1896), pp. ix–xiv, xxi, xxxiv, lxv–lxxiv. For valuable discussions, see Finucane, *Miracles and Pilgrims*, pp. 118–20; Ward, *Miracles and the Medieval Mind*, pp. 30, 68–76.

22 For the possibility that there was tension between the cathedral and the city, see N. Tanner, 'The Cathedral and the City', in *Norwich Cathedral: Church, City and Diocese, 1096–1996*, ed. I. Atherton et al. (1996), pp. 255–62, 267–68. The promotion of the cult was also anti-semitic and intended to harm and challenge the Jews, who had a privileged position in Norwich: see D.H. Farmer, 'Some Saints of East Anglia', *Reading Medieval Studies*, vol. 11 (1985), pp. 43–44; Finucane, *Miracles and Pilgrims*, p. 119; Ward, *Miracles and the Medieval Mind*, pp. 68, 76, 128. It may also have been influenced by charges of involvement in murder made by the Jews against an episcopal tenant; by the death in 1150 of Elias, prior of Norwich, who had opposed the cult; and by Thomas of Monmouth's personal ambitions: *The Life and Miracles of St William*, eds. Jessopp and James, pp. xi, xiv, xxii, 92–93, 98–110; *English Lawsuits from William I to Richard I*, ed. R. C. van Caenegem, 2 vols, Selden Society, vols. 106–7 (1990–91), no. 321; Finucane, *Miracles and Pilgrims*, p. 119.

23 Ward, *Miracles and the Medieval Mind*, pp. 68–69.

24 *The Life and Miracles of St William*, eds Jessopp and James, pp. 111–12, 172–73. For comment, see Ward, *Miracles and the Medieval Mind*, pp. 68–72. For John the sheriff, see *Sibton Abbey Cartularies and Charters*, ed. P. Brown, 4 vols, Suffolk Records Society, Suffolk Charters, vols 7–10 (1985–88), vol. 1, pp. 1–24; *The Life and Miracles of St William*, eds Jessopp and James, pp. xxxiii–xxxiv.

25 See *The Charters of Norwich Cathedral Priory*, ed. B. Dodwell, 2 vols, Pipe Roll Society, new ser., vols 40, 46 (1974 for 1965–66, and 1985 for 1978–80), vol. 1, no. 118; *English Episcopal Acta VI: Norwich 1070–1214*, ed. C. Harper-Bill (Oxford, 1990), pp. xxxii–xxxiii, no. 42A and note; H.W. Saunders, *The First Register of Norwich Cathedral Priory: A Transcript and Translation*, Norfolk Record Society, vol. 11 (1939), pp. 70–71.

26 Sibton abbey was founded on 22 February 1150, and Thomas had his first vision on Tuesday in the first week of Lent 1150: D. Knowles and R.N. Hadcock, *Medieval Religious Houses England and Wales* (2nd edn, 1971), pp. 114, 125; *Sibton Abbey Cartularies*, ed. Brown, vol. 1, pp. 1, 13–14, 17; vol. 3, nos 470–71; *The Life and Miracles of St William*, eds Jessopp and James, p. xi. For the tenurial and familial contacts that may have influenced William's choice of order, see *Sibton Abbey Cartularies*, ed. Brown, vol. 1, p. 18. In 1154 the interest of Thomas in the cult seems to have waned: Finucane, *Miracles and Pilgrims*, pp. 120, 161–62; Ward, *Miracles and the Medieval Mind*, p. 71.

27 *The Life and Miracles of St William*, eds Jessopp and James, pp. 57–88, 128–29, 132–63, 165–71, 174–83, 189–218, 222–60, 263–94.

28 Ibid., pp. 231–41.

29 Ward, *Miracles and the Medieval Mind*, pp. 37–42, 75. See also Head, *Hagiography and the Cult of Saints*, p. 290; Töpfer, 'The Cult of Relics', p. 55.

30 C. Lauranson-Rosaz, 'Peace from the Mountains: The Auvergnat Origins of the Peace of God', in *The Peace of God*, eds Head and Landes, pp. 125–27.

31 *Liber Eliensis*, ed. Blake, pp. 319, 433–35; Round, *Geoffrey de Mandeville*, p. 161.

32 *The Chronicle of Hugh Candidus*, ed. Mellows, p. 122; *The Peterborough Chronicle*, ed. Mellows, p. 65.

33 *The Chronicle of John of Worcester*, ed. McGurk, pp. 230–31. For Thurstan and the Scots, see D. Nicholl, *Thurstan, Archbishop of York (1114–40)*, (York, 1964), pp. 218–32.

34 *Recueil des Historiens des Gaules et de la France*, ed. M. Bouquet et al., 24 vols (Paris, 1869–1904), vol. 15, p. 498; *English Episcopal Acta VII: Hereford 1079–1234*, ed. J. Barrow (Oxford, 1993), no. 54. A date of June 1148 for Bishop Jocelin's letter is given by L. Grant, *Abbot Suger of St-Denis: Church and State in Early Twelfth-Century France* (1998), p. 170. This date is likely but not certain. Barrow gives dating limits between 28 June 1131 and 16 April 1148 for Bishop Robert's letter. See also L. Grant, 'Suger and the Anglo-Norman World', *Anglo-Norman Studies*, vol. 19 (1997), p. 62.

35 For Suger's life, see Grant, 'Suger and the Anglo-Norman World'; Grant, *Abbot Suger of St-Denis*.

36 See G.M. Spiegel, *The Chronicle Tradition of Saint-Denis: A Survey* (Brookline and Leyden, 1978), esp. pp. 11–13, 19–31, 34–37, 45, quotation from p. 45. I am grateful to Professor Christopher Allmand for drawing my attention to this work.

37 See Suger, *The Deeds of Louis the Fat*, trans. R.C. Cusimano and J. Moorhead (Washington, 1992), pp. 6–15; Spiegel, *The Chronicle Tradition of Saint-Denis*, pp. 30, 37.

38 See above, note 7.

39 *The Waltham Chronicle*, eds L. Watkiss and M. Chibnall (Oxford, 1994), pp. 80–84. There is no reason to believe that these miracles were invented after 1154. Hugh Thomas has shown that numerous miracle stories survive from Stephen's reign, and has convincingly argued that some were based upon actual events and can be used to throw light on secular politics and the nature of the disturbances: H.M. Thomas, 'Miracle Stories and the Anarchy of King Stephen's Reign', a paper read at the International Medieval Congress, University of Leeds, July 1997. I chaired the session in which Professor Thomas gave his paper, and am grateful to him for kindly supplying me with a copy of the paper beforehand.

40 *The Waltham Chronicle*, eds Watkiss and Chibnall, pp. 80–82.

41 Ibid., p. 80.

42 There is an extensive literature on this subject. For references, see King, 'Dispute Settlement', above, note 2.

43 *The Waltham Chronicle*, eds Watkiss and Chibnall, p. 82.

44 Humphrey was a benefactor of the house: ibid., p. 82, n. 2.

45 This was a ritual in which relics were placed on the floor and sometimes covered or surrounded with thorns and criticised or cursed. Its purpose was to encourage

the saint or God to fulfil the role of patron and protector, and to make the enemies of the church or disturbers of peace feel responsible for the humiliation and correct their ways. See Geary, *Living with the Dead*, pp. 95–124; Geary, *Furta Sacra*, pp. 20–21; Head, *Hagiography and the Cult of Saints*, p. 290; Koziol, *Begging Pardon and Favor*, pp. 144, 221–22; Abou-El-Haj, *The Medieval Cult of Saints*, pp. 102–5, 112, 118–19.

46 *The Waltham Chronicle*, eds Watkiss and Chibnall, p. 80.

47 See *Symeonis Monachi Opera Omnia*, ed. T. Arnold, 2 vols, Rolls Series, 75 (1882–85), vol. 1, pp. 3–169, 196–214, 229–61; vol. 2, pp. 333–62.

48 Richard of Hexham, *De Gestis Regis Stephani et de Bello Standardii*, in *Chronicles of the Reigns of Stephen, Henry II, and Richard I*, ed. R. Howlett, 4 vols, Rolls Series, 82 (1884–89), vol. 3, pp. 153–54.

49 Ibid., p. 154. See also Gransden, *Historical Writing*, pp. 216–18.

50 See Richard of Hexham, *De Gestis Regis Stephani* in *Chronicles of the Reigns of Stephen etc.*, ed. Howlett, vol. 3, pp. 155–56, 165.

51 Gransden, *Historical Writing*, p. 216. For the account, see Ailred of Rievaulx, *Relatio de Standardo*, in *Chronicles of the Reigns of Stephen etc.* ed. Howlett, vol. 3, pp. 181–99. For dating, see D. Baker, 'Ailred of Rievaulx and Walter Espec', *Haskins Society Journal*, vol. 1 (1989), p. 93 and n. 6.

52 See A. Squire, *Aelred of Rievaulx: A Study* (1973), pp. 76–82; Gransden, *Historical Writing*, pp. 214–15; R. Ransford, 'A Kind of Noah's Ark: Aelred of Rievaulx and National Identity', in *Religion and National Identity*, ed. S. Mews, Studies in Church History, vol. 18 (Oxford, 1982), pp. 137–46; Baker, 'Ailred of Rievaulx', pp. 91–98; B.P. McGuire, *Brother and Lover: Aelred of Rievaulx* (New York, 1994), pp. 68–70.

53 Richard of Hexham, *De Gestis Regis Stepheni*, in *Chronicles of the Reigns of Stephen etc.*, ed. Howlett, vol. 3, pp. 188–89.

54 In one of Ailred's miracle stories St Wilfrid and St Cuthbert prevented Hexham from being attacked by King Malcolm III, who is described as normally keeping the peace with Hexham out of respect for its saints. See *De Sanctis Ecclesiae Haugustaldensis*, in J. Raine, *The Priory of Hexham*, 2 vols, Surtees Society, 44, 46 (1864–65), vol. 1, pp. 173–203, esp. pp. 177–81. For commentary, see Nicholl, *Thurstan, Archbishop of York*, pp. 34–35; Squire, *Aelred of Rievaulx*, pp. 112–15; Gransden, *Historical Writing*, p. 289; M.L. Dutton, 'The Conversion and Vocation of Aelred of Rievaulx: A Historical Hypothesis', in *England in the Twelfth Century*, ed. D. Williams (Woodbridge, 1990), p. 40; McGuire, *Brother and Lover*, pp. 17–22. Ailred's concern for peace at this time was also discussed by Valerie A. Wall in a paper entitled 'The "Speculum" for Winchester: The Duel in Aelred of Rievaulx's *Genealogia Regum Anglorum*', given at the International Medieval Congress, University of Leeds, in July 1996, an abstract of which was published in *The Anglo-Norman Anonymous*, vol. 14(3), (October 1996), p. 6. See also McGuire, *Brother and Lover*, pp. 70–73.

55 See *Liber Eliensis*, ed. Blake, pp. 294–99, 314; *Historia Selebiensis Monasterii*, in *The Coucher Book of Selby*, ed. J.T. Fowler, 2 vols, The Yorkshire Archaeological and Topographical Association, Record Series, vols 10, 13 (1891 for 1890, 1893 for 1892), vol. 1, pp [33]–[44].

56 Ibid., vol. 1, pp. [33]–[34]. For a Norman example of this from 1105–6, see *The Ecclesiastical History of Orderic Vitalis*. ed. Chibnall, vol. 6, pp. 60–64, cited by C.J. Holdsworth, 'Ideas and Reality: Some Attempts to Control and Defuse War in the Twelfth Century', in *The Church and War*, ed. W.J. Sheils, Studies in Church History,

vol. 20 (Oxford, 1983), p. 65.

57 Bishop Robert's consecration of new graveyards as refuges also served to help break down the powers of the old minster parish churches by attacking their burial monopolies, one of their main financial assets: *English Episcopal Acta VII*, ed. Barrow, pp. xxxix–xl, nos 44, 50, 72, 95–96. The policy of refuge creation may have been pursued by other bishops. See *English Episcopal Acta VI*, ed. Harper-Bill, no. 139; F.M. Stenton, 'Acta Episcoporum', *Cambridge Historical Journal*, vol. 3 (1929), p. 13. For hermits, see *Wulfric of Haselbury by John Abbot of Ford*, ed. M. Bell, Somerset Record Society, vol. 47 (1933), p. lxiii; H. Mayr-Harting, 'Functions of a Twelfth-Century Recluse', *History*, vol. 60 (1975), pp. 342–43.

58 For reparation charters, see F. M. Stenton, *The First Century of English Feudalism 1066–1166* (2nd edn, Oxford, 1961), pp. 244–45; Callahan, 'Ecclesiastical Reparations', above, note 2. See also King, 'The Anarchy of King Stephen's Reign', pp. 133–53, esp. 133, 139–43, 153.

59 Attention was drawn to the importance of charters addressed to bishops in E. King, 'The Foundation of Pipewell Abbey, Northamptonshire', *Haskins Society Journal*, vol. 2 (1990), p. 170 n. 17. For examples, see BL, MS Cotton Vespasian Exx (Bardney cartulary), fo. 124r-v; *Documents Illustrative of the Social and Economic History of the Danelaw*, ed. F.M. Stenton (1920), no. 516; *The Charters of the Anglo-Norman Earls of Chester, c. 1071–1237*, ed. G. Barraclough, The Record Society of Lancashire and Cheshire, vol. 126 (1988), no. 96.

60 See, for example, *Documents*, ed. Stenton, no. 516.

61 *English Lawsuits*, ed. van Caenegem, vol. 1, no. 319.

62 *Early Yorkshire Charters*, vols 1–3, ed. W. Farrer (Edinburgh, 1914–16); vols. 4–12, ed. C.T. Clay, Yorkshire Archaeological Society Record Series, extra ser., vols 1–3, 5–10 (1935–65), vol. 3, no. 1823.

63 For the York election dispute, see D. Knowles, 'The Case of St William of York', *Cambridge Historical Journal*, vol. 5 (1936), pp. 162–77, 212–14.

64 See, for example, Koziol, 'Monks, Feuds, and the Making of Peace', pp. 239–58.

65 For large crowds coming to another cathedral city at Easter time, see *The Life and Miracles of St William*, eds Jessopp and James, p. 26. For another public reparation made before the bishop and chapter of Lincoln in the later years of the reign, see C.W. Foster, *A History of the Villages of Aisthorpe and Thorpe in the Fallows* (Lincoln, 1927), pp. 105–6; *The Charters of Norwich Cathedral Priory*, ed. Dodwell, no. 278; *English Episcopal Acta I: Lincoln 1067–1185*, ed. D.M. Smith (Oxford, 1980), no. 200.

66 *Early Yorkshire Charters*, ed. Clay, vol. 9, no. 76.

67 For Daiville, see *Charters of the Honour of Mowbray 1107–1191*, ed. D.E. Greenway (1972), p. lx. There was, however, a monk of Byland abbey with the same name: ibid., no. 77. For Robert de Alney, see Nicholl, *Thurstan, Archbishop of York*, p. 202; Gransden, *Historical Writing*, p. 291.

68 For honorial officials, see King, 'Dispute Settlement', pp. 115–18. For hermits, see P. Brown, 'The Rise and Function of the Holy Man in Late Antiquity', *Journal of Roman Studies*, vol. 61 (1971), pp. 80–101, reprinted in his *Society and the Holy in Late Antiquity* (1982), pp. 103–52; Mayr-Harting, 'Functions of a Twelfth-Century Recluse'; C. Holdsworth, 'Hermits and the Powers of the Frontier', *Reading Medieval Studies*, vol. 16 (1990), pp. 55–76, esp. pp. 59–60, 64–71. One hermit who lived through Stephen's reign, Wulfric of Haselbury, could 'resolve many tensions, and exercise all

kinds of control', and 'set a typical robber freebooter ... on the path to being abbot of Tintern': Mayr-Harting, 'Functions of a Twelfth-Century Recluse', pp. 341, 345. See also *Wulfric of Haselbury*, ed. Bell, pp. xxxiii–xxxvii, lxi–lxii.

69 *Transcripts of Charters relating to the Gilbertine Houses of Sixle, Ormsby, Catley, Bullington and Alvingham*, ed. F.M. Stenton, Lincoln Record Society, vol. 18 (1922), no. 25. It is not certain that this Robert de Alney and the hermit were one and the same man.

70 See *English Lawsuits*, ed. van Caenegem, vol. 1, no. 317; *English Episcopal Acta I*, ed. Smith, no. 83; D.B. Crouch, *The Beaumont Twins: The Roots and Branches of Power in the Twelfth Century* (Cambridge, 1986), p. 80. The saint was possibly Remigius of Rheims.

71 See, for example, *English Episcopal Acta VII*, ed. Barrow, no. 101; *The Letters and Charters of Gilbert Foliot*, ed. Z.N. Brooke et al. (Cambridge, 1967), no. 331.

72 For examples, see *English Episcopal Acta I*, ed. Smith, no. 20; *English Lawsuits*, ed. van Caenegem, vol. 1, no. 320; *English Episcopal Acta VI*, ed. Harper-Bill, no. 150; *English Episcopal Acta VIII: Winchester 1070–1204*, ed. M.J. Franklin (Oxford, 1993), no. 54.

73 *The Registrum Antiquissimum of the Cathedral Church of Lincoln*, eds C.W. Foster and K. Major, 10 vols, Lincoln Record Society, 27–29, 32, 34, 41, 46, 51, 62, 67 (1931–73), vol. 3, no. 921, and see p. 264. For a dispute settled before Robert bishop of Lincoln and an ecclesiastical assembly between 19 December 1148 and some time in 1150, see *English Episcopal Acta I*, ed. Smith, no. 137.

74 *Liber Eliensis*, ed. Blake, pp. liii, 344–62, 402–7.

75 For the Waltons, the Staffords and the foundation of Stone priory, see *VCH, Staffordshire*, vol. 3, pp. 240–41; I.J. Sanders, *English Baronies: A Study of their Origin and Descent 1086–1327* (Oxford, 1960), p. 81; G.H. Gerould, 'The Legend of St Wulfhad and St Ruffin at Stone Priory', *Publications of the Modern Language Association of America*, ed. W.G. Howard, vol. 32, new series, vol. 25 (1917), pp. 323–30. It is possible that Robert of Stafford was also acting in the capacity of sheriff. For the possibility that he was sheriff of Staffordshire in Stephen's reign: see J.A. Green, *English Sheriffs to 1154* (1990), p. 75.

76 *English Lawsuits*, ed. van Caenegem, vol. 1, no. 325.

77 Saltman, *Theobald, Achbishop of Canterbury*, pp. 58–59, 115–16, 162.

78 For France, see Rosenwein, Head and Farmer, 'Monks and their Enemies' (note 3 above), pp. 775–77.

79 For relics and altars generally, see Rollason, *Saints and Relics*, pp. 176–77. For St Wulflad and St Rufinus, see *VCH, Staffordshire*, vol. 3, p. 240; Gerould, 'The Legend of St. Wulfhad'; D.W. Rollason, 'The Cults of Murdered Royal Saints in Anglo-Saxon England', *Anglo-Saxon England*, vol. 11 (1983), p. 11; Rollason, *Saints and Relics*, pp. 119, 234. I am grateful to Dr Philip Morgan for drawing my attention to the connection of these saints with Stone and providing references. For another case of important churchmen and laymen co-operating to settle a property dispute by judicial means in the later years of the reign, see *English Lawsuits*, ed. van Caenegem, vol. 1, no. 345.

80 At times some of them provoked and engaged in controversies and violence, and even when they promoted peace they often did so to protect and to develop their own interests or those of their churches. The motives behind ecclesiastical peace-

making were complex and varied. A full consideration of them lies beyond the scope of this paper.

81 It may have been even more widespread than the examples in this paper have shown. See M. Bloch, 'La Vie de S. Édouard le Confesseur par Osbert de Clare', *Analecta Bollandiana*, vol. 41 (1923), pp. 5–131; *The Letters of Osbert of Clare Prior of Westminster*, ed. E.W. Williamson (Oxford, 1929), pp. 12–32; B.W. Scholz, 'The Canonization of Edward the Confessor', *Speculum*, vol. 36 (1961), pp. 38–60; Ridyard, *The Royal Saints*, esp. pp. 16–25, 32–36, 50–59, 72, 96–107, 113, 119–21, 130, 177–209, 253–308; R.M. Thomson, 'Two Versions of a Saint's Life from St Edmund's Abbey: Changing Currents in XIIth Century Monastic Style', *Revue Bénédictine*, vol. 84 (1974), pp. 383–408, esp. pp. 388–93; Rollason, *Saints and Relics*, pp. 138–39, 203, 206–8, 212, 219–23; *The Vita Wulfstani of William of Malmesbury*, ed. R.R. Darlington, Camden Society, vol. 40 (1928), pp. viii, xix–xxi; *Liber Eliensis*, ed. Blake; Mayr-Harting, 'Functions of a Twelfth–Century Shrine' (see note 5 above), pp. 193–206.

82 For examples of work on Martial, see Cowdrey, 'The Peace and the Truce of God', pp. 45–46, 49–52, 55–56; D.F. Callahan, 'The Sermons of Adémar of Chabannes and the Cult of St Martial of Limoges', *Revue Bénédictine*, vol. 86 (1976), pp. 251–95; Landes, *Relics, Apocalypse, and the Deceits of History*.

83 I argued that Newhouse abbey and several other religious houses were founded in Stephen's reign partly to promote peace, in a paper read at the International Medieval Congress, University of Leeds, July 1998: 'Politics, Patronage and Peace: The Foundation and Endowment of Religious Houses in Northern England in the Reign of King Stephen', an abstract of which was published in *The Anglo-Norman Anonymous*, vol. 16 (3), (October 1998), pp. 3–4. See also *Documents*, ed. Stenton, p. 166, and nos 235, 244, 247, 255, 281, 299, 303, 313; H.M. Colvin, *The White Canons in England* (Oxford, 1951), pp. 39–52; P. Dalton, 'Aiming at the Impossible: Ranulf II Earl of Chester and Lincolnshire in the Reign of King Stephen', in *The Earldom of Chester and Its Charters: A Tribute to Geoffrey Barraclough*, ed. A.T. Thacker, Journal of the Chester Archaeological Society, vol. 71 (1991), pp. 115–17; Stenton, *The First Century of English Feudalism*, pp. 48–51, 261–63.

84 See *Papsturkunden in England*, ed. W. Holtzmann, 3 vols in 4, Abhandlungen der Gesellschaft der Wissenschaften zu Göttingen, Phil.-Hist. Klasse, Neue Folge, 25, Dritte Folge, 14–15, 33 (Berlin, 1930–31), 1935–36, and Göttingen, 1952), vol. 1, nos 18, 20–21, 26–28, 30–35, 39–40, 44, 46–48, 51–53, 55–57; vol. 2, nos 18–25, 27–32, 34–36, 38, 40, 43–44, 48–58, 60–64, 66–68, 70–71, 74, 77–80; vol. 3, nos 30–32, 34–44, 46–50, 52–55, 58–59, 61–62, 64–68, 70–73, 75–78, 81, 84–89, 91, 93, 95.

Earls and Earldoms
during King Stephen's Reign

Graeme J. White

The proliferation of earldoms in the reign of King Stephen excited comment at the time and continues to exercise historians today. Largely as a result of creations by both Stephen and Empress Matilda, there were only five shires in England which did not have an earl at some point during the reign; Cornwall, Lincolnshire, Wiltshire and – arguably – Herefordshire and Norfolk had more than one at the same time, the product of rival appointments.[1] Although J.H. Round, in the 1890s, and G.H. White, in the 1920s and 1930s, made valuable contributions to our knowledge of the creation of these earldoms, they were mostly concerned with details surrounding the implementation of policy, rather than with the motivation behind it. It has been left to their successors to seek reasons for the appointment of so many earls and to argue for a good deal of coherent planning. Accordingly, R.H.C. Davis suggested that the earls were to act 'in a military capacity ... as the defenders of their counties' and were expected by both king and empress to wield executive authority on their behalf. W.L. Warren took these ideas further, seeing the appointment of an earl 'as surrogate for the king ruling an autonomous county' in the context of a deliberate policy of decentralising the government, a policy already in place before the civil war began and one which the empress 'found irresistible'.[2] Although evidence can certainly be produced in support of these claims, there were too many variations in practice between one earl and another for them to serve as all-embracing explanations, and the most recent contributors have introduced a note of caution. Thus, Keith Stringer, while agreeing that the creation of earldoms represented a planned 'decentralisation of government in the regions', has pointed out that the powers devolved by the king to his earls were generally greater in vulnerable shires than in more stable ones. In turn, Judith Green has argued that 'most of Stephen's earldoms were created for defence in border counties', while suggesting that other factors, such as the wish to control an unreliable sheriff or 'straight-forward recognition of loyalty', came into play elsewhere.[3]

If there is a consensus of opinion today, it is that, in governmental terms, the grant of an earldom in itself meant very little. What mattered was the extent to which additional powers and privileges were given away – separately from the earldom in some cases – or seized by the beneficiary.[4] But it is still worth asking how far was the position enjoyed by earls in Stephen's reign the result of careful strategic forethought, and how dependent upon their earls did king and empress become? This paper will argue that the outbreak of civil war in 1139 led to a shift in Stephen's approach to the appointment of earls, and that whereas a significant military and administrative role was normally expected of those promoted after that date, in his early years he often saw the grant of earldoms essentially as a cheap and convenient way of reinforcing baronial support. The change was by no means clear-cut, but there is enough evidence to suggest a different emphasis after 1139, as the king adjusted to the circumstances of civil war. In the event, he was soon to regret his generous distribution of earldoms, as the empress followed with creations of her own, and individual earls took opportunities to enhance their authority without reference to the crown.

Stephen presented himself at the beginning of his reign as the continuator of the liberties and good laws of his uncle Henry I, and the style of government he attempted clearly owed a great deal to his predecessor.[5] The compilation of the *Constitutio Domus Regis*, apparently at the very outset of his reign, implies an intention to model his household on that of Henry I; numismatic evidence suggests the maintenance of the policy introduced in 1125 of allowing pennies of the same Type to circulate long-term, without frequent recoinages; royal writs and charters of the period 1136–39 show substantial continuity from the previous reign in administrative personnel, in chancery practice and in the financial and judicial systems, with the king intervening in lawsuits – directly or through his justices – much as Henry I had done. There were destined to be changes in the way Stephen administered the country as a result of the recurrent crises of 1139–41, but it is in the context of initial continuity from the previous reign that we should begin to examine his creation of earldoms. Was he deliberately breaking with the past by seeking to decentralise his government, or merely developing and extending a policy towards earls which he had observed under Henry I?

Seven earldoms were bequeathed to Stephen by his predecessor, and he allowed them all to continue: Buckingham (held by Walter III Giffard), Chester (Ranulf II), Gloucester (Robert de Caen), Leicester (Robert de Beaumont), Surrey (William II de Warenne), Warwick (Roger de Beaumont), and Huntingdon/Northampton (David, king of Scots, although this Midlands earldom was granted instead to David's son Henry under the first treaty of Durham of February 1136).[6] Among these, the earl of Chester was in an exceptional position, lord of his whole shire apart from episcopal land, controlling a sheriff appointed by, and answerable to him, and in receipt of revenues which would elsewhere have come to the king.[7] But even if we put Chester to one side, it is apparent that under Henry I the powers attached to earldoms differed in several points of detail. At least two boroughs, Leicester and Warwick, were directly controlled by their local earls, who by 1130 were in receipt of the revenues as constituents of their demesnes.[8] The earl of Huntingdon/Northampton apparently received the 'third pennies' of borough revenues in Bedford and Cambridge, a privilege the earl of Surrey may also have enjoyed in Guildford and Southwark.[9] The earl of Gloucester is the only one who appears in the 1130 pipe roll as in receipt of the third penny of pleas of the shire, although later references suggest that the earls of Leicester, Surrey and Warwick may also have done so.[10] Other than Chester, earls appear to have exercised direct control over sheriffs in the years around 1100 in Warwickshire, and possibly for much of the reign in Northamptonshire, but evidence of this is lacking elsewhere.[11] As for the role played by earls within their shires, the address clauses of royal writs and charters suggest that this was neither defined nor consistent. Examples may be cited of addresses by Henry I to shire officials in Gloucestershire, Huntingdonshire, Northamptonshire, Surrey and Warwickshire to show that, while an earl was sometimes included to lend weight to the king's instructions, he was frequently omitted; he was not seen as essential either to the composition of the shire court or to local administration in general.[12] It seems clear that under Henry I most earldoms were seen – by all parties – primarily as honorific titles, coveted for the status they conferred rather than for any practical powers attached to them. Yet by the end of the reign, at least some of the holders of these titles had secured control of sheriffs, had mediatised boroughs, or had successfully laid claim to other financial perquisites. There was sufficient here to excite the aspirations of existing earls, and of magnates who wanted to be *comites* themselves.

Under Stephen, circumstances were propitious for such aspirations to be met.

A chronological approach to Stephen's creation of earldoms must begin with two creations in 1136. As count of Brittany, Alan of Richmond already bore the title *comes*, but it was as earl of Richmond that he attested two royal charters of that year. In this case, the comital title presumably acknowledged the military and administrative role Alan was fulfilling from his castle at Richmond; it implied independence from the sheriff of Yorkshire and helped to convince him of the value of remaining loyal against the Scots. While the title may not have added significantly to the authority Alan was already wielding in practice, this earldom was clearly intended to be more than honorific.[13] Elsewhere, an earldom also appears to have been conferred during the course of the year upon Simon II de Senlis, who had a hereditary claim to Huntingdon/Northampton through his mother, wife of the king of Scots. Although the two charters apparently of 1136 which show him as an earl are not above suspicion, it is likely that Simon was allowed to use the style *comes* from early in the reign, only for the title to become consistently associated with Huntingdonshire and Northamptonshire once his half-brother Henry of Scots had forfeited his tenure; this would have been by 1141 at the latest. In granting Earl Simon a title attached to this region Stephen was acknowledging an obvious aspiration, besides allowing further patronage to the influential Beaumont family, to whom Simon was related by marriage;[14] but there is no indication that his earldom initially carried any administrative responsibilities, despite the fact that he later became one of Stephen's more effective local representatives. Like Alan of Richmond he was gratified by the style *comes*, and Stephen saw no reason not to oblige him.

The next group of earldoms to consider are those created by Stephen in or about 1138, a year when, according to William of Malmesbury's *Historia Novella*, Stephen

> established many as earls who had not been earls before, with endowments of landed estates and revenues that had belonged directly to the king. They were the more greedy in asking, and he the more lavish in giving, because a rumour was flying over England that Robert, earl of Gloucester, who was in Normandy, was on the point of siding with his sister, just as soon as he had defied the king.

Robert's defiance duly followed in June 1138, although the predictable sequel, a military invasion of England, did not come until 15 months later.[15]

William of Malmesbury's comments are useful in suggesting a date, and a possible political context, for some of Stephen's early grants of earldoms, but they certainly should not be accepted without reservation. For a start, at least one new earl at this time, Waleran of Worcester, was outside the ranks of those 'who had not been earls before' (*comites, qui ante non fuerant*), because he was already count of Meulan.[16] The association with Robert earl of Gloucester's impending defection is inappropriate in the cases of William of Aumale and Robert de Ferrers, who were given their earldoms of York and Nottingham/Derby after the battle of the Standard in August 1138, as reward for their contribution to the defeat of the Scots.[17] As for the distribution of lands and revenues, this was patronage which all Anglo-Norman kings had to engage in. One earl whom William of Malmesbury probably had in mind was Waleran of Meulan, who had already received the city of Worcester, the saltworks in Droitwich and several royal manors in Worcestershire, besides new holdings in Normandy, before receiving his earldom of Worcester. Similarly his brother Hugh le Poer had already been given the town of Bedford and the heiress of the Bedfordshire baron Simon de Beauchamp in marriage, before his creation as earl.[18] William of Aumale's acquisition of nearly all the important royal manors in Yorkshire may well have been by the king's grant during the course of 1138, but he was possibly in control of the city of York sometime before he became earl, and his management of royal forests in the shire also seems to have been distinct from his earldom.[19] There were strategic considerations behind all this patronage – the wish to enhance the position of the trusted Beaumont family in the Midlands; a concern to balance the favour shown in Yorkshire to Alan of Richmond and William of Aumale – but the grant of comital titles was only one element within it.

It would, however, be wrong to dismiss William of Malmesbury's comments altogether. A concern to provide a military bulwark against Robert earl of Gloucester may well have been in mind when Stephen established Waleran of Meulan in Worcestershire, culminating in the grant of the earldom.[20] The impression conveyed in the *Historia Novella* of a 'snowball effect', of the king yielding to increasing demands, also rings true, for besides those already mentioned, 1138 certainly saw the creation of a new earl of Pembroke (Gilbert fitz Gilbert) and was probably also the year when Gilbert fitz Richard, William de Roumare and William d'Aubigny *pincerna* became earls of Hertford, Cambridge and Lincoln respectively.[21] Doubtless there were particular circumstances underlying some of these grants, such as the need to elevate William d'Aubigny to a status in keeping with his brilliant marriage to Henry I's widow Adeliza, but there is a general impression here of magnates already in the king's favour who saw no reason why they should be left out of the queue for comital titles. With the looming threat of invasion led by Robert earl of Gloucester, Stephen probably felt it unwise to refuse their requests.

We still have to ask, however, what role the earldoms created around 1138 were supposed to fulfil. Waleran of Meulan may well have been expected to defend his shire militarily not only against the earl of Gloucester but also against the Welsh, although as we have seen the landed resources to help him to do so had already been given in advance of the earldom. Robert de Ferrers and William of Aumale were doubtless expected to counter an advance by the Scots, although they had already helped to win the battle of the Standard before their promotion as earls. A military purpose underlying the grant of the earldom of Pembroke to Gilbert fitz Gilbert, at a time of Welsh resurgence, seems incontrovertible, although it was not until 1145 that he actually campaigned in south Wales, having spent much of the intervening period with Stephen in England.[22] If we look for administrative responsibilities, it is clear that by 1137 and 1139 respectively the shrievalties of Warwickshire and Worcestershire were controlled by their earls, Roger de Beaumont and Waleran of Meulan.[23] A good case has been made for regarding William of Aumale as having been entrusted by Stephen with wide-ranging powers in Yorkshire, including control of the sheriff, at a time of military and administrative crisis in 1138, although we cannot be sure that some of his privileges were not acquired later.[24] These examples suggest that, even before the empress's arrival in the kingdom in September 1139, Stephen viewed some earldoms as carrying considerable governmental responsibilities – military, administrative, or both – and, as Judith Green has pointed out, these tended to be located in shires close to the frontiers of the kingdom. But they do not constitute a general policy on the subject, for other potentially vulnerable shires bordering on the earl of Gloucester's lands, such as Herefordshire, Wiltshire and Somerset, and those on the south coast which might have to face invasion from across the Channel, were left without an earl in this period. Elsewhere, we may safely treat Stephen's grant of the earldom of Northumberland to Henry of Scots, under the second treaty of Durham of April 1139, as a special case; in commanding the barons of Northumberland to do homage to Earl Henry, Stephen was accepting a transfer of control.[25] Beyond this, however, it is hard to see the earldoms granted in these early years to Simon II de Senlis, Hugh le Poer, William de Roumare, Gilbert fitz Richard and William d'Aubigny *pincerna* – all in shires under no particular military threat – as intended other than as honorific titles, even if the first three were prompted at least in part by a wish to bolster loyal support in the Midlands as a counter to the Scots.

As a favoured member of Henry I's court, Stephen had been accustomed to earldoms which occasionally carried local governmental responsibilities (and in Chester's case a military role and a measure of autonomy) but in the main were honorific, with no obvious threat to the powers of the crown. In the late 1130s, when he needed to secure the loyalty of his magnates, it was all too tempting to maintain Henry I's policies and take them further: to continue to grant out coveted titles, but to be liberal where he had been sparing, and where it seemed appropriate to add military and governmental duties as well. This must have seemed an inexpensive way of pandering to magnates' aspirations, one which occasionally involved some devolution of power but which could work to the king's advantage if the beneficiaries remained loyal and efficient. Continuity from Henry I's time is implied by the address clauses of Stephen's writs and charters, issued to shires which had earls in the late 1130s, for these show the same inconsistency in formulae as in the previous reign: even earls such as Roger of Warwick and Waleran of Meulan of Worcester, who had subordinate sheriffs to give effect to their authority, were as likely to be omitted as to be included when the king demanded local action.[26] But whatever Stephen's view of the earls he had created, the fundamental problem was that once a baron became a *comes* he was liable to dream of the power and autonomy enjoyed by the greatest to hold the title, including those in north-west France such as the *comites* of Anjou and Blois. Herein lay a potent threat to the efficacy of royal government in England, once the civil war had begun.

Even after Empress Matilda's invasion, some of Stephen's new earldoms continued to be primarily honorific in purpose. At the close of 1140, the king visited Lincolnshire to make a pact with William de Roumare and his half-brother Ranulf II earl of Chester, and – in the words of William of Malmesbury – 'added to their honours'. It was probably on this occasion that William was given the earldom of Lincoln (in place of his previously held Cambridge), but although he continued to be styled earl of Lincoln for the rest of the reign, there is no evidence that he acted in an administrative capacity here either for Stephen or the Angevins, and he spent much of his time thereafter in Normandy. Stephen's grant evidently did not include Lincoln castle – as it surely would have done if a military role was envisaged – and it was in an attempt to recover this from the brothers that the king was captured in battle in February 1141.[27] The previous earl of Lincoln, William d'Aubigny *pincerna*, may well have been given the alternative earldom of Sussex (which he held by Christmas 1141) so that Lincoln could be conferred upon William de Roumare. Sussex at least had the benefit, unlike Lincolnshire, of being a shire in which he held estates, his wife's honour of Arundel. But his readiness to use a variety of names for his earldom – Arundel, Chichester, Sussex and Aubigny – suggests that it was the comital style itself, not its association with particular local administrative duties, which mattered most to a man described in the *Waltham Chronicle* as being so 'arrogant and inordinately conceited' that 'he could not bear anyone being his equal'.[28]

These cases notwithstanding, Empress Matilda's arrival in England in September 1139, ready to fight her way to the throne, led to a new phase in the creation of earldoms. Her appearance was followed by the establishment of an alternative royal administration, initially based in Bristol and Gloucester, to which disaffected barons and *curiales* could turn, and created a climate of conflict and instability which made it more difficult for the king to enforce his will. As the northern writer John of Hexham put it, the empress's arrival 'caused very grave disturbance in England and undermined the stability of Stephen's kingdom'.[29] William of Malmesbury was another who explicitly linked the onset of suffering to the outbreak of war, following hard upon the empress's invasion. 'That whole year was troubled by the brutalities of war', he wrote of 1140 in the aftermath of Matilda's arrival: 'knights from the castles ... after plundering the dwellings of the wretched countrymen ... bound the owners and ... did not let them go until they had spent for their ransom all they possessed.'[30] This was the year when Stephen was obliged to campaign in the fens against the rebellious Nigel bishop of Ely, and when the notorious Robert fitz Hubert – a prime example of an extortionate 'castle-knight', famed for smearing prisoners with honey and leaving them to be stung under the heat of the sun – took Devizes castle, only to be captured by John fitz Gilbert and hanged by the earl of Gloucester.[31] It was sometime in 1140, probably arising from the bishop of Ely's rebellion, that Stephen ordered two local landholders, Hugh and Stephen de Scalers, to restore the 'farm' they were withholding from the monks of Ely, only then to find himself obliged to turn to Geoffrey de Mandeville – as yet without a comital title – to constrain them to obey.[32] In circumstances such as these, when the presence in the country of a challenger for the throne could lend some justification to resistance to the king, and when local magnates often seemed better placed than the king to maintain law and order, it must have appeared sensible to appoint more earls as the king's representatives in the shires, and to entrust them with administrative, executive and military authority to act on his behalf.

Two new creations by Stephen during the course of 1140, both certainly intended to provide a military challenge to the empress's supporters, were those of Hervey Brito as earl of Wiltshire and Alan of Richmond as earl of Cornwall: the *Gesta Stephani* tells us that Hervey was granted Devizes castle, from where he fought 'obstinate and unceasing warfare with the king's assailants', while Alan was given Cornwall with specific instructions to 'wage continual warfare' against the Angevin party.[33] Both men doubtless hoped that success would bring its own rewards at the expense of the defeated. The king's grant hereditarily of the *totus comitatus* of Herefordshire to Robert earl of Leicester, almost certainly in the same year, presumably had similar considerations in mind, given the Angevin dominance of this part of the country. Robert received the borough and castle of Hereford, and lordship of all fiefs in the shire with certain exceptions; in other words, he was given the resources and the incentive to fight Stephen's enemies in Herefordshire, and so make good the terms of the king's charter. One clause specifically referred to this, saying that he could have lordship of one of the excluded fiefs, that of Josce de Dinan, if he could induce Josce to hold it from him.[34] Elsewhere, the charter announcing Geoffrey II de Mandeville's creation as earl of Essex, also in 1140, gave no details of what the title implied – he was to hold his earldom hereditarily, with the same dignities, liberties and customs as other earls enjoyed – but since he had a hereditary claim to the shrievalty and had apparently served in an administrative capacity within the shire already, it is reasonable to believe that he, too, expected to wield considerable authority in practice. There may also have been military factors in his appointment, given that Hugh Bigod's revolt in the summer of 1140 obliged Stephen on two occasions to lead an army into East Anglia.[35]

As for the king's opponents, there can be no doubt that most of the earls appointed by Empress Matilda were expected to maintain the Angevin cause in their shires, by force of arms and by such administrative expedients as were required. The success of her half-brother Reginald de Dunstanville in gaining a foothold in Cornwall during the course of 1140 was seized upon by the empress who duly recognised him as her earl, although in this case it may have been Robert earl of Gloucester who was initially responsible for the creation.[36] In the following year, while Stephen was in captivity, Geoffrey II de Mandeville became her earl of Essex, Baldwin de Redvers her earl of Devon, William de Mohun her earl of Somerset, Miles of Gloucester her earl of Hereford, and Aubrey III de Vere her earl of Oxford, a list to which should probably be added Hugh Bigod as earl of Norfolk.[37] The terms of three of these grants survive, and two of them demonstrate the empress's readiness to devolve wide-ranging powers to her earls. Geoffrey II de Mandeville, already earl of Essex by virtue of Stephen's creation, won a series of concessions which reinforced his military and administrative authority. The empress's 'first charter' included the shrievalty and justiciarship of Essex, the third penny of pleas, custody of the Tower of London and various lands and lordships. Her 'second charter' added the shrievalties of London/Middlesex and Hertfordshire, and several other benefits, including the right to retain and fortify certain castles.[38] For his part, Miles of Gloucester, besides receiving portions of royal demesne in Herefordshire and lordship of three named vassals, was granted the castle of Hereford, the third penny of borough revenues and the third penny of pleas of the shire. He was familiar as an administrative official in Herefordshire and may already have held the office of sheriff, so a significant military and administrative role was clearly implied here also.[39] Yet the empress's charter for Aubrey III de Vere, while generous in many respects to Aubrey and his family, was tentative and vague when it came to the earldom. He was given Cambridgeshire 'with the third penny as an earl ought to have', but only if the king of Scots did not hold it. Failing Cambridgeshire, he was to become earl of whatever shire he chose, out of Oxfordshire, Berkshire, Wiltshire and Dorset; yet he had no lands in any of them, and although he was assured that he would hold his earldom as well as any earl did, this was an empty promise without the local offices, lands and castles which the empress's other earls were coming to acquire. Aubrey's choice of Oxfordshire was sensible: the charter was issued at Oxford, where the empress's subsequent residence and effective authority over the surrounding area made the grant of further comital powers a realistic prospect. But without them, it is hard to see this particular earldom as other than an honorific title, and it certainly proved insufficient to retain Aubrey's allegiance once Angevin fortunes in England declined, for he had deserted to Stephen by 1145.[40]

In abandoning the empress, he was not alone among her chosen earls, for Geoffrey II de Mandeville and William de Mohun also returned to Stephen's allegiance, the former by September 1141, the latter by 1144.[41] The king himself learned a salutary lesson from the political upheavals of 1141, as his earls of Lincoln, Worcester, Warwick, Pembroke and Essex committed themselves to the Angevin cause (albeit temporarily in the last three cases) and those of Bedford, Cornwall and Wiltshire failed to maintain their positions in their respective shires.[42] The experience led both Stephen and the empress to put less faith in their earls thereafter, although each of them was to make one further appointment which can be seen as carrying significant local responsibilities. In the mid-1140s the empress created Patrick of Salisbury, drawn from a family well-established as sheriffs, as her earl of Wiltshire; Patrick was clearly an active administrator, and he accounted for the sheriff's farm here from 1153 to 1160.[43] For his part, about 1149, Stephen made the Lincolnshire landholder Gilbert de Gant earl of Lincoln, in succession to the defector William de Roumare; here, the expectation seems to have been that Gilbert would defend the shire against Ranulf II earl of Chester, by then the king's implacable enemy.[44] There were other cases in which succession was allowed following the deaths of incumbent earls – to Pembroke and Surrey on Stephen's side, to Gloucester and Hereford among the Angevins – and there were to be two further grants of *totus comitatus* in 1153, to the earl of Chester in Staffordshire and to the earl of Surrey (Stephen's own son William) in Norfolk.[45] But these should be set against the fact that the empress appointed no successor to William de Mohun as earl of Somerset, and that Stephen chose not to replace Hugh le Poer, Alan of Richmond, Geoffrey II de Mandeville, Hervey Brito and Waleran of Meulan as earls of Bedford, Cornwall, Essex, Wiltshire and Worcester. All in one way or another had proved grave disappointments, while Waleran and Geoffrey, especially, had demonstrated the dangers inherent in the creation of earldoms, that over-ambitious *comites* would seek to accumulate too much autonomous power.[46] Accordingly, king and empress were left to govern those limited parts of the country where their authority was recognised and deal as best they could with the earls who remained.

The evidence of surviving writs and charters supports the contention that after 1141 neither king nor empress relied heavily on their earls as local representatives in the shires. Among the king's writs and charters directed to specific shires, and datable with virtual certainty to the period between his release from captivity and the eventual peace settlement, there are only two examples of addresses to named earls. One, a writ ordering Geoffrey earl of Essex and the (unnamed) sheriff of London to ensure that the canons of St Martin's le Grand hold their land outside Cripplegate in peace, appears to have included Geoffrey because of his role as justiciar of London rather than as earl of Essex. The other, a charter concerning the gift of estovers in the forests of Yorkshire to St Peter's Hospital, York, was addressed to William count of Aumale but did not describe him as earl of York; the omission may be significant, implying that he had custody of the forests in a capacity distinct from the earldom.[47] Even if we adopt a more liberal approach to dating, considering examples which may well date to 1141–53 but could possibly be earlier or later, we still find earls largely ignored: royal writs and charters addressed to shire officials in Buckinghamshire, Hertfordshire, Leicestershire, Lincolnshire, Nottinghamshire, Sussex, Warwickshire and Yorkshire can all be cited to demonstrate the point that incumbent earls were more often omitted than included.[48] The only earl who appeared with any frequency in Stephen's address clauses, in company with the shire officials of Huntingdonshire or Northamptonshire, was Simon II de Senlis; in this case, the king does seem to have had faith in the earl to act on his behalf.[49] But the evidence as a whole – Earl Simon and perhaps Earl Gilbert de Gant notwithstanding – does little to suggest a significant role for earls as the king's representatives in local administration. Stephen might occasionally acknowledge an earl by including him to add lustre to an address clause, much as Henry I had done, but he usually looked elsewhere for effective action. Indeed, he almost certainly came to see most of his earls more as obstacles to his government of the shires than as vehicles for enforcing his will. The number of writs and charters known to have been addressed by Stephen in the years following his release from captivity to the Midlands shires of Leicestershire, Nottinghamshire and Warwickshire stands in single figures, despite the presence of nominally loyal earls in the first two for the entire period to 1153, and in the third from the mid-1140s onwards.

Conversely, over 20 royal writs and charters are known to have been addressed to the king's officials in Essex in the period after the fall of Geoffrey II de Mandeville, an event which allowed the king to govern without the intervention of an earl.[50]

As for the empress, there are isolated examples of a charter of restitution in favour of Cirencester Abbey addressed among others to William de Mohun as earl of Somerset, and of a notification of a grant in Warwickshire addressed to Roger earl of Warwick,[51] but otherwise she also attempted to govern with little reference to her earls as heads of shire administration. On the one hand, although she is known to have addressed five writs and charters to her officials in Oxfordshire, all in 1141 or 1142, not one included her earl Aubrey de Vere.[52] On the other hand, we have no writs and charters at all from the empress to Devon and Cornwall:[53] a sign that, whatever the political contribution of earls Baldwin de Redvers and Reginald de Dunstanville in resisting the king's authority here, her own influence in these shires was minimal. Much the same could be said of her son, the future Henry II. The only shire officials he certainly addressed in the period before the peace settlement of 1153 were those of Gloucestershire, in one case including anonymous 'earls' with archbishops and bishops in the plural, in another Roger earl of Hereford alongside the sheriff of Gloucestershire and others: a combination of evidence which scarcely suggests reliance upon the incumbent earl William.[54] The absence of addresses by Henry to any other earls in the 'Angevin' south-west strengthens the impression that, in practical terms, at least until 1153, they acted independently of him.

This is not the place to explore in detail the extent to which earls took opportunities presented by weakened royal government from 1141 onwards to acquire additional powers for themselves. By the close of Stephen's reign, the earls of Devon, Gloucester, Hereford, Leicester, Nottingham–Derby, Northampton and Wiltshire were clearly controlling the shrievalties of their respective shires;[55] during the course of it, the earls of Worcester and Warwick ordered quittances from danegeld,[56] the earl of Gloucester levied scutage,[57] the earls of Cornwall and Devon assumed the right to hear crown pleas,[58] the earls of Gloucester, Leicester, Lincoln, Northampton, Nottingham–Derby, Wiltshire and York seem to have issued their own coins [59] and several earls, among them those of Devon, Gloucester, Hereford, Lincoln and Northampton, took control of boroughs previously accountable directly to the king.[60] Although Stephen had certainly envisaged some devolution of authority to favoured individuals in the late 1130s, in the context of granting out largely honorific titles, this was decentral-isation of government out of all proportion to that originally intended. Government in the hands of earls was not necessarily reprehensible, despite the tendency of contemporary writers to stereotype them as self-seeking oppressors. Whenever they initiated a court case, autho-rised the minting of coins, or ordered exemption from taxation, they were – in a sense – providing a service the king was currently unable to offer. And the various treaties into which they entered with one another, although undoubtedly motivated primarily by self-interest, can be regarded in broad terms as promoting a measure of stability.[61] But the transfer of power away from the king, which all this repre-sented, would obviously be an issue for urgent resolution once the civil war was over.

If the arguments set out here are accepted, we have in Stephen's reign earldoms which differed in their implications, one from another. Until 1139, as he sought to govern on the model bequeathed to him by Henry I, Stephen saw the grant of the title *comes* as an inexpensive means of patronage which would rally support against an impending threat to his throne. There was some readiness to devolve executive authority in vulnerable shires, but no consistent policy. The coming of civil war, however, led Stephen, and the empress in her turn, to see the appointment of active local representatives as imperative; as a result, most earldoms created during 1140 and 1141 carried considerable mil-itary and administrative powers. Thereafter, as several earls proved disloyal and many sought to administer their shires independently of higher authority, practice changed again: further creations of earls were exceptional, and king and empress often preferred to govern without them.

A glance ahead to the reign of Henry II shows us a king commit-ted to restoring the conditions of his grandfather's reign and – accord-ingly – to stripping the earls of the power and independence they had enjoyed under Stephen. Some titles, such as those of Waleran of Meu-lan at Worcester and William of Aumale at York, were withdrawn almost immediately;[62] some, such as those of Roger at Hereford, and Gilbert de Gant and William de Roumare at Lincoln, were allowed to lapse on death;[63] others – among them the earldoms of Derby, Devon, Essex, Norfolk, Oxford and Sussex – were permitted to continue and, in most cases, eventually to be passed on to heirs.[64] Where we have details of the terms under which earldoms were held or renewed, the only consistent privilege appears to have been entitlement to the third penny of pleas of the shire.[65] Although a few earls, notably Patrick of Salisbury in Wiltshire and Baldwin de Redvers' son Richard in Devon, retained shrievalties through the earliest years of the reign,[66] and although Cheshire and (until Earl Reginald's death in 1175) Cornwall remained bastions of comital control,[67] the new king was generally successful in ensuring – almost from the outset – that sheriffs and other local officials answered directly to him and that earls ceased to function in any practical sense as intermediaries between the king and the shires. Even in the first few years of Henry II's reign, royal writs directed to specific shires were almost invariably addressed to the sheriff, and sometimes to the bishop, a justice and local officials in general, rather than to earls. Indeed, there seems to have been greater consistency in ignoring the earls when addressing shire officials than had been the case under Henry I.[68]

But if this fairly describes Henry II's approach to his earls, how much of a contrast is it to what had gone before? In practice, as we have seen, both Stephen and the empress had sought to administer the shires with little reference to their earls after 1141. And once the civil war had ended with the treaty of Winchester in November 1153, Stephen had effectively reverted to the practice of his early years as king: that of flattering his barons with comital titles but treating these, essentially, as honorific. He now recognised the earldoms held by former Angevin adherents, among them Hugh Bigod in Norfolk and Patrick of Salisbury in Wiltshire, who for the first time witnessed his charters duly styled as earls.[69] But his interventions in local government consistently looked to others to represent him: although the shire officials of Hampshire, Lincolnshire, Wiltshire and Yorkshire were all addressed by the king in this period, there is only one known example of an address to a named earl, and that may predate the peace treaty in any case.[70] Among charters which appear to show some administrative recovery, Stephen's assignment to St Peter's Hospital, York, of 40 shillings per annum from the farm of the city of York, half at each of the exchequer terms, was addressed to the archbishop of York and the local justice and sheriff, not to Earl William of Aumale. And although his appointment of the bishop of Lincoln as 'my justice of Lincoln and Lincolnshire' was addressed to anonymous earls, barons, abbots, sheriffs, ministers, citizens and faithful men of the shire, this was to order them to attend the royal justice's pleas on pain of forfeiture of chattels.[71] Both charters were issued in the summer of

1154, and in effect they were signalling that earls had little part to play at local level in the restoration of royal authority which was now under way. In this respect, as in others, Henry II's governmental achievement in the first decade of his reign was to be based upon a continuation of policies which Stephen had already put in motion.

NOTES

1 R.H.C. Davis, *King Stephen, 1135–1154* (3rd edn, 1990), pp. 125–41. Davis argues that grants of a 'whole county' (*totus comitatus*), which included Herefordshire to Robert earl of Leicester (probably in 1140), Norfolk to William IV de Warenne earl of Surrey, and Staffordshire to Ranulf II earl of Chester (both in 1153), represented 'second earldoms' for those who held one already. My own view accords with that set out in P. Latimer, 'Grants of *totus comitatus* in Twelfth-century England: Their Origins and Meaning', *BIHR*, vol. 59 (1986), pp. 137–46, where *totus comitatus* is explained not as the earldom, but as the king's collective rights in the shire. Even so, earls in receipt of such grants were, in practice, being invited to exercise authority in more than one shire; in that sense, a shire which featured in a grant of *totus comitatus* did acquire an earl.

2 J.H. Round, *Geoffrey de Mandeville* (1892), pp. 267–77; G.H. White, 'King Stephen's Earldoms', *TRHS*, 4th ser., vol. 13 (1930), pp. 51–82 [read 1929]; White, 'The Career of Waleran, Count of Meulan and Earl of Worcester (1104–1166)', ibid., 4th ser., vol. 17 (1934), pp. 19–48 (at pp. 27–29); Davis, *King Stephen*, pp. 125–28 (originally in the first edition of 1967, pp. 129–32); W.L. Warren, *The Governance of Norman and Angevin England, 1086–1272* (1987), pp. 92–94.

3 K.J. Stringer, *The Reign of Stephen* (1993), pp. 53–55; J.A. Green, *The Aristocracy of Norman England* (Cambridge, 1997), pp. 298–305.

4 For example, E.J. King, 'Waleran, Count of Meulan, Earl of Worcester (1104–1166)', in *Tradition and Change*, eds D. Greenway, C. Holdsworth and J. Sayers (Cambridge, 1985), pp. 165–81 (at pp. 168–69); P. Dalton, *Conquest, Anarchy and Lordship: Yorkshire, 1066–1154* (Cambridge, 1994), pp. 145–47, 152–57.

5 For what follows, see J. Bradbury, 'The Early Years of the Reign of Stephen', in *England in the Twelfth Century*, ed. D. Williams (Woodbridge, 1990), pp. 17–30; G.J. White, 'Continuity in Government', in *The Anarchy of King Stephen's Reign*, ed. E.J. King (Oxford, 1994), pp. 117–43 (at pp. 118–22).

6 G.E. Cokayne, *C[omplete] P[eerage]*, ed. V. Gibbs et al., 13 vols (1910–59), vol. II, pp. 386–87; III, pp. 164–67; V, p. 683; VI, pp. 838–42; VII, pp. 523–27; IX, pp. 662–64; XII (i), pp. 493–96; XII (ii), pp. 357–62, and appendix A, pp. 2–3; *Regesta Regum Scottorum*, vol. I, ed. G.W.S. Barrow (Edinburgh, 1960), pp. 99–102.

7 *VCH, Cheshire*, vol. II, ed. B.E. Harris (Oxford, 1979), pp. 1–8; J.A. Green, *English Sheriffs to 1154* (1990), p. 32.

8 No *auxilia* were rendered for these boroughs, as they were from other centres of

shire administration (*P[ipe] R[oll] 31 Hen[ry] I*, ed. J. Hunter, Record Commission, (1833), pp. 88–89, 108). [Later Pipe Rolls published by Pipe Roll Society from 1884, except *PR 2–4 Hen. II* published by Record Commission (1844).] F.M. Stenton, *The First Century of English Feudalism* (2nd edn, Oxford, 1961), p. 234 and n. 2 includes Gloucester as one of those mediatised to the local earl, but an *auxilium* is recorded at *PR 31 Hen. I*, p. 80.

9 *Regesta Regum Scottorum*, vol. I, nos 203–4; G.H. Fowler, 'The Shire of Bedford and the Earldom of Huntingdon', Publications of the Bedfordshire Historical Record Society, vol. 9 (1925), pp. 23–34; *Liber Memorandum Ecclesie de Bernewelle*, ed. J.W. Clark (Cambridge, 1907), p. 93; P. Latimer, 'The Earls in Henry II's Reign' (unpubl. PhD thesis, University of Sheffield, 1982), p. 129.

10 *PR 31 Hen. I*, p. 77; Latimer, 'The Earls in Henry II's Reign', pp. 135–36.

11 D. Crouch, 'Geoffrey de Clinton and Roger Earl of Warwick: New Men and Magnates in the Reign of Henry I', *BIHR*, vol. 55 (1982), pp. 113–24 (at p. 115); Green, *English Sheriffs*, pp. 17, 63, 83; *Early Scottish Charters*, ed. A.C. Lawrie (Glasgow, 1905), nos. 56, 60.

12 *R[egesta] R[egum] A[nglo–]N[ormannorum]*, vol. II, eds C. Johnson and H.A. Cronne (Oxford, 1956), nos 1657, 1681 (Gloucs.), 1064, 1468, 1659, 1666 (Hunts.), 996–7, 1244 (Northants.), 639, 1350, 1435 (Surrey), 1415, 1636 (Warwicks.); J.A. Green, *The Government of England under Henry I* (Cambridge, 1986), p. 119; White, 'Continuity in Government', p. 125; but cf. Davis, *King Stephen*, p. 127.

13 *RRAN*, vol. III, eds H.A. Cronne and R.H.C. Davis (Oxford, 1968), nos. 204, 949; Davis, *King Stephen*, p. 141; Dalton, *Conquest, Anarchy and Lordship*, pp. 73–74, 166–67.

14 *RRAN*, vol. III, nos 284, 945; *Regesta Regum Scottorum*, vol. I, p. 102; *CP*, vol. VI, pp. 638–45; Davis, *King Stephen*, pp. 129–31; D. Crouch, *Beaumont Twins* (Cambridge, 1986), pp. 41, 84.

15 William of Malmesbury, *Historia Novella*, ed. E.J. King (Oxford, 1998), pp. 40–41 and n. 104.

16 Davis, *King Stephen*, pp. 132–33; Crouch, *Beaumont Twins*, p. 39; White, 'King Stephen's Earldoms', pp. 56–72; White, 'The Career of Waleran', esp. p. 23 (although King, 'Waleran, Count of Meulan', p. 168, favours 1139 as the date for the conferment of the earldom of Worcester). William of Aumale may also have been styled count of Aumale before 1138, but this is uncertain: see B. English, *The Lords of Holderness, 1086–1260* (Oxford, 1979), p. 18; cf. Dalton, *Conquest, Anarchy and Lordship*, p. 146.

17 John of Hexham, *Historia*, in Symeon of Durham, *Opera Omnia*, ed. T. Arnold, Rolls Series (1885), vol. II, pp. 293–95; Richard of Hexham, *Historia*, in *Chronicles of the Reigns of Stephen, Henry II and Richard I*, ed. R. Howlett, Rolls Series (1884–89), vol. III, pp. 164–65.

18 Crouch, *Beaumont Twins*, pp. 30, 41; Orderic Vitalis, *Ecclesiastical History*, ed. M. Chibnall (Oxford, 1969–80), vol. VI, p. 510.

19 Dalton, *Conquest, Anarchy and Lordship*, pp. 153–59.

20 R.B. Patterson, 'William of Malmesbury's Robert of Gloucester: A Re-evaluation of the "Historia Novella"', *American Historical Review*, vol. 70 (1965), pp. 983–97 (at pp. 990–91); Crouch, *Beaumont Twins*, pp. 30–31, 39–41.

21 Davis, *King Stephen*, pp. 133–35.

22 *Brut y Tywysogion, Red Book of Hergest Version*, ed. T. Jones (2nd edn, Cardiff,

1973), pp. 120–21; D. Crouch, 'The March and the Welsh Kings', in *Anarchy*, ed. King, pp. 255–89 (at pp. 274–75).

23 Crouch, 'Geoffrey de Clinton and Roger Earl of Warwick', p. 122; Crouch, *Beaumont Twins*, pp. 39–40.

24 Dalton, *Conquest, Anarchy and Lordship*, pp. 148–57.

25 Richard of Hexham, *Historia*, p. 177; G.W.S. Barrow, 'The Scots and the North of England', in *Anarchy*, ed. King, pp. 231–53 (at pp. 247–48).

26 White, 'Continuity in Government', pp. 127–28.

27 *Historia Novella*, pp. 80–81; Davis, *King Stephen*, pp. 134–35.

28 *Waltham Chronicle*, eds L. Watkiss and M. Chibnall (Oxford, 1994), pp. 76–77; Davis, *King Stephen*, pp. 135–36.

29 John of Hexham, *Historia*, p. 302.

30 *Historia Novella*, pp. 70–73; Henry of Huntingdon's poem lamenting the country's 'Stygian gloom' was also placed in the year 1140: see Henry, Archdeacon of Huntingdon, *Historia Anglorum*, ed. D. Greenway (Oxford, 1996), pp. 724–25.

31 *Gesta Stephani*, pp. 98–100, 105–9; *Chronicle of John of Worcester*, vol. III, ed. P. McGurk (Oxford, 1998), pp. 286–91; *Historia Novella*, pp. 74–77.

32 *RRAN*, vol. III, nos. 264–65, and generally on Stephen's difficulties at this time, Davis, *King Stephen*, pp. 41–48, and White, 'Continuity in Government', p. 124.

33 *Gesta Stephani*, pp. 102–3, 108–9; Davis, *King Stephen*, pp. 136–37.

34 *RRAN*, vol. III, no. 437; Crouch, *Beaumont Twins*, pp. 48–49; M. Chibnall, *The Empress Matilda* (Oxford, 1991), p. 124. For grants of *totus comitatus*, see above, n. 1.

35 *RRAN*, vol. III, no. 273, cf. nos 40, 543; 'Annals of Waverley', in *Annales Monastici*, ed. H.R. Luard, Rolls Series (1854–69), vol. II, p. 228; C.W. Hollister, 'The Misfortunes of the Mandevilles', *History*, vol. 58 (1973), pp. 18–28; Green, *English Sheriffs*, pp. 39–40; Davis, *King Stephen*, pp. 42, 136.

36 *Gesta Stephani*, pp. 100–3; *Historia Novella*, pp. 72–75; Davis, *King Stephen*, p. 136; Chibnall, *Empress Matilda*, p. 89.

37 *RRAN*, vol. III, nos. 274–75, 393, 634 (which implies, by offering Dorset, that William de Mohun was not considered to be earl of that shire, despite *Gesta Stephani*, p. 128).

38 *RRAN*, vol. III, nos. 274–75; Chibnall, *Empress Matilda*, pp. 109–11; M. Chibnall, 'The Charters of the Empress Matilda' in *Law and Government in Medieval England and Normandy*, eds G. Garnett and J. Hudson (Cambridge, 1994), pp. 276–98 (at pp. 281–82).

39 *RRAN*, vol. III, no. 393, cf. no. 382; D. Walker, 'Miles of Gloucester, Earl of Hereford', *Transactions of the Bristol and Gloucestershire Archaeological Society*, vol. 77 (1958), pp. 66–84; Green, *English Sheriffs*, p. 46.

40 *RRAN*, vol. III, no. 634; Stenton, *The First Century of English Feudalism*, pp. 233–34; Davis, *King Stephen*, pp. 137–38; Chibnall, *Empress Matilda*, pp. 111–12; Chibnall, 'The Charters of the Empress Matilda', pp. 282–83.

41 Davis, *King Stephen*, pp. 136, 138, 157–60.

42 *Gesta Stephani*, p. 116; Davis, *King Stephen*, pp. 131–33, 136–37.

43 Ibid., p. 137; Chibnall, *Empress Matilda*, p. 126; *Red Book of the Exchequer*, ed. H. Hall, Rolls Series (1896), vol. II, p. 649; *PR 2 Hen. II*, pp. 56–57 to *PR 6 Hen. II*, p. 15; Green, *English Sheriffs*, pp. 85–86.

44 *RRAN*, vol. III, nos. 123, 414, 736, 738, 861–62; Davis, *King Stephen*, p. 135;

P. Dalton, 'Aiming at the Impossible: Ranulf II Earl of Chester and Lincolnshire in the Reign of King Stephen', in *The Earldom of Chester and its Charters*, ed. A.T. Thacker (Chester, 1991), pp. 109–34 (at pp. 121–25).

45 *RRAN*, vol. III, nos. 180, 272; *CP*, X, pp. 352–53; XII (i), pp. 497–98; Davis, *King Stephen*, pp. 129, 131, 133, 137. The earldom of Surrey passed by marriage to Stephen's son William, sometime after the death of William III de Warenne in January 1148.

46 Contemporary comments on the threats posed by these earls' excessive power occur in *Gesta Stephani*, pp. 72–75, 160–63, and Henry of Huntingdon, *Historia Anglorum*, pp. 742–43, 754–55.

47 *RRAN*, vol. III, nos 533, 992, cf. p. xxv; Dalton, *Conquest, Anarchy and Lordship*, pp. 147, 153, 155.

48 Cf. *RRAN*, vol. III, nos 589, 649 (Bucks.), 219, 510, 858, 860 (Herts.), 682 (Leics.), 125, 414, 471, 605–6 (Lincs.), 737–38 (Notts.), 448 (Sussex), 570, 687, 689 (Warwicks.), 101, 109, 123–24, 984, 987–88, 991 (Yorks.).

49 Ibid., vol. III, nos 612, 657, 671, 884, although he is not addressed in no. 660.

50 White, 'Continuity in Government', p. 133 and n. 102; Davis, *King Stephen*, pp. 131–33, 142–43.

51 *RRAN*, vol. III, nos 190, 597.

52 Ibid., vol. III, nos 295, 368, 644, 647, 697.

53 Only one of the empress's charters (addressed generally) related to property in these shires: a confirmation of a gift by Earl Baldwin to the priory of St Martin-des-Champs, Paris (ibid., vol. III, no. 651).

54 Ibid., vol. III, nos 362a, 420, 901. On Earl William's position late in Stephen's reign, cf. R.B. Patterson, 'An Un-edited Charter of Henry fitz Empress and Earl William of Gloucester's Comital Status', *EHR*, vol. 87 (1972), pp. 755–57, and D. Crouch, 'Earl William of Gloucester and the End of the Anarchy: New Evidence Relating to the Honour of Eudo Dapifer', *EHR*, vol. 103 (1988), pp. 69–75.

55 Green, *English Sheriffs*, pp. 13, 21, n. 52.

56 H.W.C. Davis, 'Some Documents of the Anarchy', in *Essays in History presented to R.L. Poole* (Oxford, 1927), pp. 170–71; *Cartulary of Worcester Cathedral Priory*, ed. R.R. Darlington, Pipe Roll Society (1968), no. 9.

57 *Gesta Stephani*, pp. 150–51.

58 *Charters and Documents of Salisbury*, ed. W.D. Macray, Rolls Series (1891), pp. 23–24; *Charters of the Redvers family and the Earldom of Devon, 1090–1217*, ed. R. Bearman, Devon and Cornwall Record Society, new ser., 37 (1994), no. 34.

59 The evidence for this is firmer in some cases than others: see M. Blackburn, 'Coinage and Currency', in *Anarchy*, ed. King, pp. 145–205 (esp. pp. 167–93), and E.J. King, 'Economic Development in the Early Twelfth Century' in *Progress and Problems in Medieval England*, eds R. Britnell and J. Hatcher (Cambridge, 1996), pp. 1–22 (at p. 16).

60 *Charters of the Redvers family*, ed. Bearman, pp. 8, 31; *Charters of the Earldom of Hereford*, ed. D. Walker, Camden Miscellany, vol. XXII (1964), nos. 5, 39, 42; Dalton, 'Aiming at the Impossible: Ranulf II Earl of Chester and Lincolnshire', pp. 111–12; *VCH, Northamptonshire*, vol. III, ed. W. Page (1930), pp. 3–4.

61 For general criticism of earls, see e.g. Henry of Huntingdon, *Historia Anglorum*, pp. 728–35; *Gesta Stephani*, pp. 102, 158–60, 164, 214; Robert de Torigni, *Chronica* in *Chronicles of the Reigns of Stephen*, ed. Howlett, vol. IV, p. 183. On treaties between them, see e.g. R.H.C. Davis, 'Treaty between William Earl of Gloucester and Roger Earl of Hereford', in *Medieval Miscellany for D.M. Stenton*, eds P.M. Barnes and C.F. Slade, Pipe Roll Society (1968), pp. 139–46; E.J. King, 'Mountsorrel and its Region in King Stephen's Reign', *Huntington Library Quarterly*, vol. 44 (1980), pp. 1–10; Davis, *King Stephen*, pp. 108–11.

62 Crouch, *Beaumont Twins*, pp. 74–76; Dalton, *Conquest, Anarchy and Lordship*, pp. 155–56. No 'third pennies' were allowed to earls of Worcester or York in Henry II's pipe rolls. Other earldoms apparently withdrawn very early in Henry II's reign were those of Pembroke (M.T. Flanagan, 'Strongbow, Henry II and the Anglo-Norman intervention in Ireland', in *War and Government in the Middle Ages*, eds J. Gillingham and J.C. Holt (Woodbridge, 1986), pp. 62–77 (at p. 64) and, by negotiation with the Scots in 1157, Northumberland (W.L. Warren, *Henry II* (1973), p. 182).

63 *CP,* VII, pp. 669–75; Crouch, 'The March and the Welsh kings', in *Anarchy*, ed. King, pp. 284–86. See also *CP,* II, p. 387, for the withdrawal of the earldom of Buckingham after Walter III Giffard's death in 1164.

64 Others in this category were Hertford, Wiltshire and Richmond, although the latter may have been a revival by Henry II, since Conan, successor to Earl Alan (d. 1146), does not occur in Stephen's charters (*CP*, I, pp. 233–35; IV, pp.191–93, 312–13; V, pp. 116–18; VI, pp. 499–501; IX, pp. 584–87; X, pp.199–208, 791–94; XI, pp. 375–77). On the complicated succession to Huntingdon–Northampton, see *CP*, VI, p. 645; IX, p. 664 note (c); K.J. Stringer, 'A Cistercian Archive: The Earliest Charters of Sawtry Abbey', *Journal of the Society of Archivists*, vol. 6 (1980), pp. 325–34; J.C. Holt, '1153', in *Anarchy*, ed. King, pp. 305–6.

65 *CCR*, IV (1903–27), p. 257; *Cartae Antiquae Rolls 11–20*, ed. J.C. Davies, Pipe Roll Society (1960), pp. 157–58; Round, *Geoffrey de Mandeville*, pp. 235–36; *Sir Christopher Hatton's Book of Seals*, eds L.C. Loyd and D.M. Stenton, Northamptonshire Record Society (1950), no. 40. On the issue of 'third pennies' generally, see Latimer, 'The Earls in Henry II's Reign', pp. 121–58.

66 For Patrick earl of Wiltshire see above, n. 43; for the Redvers interest *Red Book of the Exchequer*, II, p. 653; *PR 2 Hen. II*, p. 46; *PR 3 Hen. II*, p. 74; cf. *PR 4 Hen. II*, pp. 157–58.

67 *VCH, Cheshire*, vol. II, pp. 1–8; A.T. Thacker, 'Introduction', in *Earldom of Chester*, pp. 7–21; D.B. Crouch, 'The Administration of the Norman Earldom', ibid., pp. 69–95; *Pleas before the King or his Justices*, ed. D.M. Stenton, Selden Society (1952–53), vol. II, pp. 117–18; *Cartulary of Launceston Priory*, ed. P.L. Hull, Devon and Cornwall Record Society (1987), p. xx.

68 For example, *Royal Writs in England from the Conquest to Glanvill*, ed. R.C. van Caenegem, Selden Society (1959), nos 18, 90, 93, 152, 168, 170, 194–95; cf. Davis, *King Stephen*, p. 127.

69 *RRAN*, vol. III, no. 896; G.J. White, 'King Stephen, Duke Henry and Ranulf de Gernons Earl of Chester', *EHR*, vol. 91 (1976), pp. 555–65 (at p. 565).

70 *RRAN*, vol. III, nos 129, 258, 490, 664, 797, 923, 993, and for a writ addressed to William earl of Gloucester no. 344; in view of the earl's ambivalent loyalties in the early 1150s, this does not necessarily postdate the peace treaty. It is true that, in addressing the sheriff of Wiltshire, Stephen was in reality addressing Earl Patrick, but in his capacity as sheriff not as earl.

71 Ibid., vol. III, nos. 490, 993.

The Impact of 'Foreign' Troops in the Civil Wars of King Stephen's Reign

Matthew Bennett

Civil wars tend to encourage one side or the other – usually both – to bring in forces from outside the riven polity. Mercenaries from abroad can be expected to be loyal to their paymaster and not to have political sympathies which might align them with the opposition. Neighbouring territories may also prove rich recruiting grounds by reason of alliance or allegiance. So, in the medieval British Isles, the Scottish kingdom, the Welsh principalities and Ireland often provided additional forces. Troops from all these sources also brought with them specific skills which could prove useful to whoever wished to employ them. In Stephen's reign there are many examples of 'foreign' troops being used. Flemish mercenaries were employed by both sides, although King Stephen's employment of William of Ypres is best known. Today the word 'mercenary' has a more pejorative sense than it necessarily had at the time.[1] It is true, though, that contemporaries were critical of both their employment and their behaviour. The Welsh troops recruited by Robert of Gloucester and other Marcher barons opposed to the king received a similarly bad press. Worst of all, in English eyes, were the barbarian Scots who were allied to the Angevin cause. This paper seeks to investigate the impact of these outsiders on the English military scene during Stephen's reign, considering what made them seem 'foreign' and how they were viewed by contemporaries.

On 2 February 1141, Stephen, king of England, was taken prisoner in a battle fought outside the western wall of Lincoln. The circumstances of his capture are interesting. He was fighting dismounted, supported by only a few loyal nobles and household knights, his cavalry having fled earlier in the encounter. The rebel forces of his opponents 'attacked on all sides as if they were storming a castle'.[2] He swung a long Norse axe and kept them at bay until it was broken.

Eventually, he was felled by someone throwing a stone – an unchival-rous act, as historians have pointed out. The rebels numbered many Welsh troops in their forces and it could have been one of them who hurled the missile. Then a knight named William de Cahagnes seized Stephen, shouting: 'Here, everyone, here; I have taken the king!' The king was then handed over to the leading rebel, Robert earl of Gloucester, who took him prisoner.[3] This vivid anecdote illustrates two initial points about the role of 'foreign' troops in Stephen's reign: that they played an important, though often unclear, role in the war-fare of the period, and that the spoils fell not to them, but to the estab-lished aristocracy.

The first question that might occur to anyone considering the inci-dent is: 'What were Welshmen doing at Lincoln?' which is, after all, on the far side of England. The answer makes a third point, because they were serving Robert of Gloucester, already mentioned, and Ran-ulf aux Grenons, earl of Chester, both of whom, as their titles suggest, held territories in the Marches. Ranulf was also involved because his half-brother, William de Roumare, earl of Lincoln, had seized its cas-tle and was holding it against the king. This relationship, with all it implied in terms of family, politics and claims to control lands and cas-tles, serves to exemplify a fourth point about the nature of the civil war in the twelfth century. There was no simple dichotomy between the royalists and their opponents; instead there was a tortuous mesh of allegiances and alliances, which meant that barons could not be relied upon to support one warring party or the other wholeheartedly. In such a situation, foreign troops, especially mercenaries, might prove much more reliable than those raised by feudal obligation.

A brief survey of the 18 years of war during Stephen's reign will help to set the context for the military operations. At its root was the succession crisis brought about by the death of Henry I's heir William, drowned in a cross-channel shipping disaster in 1120. Although the king remarried, and despite his renowned fertility (he fathered no less than 21 bastards), Henry was unable to achieve a male heir. As a result, he forced his nobility to swear an oath that they would accept his daughter Matilda (known as the Empress because of her previous mar-riage to Henry V, king of Germany and Holy Roman Emperor) as his heiress.[4] Unfortunately for his plans, the contemporary baronage were unhappy at the idea of a female ruler who could be married out to a for-eign dynasty. So, when upon Henry's death his nephew Stephen, count of Boulogne, seized the throne and had himself crowned at

Westminster on 22 December 1135, it looked as if the issue was settled in favour of the new king.[5] But Matilda had actually been re-married to count Geoffrey of Anjou in 1128, and Geoffrey was a staunch opponent of Stephen in his new role as duke of Normandy. As a result, the so-called Angevin party developed, prepared to fight for Matilda's right to the crown. Its initial objective was rather more limited: the conquest of the old rival Normandy. Geoffrey launched his first attack in 1137, although with little success. Stephen responded by taking troops into the duchy, but his strategy was nullified by disputes within his own army, resulting in a stalemate. This was actually his last intervention across the Channel, and Normandy did eventually fall into Geoffrey's hands by 1144.

In England, civil war did not break out until 1138. Prior to that there had been some serious problems for Stephen's regime. In 1136, a Welsh revolt began which undermined English authority in Wales and led to the defeat and death of some of the prominent colonising lords.[6] In 1138, a series of related but poorly co-ordinated rebellions broke out in England itself. These took place first at Bampton and Exeter, in Devon. Throughout the long war that followed, the West Country was to be the heartland of Angevin resistance to Stephen. Most seriously, though, Robert of Gloucester, a bastard son of Henry I, took the part of his half-sister Matilda and also raised the standard of rebellion. In addition, David, King of Scots, launched three invasions during 1138, which brought his forces deep into Yorkshire. Stephen reacted quickly and effectively. He recovered Hereford and Shrewsbury in August, while his northern forces decisively defeated the Scots at Northallerton (at the battle of the Standard, 22 August). In 1139, Stephen took Ludlow and gradually isolated the rebel city of Bristol by taking the castles surrounding it. Other rebellions broke out behind him. Dover castle was held against him, although it was neutralised by a besieging force headed by his wife Queen Matilda. A factor in the king's favour was that the leaders of the Angevin party, Robert of Gloucester and the Empress Matilda, did not actually arrive in England (at Arundel) until September 1139, and then brought only a small force with them. While Robert slipped through the royalist lines to Bristol, Matilda remained in Sussex. Stephen did allow her safe conduct to join the western rebels. This can be seen as an illustration of the chivalrous nature of warfare at the time, but may also indicate that the surrounding parties did not consider the breach irremediable.[7] Despite royalist pressure, the Angevins hung on in the west, and established a powerful bridgehead at the strategically placed Wallingford castle (which they never relinquished).[8] The revolt of Nigel, bishop of Ely, in the Fens was easily crushed, and the rebels were restricted to destructive raids upon Worcester and Nottingham. Attempts at peace-brokering by Henry, bishop of Worcester, in 1140, came to naught, and the castle war continued until a decisive point was reached at the battle of Lincoln on 2 February 1141.

Lincoln was the only large-scale battle of the war, resulting, as we have seen, in the defeat and capture of the king. This should have been catastrophic for his cause, but the Empress Matilda proved incompetent in victory. She advanced upon London, since holding the capital was a necessary prerequisite for coronation; but she completely failed to win over its citizens. They were stout supporters of the king, from whom they had received extensive privileges. Matilda's demand for taxes, combined with menacing the city with her troops, so enraged the Londoners that they rose in arms and the Empress was lucky to escape with her life.[9] She retreated to Oxford, leaving her namesake, Queen Matilda, to take over the city. The Angevins' next move was to attack Winchester, besieging the castle of its bishop, the king's brother, Henry of Blois. This they did by the end of July, but in August they were themselves besieged by Queen Matilda and Stephen's 'mercenary captain', William of Ypres.[10] Deprived of supplies, the Angevins became increasingly hard-pressed and in mid-September Matilda made a run for it, forcing Robert of Gloucester to fight a fierce rearguard action during which he was captured. The 'Rout of Winchester' evened up the stakes for the warring parties. On 1 November Robert and Stephen were exchanged.[11]

The first part of 1142 was quiet, with both Matilda and Stephen falling ill. By Easter it looked as if the king might die; but he recovered, and, as Robert of Gloucester had returned to Normandy to try to encourage Geoffrey of Anjou to provide more substantial support, the royalists resumed the offensive. They seized Wareham and, at the end of September, surrounded Oxford, seeking to capture the Empress. A bitter siege followed, with Matilda famously escaping through the winter snows, clad in a white cloak as camouflage, alone and humiliated. Meanwhile, Robert of Gloucester had returned with 300 knights (a sizeable force) and retaken Wareham. Towards the end of 1142, he besieged Wilton and drove off Stephen's attempted relief of the castle, the king being lucky to escape capture once more. The years 1143-44 saw the rebellion and death of Geoffrey de Mandeville, earl of Essex, which was a significant victory for Stephen. But this was followed in 1144 by another failed attempt to besiege Lincoln. Also in that year, Stephen besieged Tetbury, only to retire in haste before Robert of Gloucester's relief force. The king had learnt the risks of battle. Such warfare did not seem likely to produce a favourable result one way or the other. In 1145, the royalists captured Faringdon, which contemporaries noted as a turning point in the war, signalling the inevitability of a royal victory.[12] In 1146, Ranulf of Chester made peace with the king, then fell out with him again and joined the Angevin cause, reviving its fortunes for a while. In the same year Stephen finally captured Lincoln. In 1147 Robert of Gloucester died, and in 1148 the Empress Matilda retired dispirited to Normandy (held by her husband Geoffrey since 1144).

The Angevin candidate was now young Henry Plantagenet. He had brought forces with him to England in 1147, but he lacked the money to support them, since apparently they were mercenaries. So Stephen paid them off and sent Henry back to Normandy.[13] In 1149, Henry returned, now old enough to be knighted, and he chose the court of his great-uncle, David, king of Scots, for the ceremony. This revived the threat of 1138, and the Angevins were made stronger still by the support of Ranulf, earl of Chester; but an attempt on York was forestalled by Stephen, and Henry retired once more to Normandy. When he came back in 1153 he was much more of a match for the king. He was now count of Anjou and had just married Eleanor of Aquitaine, the divorced wife of the French king Louis VII, who brought him extensive territories. He was clearly a young man with a future and he found it easier to win support than on his previous expeditions. The denouement occurred near Wallingford, that thorn in Stephen's side for so long. In August 1153, the two sides faced each other across a stream, but neither leader could get his followers to engage. They made a truce, which did not stop the 'castle war' from dragging on. At Winchester in November, though, the truce became a treaty, confirmed in a Westminster charter in December. This so-called 'Barons' Peace' effectively ended the war. Stephen's elder son, with whom he had associated the crown, died in August, and the terms of the agreement now made Henry his heir. The king himself died in 1154, physically and emotionally exhausted after so many wounds and the death of his wife, son and closest supporters.

So what conclusions can we draw from this brief survey of the war? First, although the reason for the warfare – a succession dispute – was not unusual, the intensity and duration of the fighting was. There is no internecine conflict to compare with that of Stephen's reign until the British civil wars of the seventeenth century: not the 'Barons' Wars' of the early and middle thirteenth century, nor the sporadic rebellions during the reigns of Edward II and Henry IV, nor even the brief campaigns grouped together under the rather misleading heading of the 'Wars of the Roses' in the fifteenth century.[14] Secondly, the territories held by the competing parties, royalist and Angevin, were established early in the war and sustained throughout. Stephen's base of London was only briefly in enemy hands and the royalists were not able to push west of Oxford before the capture of Faringdon in 1145.[15] In this respect the war resembled closely the positions of parliament and the king 500 years later, a direct result of the strategic geography of England. Thirdly, the participants did *not* seek battle to resolve the issue. The combats at Lincoln and Winchester (1141) and Wilton (1142) came about as the result of sieges. At Wallingford in 1153, the barons of both sides persuaded their principals not to engage in battle. The war was one of sieges of fortresses, ranging in scale from outpost forts to cities, at a time when fortifications held an advantage over techniques of attack. This kind of warfare places an emphasis upon reliable, long-serving troops for both the garrisons and the besiegers. Experience and specialist skills are at a premium; short-service local levies a liability. There was the continuing problem of how to keep troops in the field for such operations. Periods of military obligation were generally short – no more than one or two months, after which the troops had to be paid anyway. In such circumstances hired professionals were more useful than the landed gentry in arms.[16]

Fourthly, it is important to remember just how small military forces were in this period. Although chroniclers' numbers are notoriously unreliable and we lack the financial records for Stephen's reign, we can be sure that most forces were numbered in scores and hundreds rather than in thousands. Large numbers of infantry could only be gathered from urban centres, notably London, and were not always of dependable training or morale or appropriately equipped. Fifthly, the conflict was fought – mostly – according to chivalric conventions. To a modern audience Stephen's safe-conduct given to Empress Matilda in 1139, or his paying-off Henry's mercenaries in 1147, may seem extraordinary; but these actions are explicable in the context both of contemporary mores and pragmatic policy. Put simply, it would have caused more difficulties *not* to have done what Stephen did on these occasions. Finally, warfare revolved around the king or great lord with his immediate military household, and only where these households went was there any hope that military objectives could be achieved. It is in the context of these factors that I come to the issue of the use of foreign troops in Stephen's reign.

THE FLEMINGS

Stephen is well-known for his reliance upon Flemish mercenaries, whose most prominent captain was William of Ypres.[17] William was well-born, the son of Philip, count of Ypres and grandson of Robert, count of Flanders, a hero of the First Crusade. It used to be thought that he was illegitimate, although this was probably not the case, but he certainly lacked an inheritance. After the assassination of Charles, count of Flanders, at Bruges on 2 March 1127, he made a bid for the comital title. He was to be disappointed though, because King Louis VI of France adjudged the fief to William Clito, son of Robert, duke of Normandy. This did not suit Henry I of England, who sent over his nephew Stephen, count of Boulogne, to challenge the decision with arms. William of Ypres was captured in his own city and imprisoned by William Clito, only to be released in order to help his former captor fight against another claimant, Thierry of Alsace. After Clito was killed in battle on 27 July, William of Ypres served Thierry for a while, being related to the new count's wife. But the relationship was not harmonious and, after her death in 1130, William lost favour. In 1133, he sought refuge in England, where he joined the household of Stephen of Boulogne. Following Stephen's coronation in December 1135, he seems to have been made head of some Flemish mercenaries whom the king had recruited. William led them on the ill-fated Normandy campaign of 1137. In the course of this campaign he was accused of having tried to ambush Robert of Gloucester (at this time still loyal to the king), although whether this was at Stephen's behest is uncertain. William led a force in Normandy again in the following year, but after that was engaged in the civil war in England.[18]

Contemporary chronicles do not treat him favourably. Modern historians have picked up twelfth-century prejudices and tend to repeat them uncritically. Of course, modern members of nation states with their own standing armies, mostly recruited from their own citizens possessing suffrage rights, are very unsympathetic to the idea of mercenaries. Political units of what can accurately be called the *ancien régime* were much more tolerant of such troops and indeed favoured them.[19] Also, William was related to Stephen (descended from the king's great uncle) and was suffering political exile from Flanders. What could be more natural than that he should lead knights recruited from the county who were serving in England? There was a long tradition of Flemings coming to England. Not only had there been close contacts before the Conquest, but many Flemings followed Duke William in 1066, not least because his wife was daughter of the then duke of Flanders, Baldwin V. In the reign of Henry I there had been a deliberate policy of establishing Flemish colonies along the southern Welsh coast as far as Pembrokeshire. While the Flemings were there as townsmen and farmers, they also proved themselves effective in the military defence of the new plantations. Flemish spearmen already had a reputation, which was enhanced in the thirteenth century and in the Flemish wars against the French after 1300, as specialist infantry.

In addition, there had been a formal relationship established in directly financial terms in the previous reign. In 1101, Henry I had drawn up a treaty by which the count of Flanders received a money fief of £500 per annum. In return the count promised to provide '1,000' knights to serve in England or Normandy or '500' knights for service in the county of Maine, and to compensate for their losses (which usually meant the replacement of horses). This agreement was reconfirmed in 1110, and in 1120 Henry granted a similar amount of money to the count of Hainault (although the exact terms are unknown). Writing of the royal military household, John Prestwich comments on its impressive strength:

> Its officers included the constables, the master marshal and the deputy marshals; its members received bonus payments, regular wages and compensation for losses when on service; and it attracted men from outside Henry's dominions who were retained by annual fees. Moreover Henry envisaged that it could be expanded into a very large force, absorbing 500 or even 1000 knights from Flanders alone.[20]

So William of Ypres' position was not so exceptional as modern historians might assume. (Certainly, English kings continued to recruit in Flanders throughout the medieval period and later.)[21] It is true, however, that Flemings received the opprobrium of most contemporaries. Typically, Gervase of Canterbury has some resounding criticisms of them, again focused on William of Ypres:

Flemings were called to England by the king [Stephen], and they, envying the long-time inhabitants of the land, having left their native soil and the job of weaving, flocked to England in troops, and like hungry wolves proceeded energetically to reduce the fecundity of England to nothing. One of these men was William of Ypres, to whom the king gave custody of all Kent. Wherefore the natives, greatly stirred up, tried to expel the king from the kingdom.[22]

But actually, this passage is not strictly contemporary, being written 50 years later, and serves to show how the Flemings became stereotyped by later twelfth-century writers. The men 'who left the job of weaving' were foot-soldiers – routiers – and their misdemeanours are then used to represent *all* Flemings, of whatever standing. Of course, it is possible to find cases of 'bad behaviour' by knightly mercenaries of Flemish extraction who performed selfishly or cruelly during the civil wars: for example, Robert fitz Hubert, who seized Malmesbury castle in 1139. The king had to besiege the place for a fortnight, and William of Ypres, his kinsman, was required to negotiate before Robert would give up his prize.[23] He then promptly defected to the Angevin cause; and then played the same trick again at Devizes in the following year, bringing in 'a large body of his own people' to garrison the castle.[24] He was outsmarted by John Marshal at Marlborough, captured and handed over to Robert of Gloucester, who hanged him in front of his countrymen at Devizes. This still did not make them submit, and eventually they had to be bought out by King Stephen. His choice for the new castellan was another 'foreigner', Hervey the Breton, apparently his son-in-law, who proved incapable of holding the castle against local resistance and was forced to flee abroad.

Nor should historians discount the propaganda aspects of the authors whom they read. William of Malmesbury had Robert, earl of Gloucester, for a patron; obviously William is going to praise him and decry his enemies. But let us take a specific example of William of Ypres' alleged brutality, his burning of the nunnery at Wherwell. This might seem a prime example of breaking the laws of war as they were conceived at the time; yet the passage needs to be placed in context. By the late summer of 1141, Queen Matilda's forces were attempting the relief of Winchester. Bishop Henry was holed up in his castle, while the Angevins held the other castle in the city and were pressing the siege hard. The defenders of the bishop's castle hurled incendiaries at the buildings of Winchester, to keep the attackers at bay. As a result of this bombardment the nunnery within the city and Hyde abbey outside the walls both caught fire. Then, William of Malmesbury informs us: 'Also the nunnery of Wherwell was burnt by a certain William of Ypres, a wicked man [*homine nefando*], who feared neither God nor men, on the grounds that some of the Empress's adherents had taken refuge in it.'[25] While no-one at the time would have argued that an undefended abbey was a legitimate target, one that had been fortified and garrisoned against the king could be seen as such.[26] A comparison might be made with William the Conqueror's attack on Ely in 1071, after its seizure by English rebels (who included that Victorian hero, Hereward the Wake).[27] William of Malmesbury is critical of the burning of the other religious houses by Henry of Blois' men, and accuses the bishop of using gold and silver ornaments melted down in the fire for paying his soldiers.[28] Yet he reserves especial opprobrium for William of Ypres' attack on Wherwell. Clearly, it looked bad for the royalist cause if such insults were offered to monastic buildings; yet if the actions cannot be entirely excused they can be explained as what is known today as 'collateral damage'. We should perhaps beware of modern historians, reading the chronicles too literally and led by them to distinguish between loyal servants of the crown and dangerous 'mercenaries'.

There does remain the striking example of William of Ypres' apparent defection at the battle of Lincoln, with which I began this paper. Both the commanders of King Stephen's cavalry wings 'fled before coming to close quarters'. Of William it was said by the chronicler Henry of Huntingdon (who gives the fullest account of the engagement) that 'as an experienced commander he recognised the impossibility of supporting the king'. There are some mitigating circumstances for this apparent betrayal, not least that the royalist earls had simply not brought enough knights with them to make battle a feasible option and that King Stephen was rash to offer it. An alternative interpretation might be connected to Henry's ironical strain of description, identified by his most recent editor.[29] Perhaps this is a tongue-in-cheek statement. Certainly Stephen seems to have borne no grudge against William of Ypres. The Fleming served Queen Matilda well in the campaigns of 1141, which restored the royalist cause and resulted in the king emerging from captivity in November. William remained as Stephen's right-hand man throughout the rest of his reign, and there is no reason to doubt either his loyalty or his competence as a military commander. Only when he became blind, towards the end of his life, did he lose his crucial role. It is difficult to say when this happened. It may have occurred after the Angevin cause was triumphant, but if it was as early as 1148, when he last attests a charter for Stephen, then his incapacity may have had a serious impact on the eventual outcome of the war.

Another Fleming who played a prominent role in Stephen's military affairs, but escaped notoriety, was Faramus of Boulogne.[30] He was 'a kinsman of Stephen's queen' and castellan of Dover and, according to John of Hexham, 'ran King Stephen's household' in conjunction with William of Ypres during the king's captivity. He is not mentioned as conducting military operations for the king, although the 1156 Pipe Roll records a *destructio Faramusi* in Cambridgeshire. Despite this apparent evidence of ravaging, Faramus is not pilloried by chroniclers for this activity in the same way as other Flemings. This may be due to the way in which he made a smooth transition into favour in the next reign. Henry II took Dover castle back into his own hands, but Faramus was well compensated with lands in Buckinghamshire, which he held for 30 years until his death and which passed to his heir. So there is another 'type' of Fleming to be considered during Stephen's reign: a loyal servant who performs unimpeachable service to one king which he then transfers to another. Yet who is to say that, if William of Ypres had not been incapacitated and had retained his usefulness, Henry II might not have accommodated him too?[31] Although the new king did not employ Flemings within England, he had no hesitation about using them in Aquitaine.

THE WELSH

What about the Welsh, with whom we started this investigation of foreign troops? English chroniclers are as universally scathing of them and their military virtues as they are critical of the greedy Flemings. When Henry of Huntingdon puts scornful words of criticism in the mouths of the royalist speech-makers before the battle of Lincoln, he is merely conforming to a contemporary racial stereotype: 'You may despise the Welsh he [Robert of Gloucester] has brought with him, for they prefer the rash bravery of the unarmed to proper fighting and, lacking both the knowledge and techniques of battle, they rush like wild beasts upon the hunters' spears.'[32]

There is actually an underlying, perhaps even an apparent, sense of fear in this statement. This was a product of the Welsh revolt of 1136–38, which seriously threatened the English supremacy in southern Wales.[33] Stephen was either unlucky or inept in his management of the Welsh.[34] Henry I kept them in check 'by playing off one kinglet against another': a chronicler of the rulers of Powys commented on the dynasty that 'they were all for killing one another'.[35] But by the mid-1130s Madog ap Maredudd had established himself as an effective ruler. David Crouch points out that he and contemporary kings possessed mounted households (*teulu*), some of whom were armoured, and that 'trained troops in some numbers were always at the disposal of Welsh kings. ... It made possible the Welsh mercenary, with his king as his contractor.'[36] Although the role of the Welsh at Lincoln is disputed, the presence of three kings and their *teuloedd* may well have swung the balance. The English Marcher lords were accompanied by Madog ap Maredudd of Powys, Cadwaladr ap Cynan of Gwynedd and Morgan ab Owain of Glamorgan, a wide geographical spread of allies. Orderic Vitalis is critical of Robert of Gloucester for bringing in the Welsh:

> More than 10,000 barbarians (as they are called) were let loose over England and they spared neither hallowed place nor men of religion, but gave themselves up to pillage and burning and massacre. I cannot relate what sufferings the Church of God endured in her sons, who were daily slaughtered like cattle by the swords of the Welsh.[37]

William of Malmesbury, as one of Robert's supporters, has no such criticisms; in fact he discreetly omits to mention the Welsh at all!

It might be asked what the Welsh princes were going to get out of their campaigns deep within the English kingdom.[38] Contemporary chroniclers claim that they were merely there for plunder. This seems a fair enough assessment: apart from the status accruing to princes for conducting such grand-scale raids into enemy territory, they also assured their positions precisely by providing booty and largesse to their followers. Presumably, the deeper they penetrated into agrarian England the greater the opportunity for such rewards for leaders and followers alike. How much of this booty came from religious properties cannot be certain, because of the black propaganda aspects of the chroniclers' assertions that it mostly did. There were strategic and territorial implications as well. First, a Welsh king made wealthy by plundering England had more opportunities to create a stronger position at home. Secondly, there is no doubt that the confusion in England made it easier for the Welsh to assert their authority: the classic example is King Stephen's failure to support Ranulf of Chester's expedition in 1146. The Welsh could readily read such signals and took the opportunities that the absence of reprisals offered.[39]

THE SCOTS

One group of foreigners I have not yet discussed are the Scots. The Scottish kings had been quicker than the Welsh princes to adopt the military style of northern France and, being richer, attracted Norman and other French nobles to their courts. At the battle of the Standard, King David led a force which contained a small component of well-armed knights. These he put under the command of his son Henry, earl of Huntingdon and already Anglicised by time spent at Henry I's court.[40] The Scottish forces included another significant element, though: the Galwegians. They were regarded by the monastic chroniclers of northern England with horror: 'more atrocious than the whole race of pagans, neither fearing God nor regarding man' and acting 'in the manner of beasts', as John of Hexham puts it.[41] They do seem to have behaved in a barbaric manner (as contemporaries viewed it), breaking rules of warfare that had long been agreed in the south.[42] Henry of Huntingdon's atrocity story can stand for all the descriptions:

> They ripped open pregnant women, tossed children on the points of spears, butchered priests at their altars, and, cutting off the heads from images of crucifixes, placed them on the bodies of the slain, while in exchange, they fixed on the crucifixes the heads of their victims. Wherever the Scots came, there was the same scene of horror and cruelty; women shrieking, old men lamenting, amid the groans of the dying and the despair of the living.[43]

This is clearly a piece of black propaganda (rather like the 'babies on bayonets' atrocities attributed to the Germans in the First World War), but there were factors that made the Scots different.[44] First, they were most ruthless ravagers. Not that they were alone in this, since most medieval warfare revolved around the destruction of enemy territory; but they went further in their attacks upon church properties and their inhabitants, which should have been sacrosanct. Moreover, like the Welsh they were engaged in border warfare, which included a component of slaving. This aspect has been well studied by Matthew Strickland. For example, in 1138 Alberic, cardinal bishop of Ostia, the papal legate sent to broker peace between King David and the English, made the Galwegians pledge to return all 'girls and women' held captive at Carlisle, but it is far from certain that this restitution actually took place.[45]

The Borders were always a dangerous place for the unarmed population, but the outcry by chroniclers does seem fairly sustained, even by the standards of the time. John Gillingham has pointed out that in the British Isles around 1100 attitudes to warfare were changing, and has even gone so far as to talk about the 'introduction of chivalry' in 1066 which heralded this transformation. French customs of ransoming and honouring a knightly opponent were apparently unknown in the mid-eleventh-century wars fought by the English and their Celtic opponents alike. The execution of prisoners was commonplace, as was the killing of enemy leaders. In 1053, Harold received the head of a Welsh king from his followers; while in 1071, one of the last English resisters to William the Conqueror was betrayed by followers and his head was also handed over to the king. In stark contrast, when Henry I defeated his brother Robert, duke of Normandy, at Tinchebrai in 1106, he imprisoned him (admittedly for life). Execution was out of the question. On the fringes of the English kingdom, though, old customs still carried on, making the behaviour of the Scots and the Welsh even more foreign.

Reviewing the evidence for the impact of foreign troops, I do feel that perhaps it has been exaggerated by contemporary writers for political reasons and by modern historians out of prejudice. As my outline of the war suggests, the campaigns largely revolved around the defence and besieging of castles. In this warfare, the knights had the greatest role to play. They were both mobile enough, as mounted men, to raid and blockade; and well-armed enough to defend fortifications, almost for as long as was necessary. The Flemings who came into the country fought in the northern French, chivalric, manner, and although there were some bad eggs amongst them, their behaviour was more in keeping with that of the native barons than modern studies have tended to suggest.[46] The 'barbarian' types from the Celtic periphery did not actually make any very substantial impact on the long course of the civil war, although they did briefly play important roles.[47] There is no doubt that the Angevin cause would have been the weaker without them. What is significant is that the nature of warfare was changing throughout the British Isles, and the civil wars of Stephen's reign played a part in bringing the different military cultures together. Across the water in Ireland things were still different, but it was to be another generation before men fighting in the French style were to make their mark there.[48]

NOTES

1 Mercenaries, and the payment of troops generally, in the twelfth century have been extensively studied by historians. See J. Boussard, 'Les mercénaires au xiie siècle: Henri Plantagenet et les origines de l'armée de métier', *Bibliothèque de l'École des Chartres*, vol. 106 (1945–46), pp. 189–224; J.O. Prestwich, 'The Military Household of the Norman Kings', *EHR*, vol. 96 (1981), pp. 1–37; M. Chibnall, 'Mercenaries and the *Familia Regis* under Henry I', *History*, vol. 62 (1977), pp. 15–23; S.D.B. Brown, 'The Mercenary and his Master: Military Service and Monetary Reward in the Eleventh and Twelfth Centuries', *History*, vol. 74 (1989), pp. 20–38.

2 This description of Stephen's heroic resistance to capture is neatly summarised by J. Bradbury, *Stephen and Matilda: The Civil War of 1139–53* (Stroud, 1996), p. 97, taken from the slightly differing accounts of the main narrative sources. Those used in this paper are: Henry, archdeacon of Huntingdon, *Historia Anglorum*, ed. D. Greenway (Oxford, 1996), author of the quoted phrase (on p. 736); *Gesta Stephani*, ed. K.R. Potter (Oxford, 1976); William of Malmesbury, *Historia Novella*, ed. E.J. King (Oxford, 1998); Orderic Vitalis, *Ecclesiastical History*, ed. M. Chibnall, 6 vols (Oxford, 1969–80); John of Hexham, *Historia Johannis, Prioris Haugustaldensis Ecclesiae*, in *The Priory of Hexham, its Chroniclers, Endowments and Annals*, ed. J. Raine, Surtees Society, vol. 44 (Durham, 1864). For a fuller list of narrative and documentary sources for the period see *The Anarchy of King Stephen's Reign*, ed. E.J. King (Oxford, 1994).

3 Henry of Huntingdon is the only author to identify King Stephen's captor in his *Historia Anglorum*, ed. Greenway, p. 738; Orderic records his surrender to Earl Robert in his *Ecclesiastical History*, ed. Chibnall, p. 544.

4 This took place on at least three occasions: in 1126, 1128, and 1131. See R.H.C. Davis, *King Stephen* (1967), pp. 6, 14–15; Bradbury, *Stephen and Matilda*, p.12; M. Chibnall, *The Empress Matilda* (Oxford, 1991).

5 Stephen's position was bolstered by the testimony of Hugh Bigod, who claimed that Henry had declared Stephen his heir in a death-bed statement: Bradbury, *Stephen and Matilda*, p. 18.

6 D. Crouch, 'The March and the Welsh Kings', in *The Anarchy*, ed. King, pp. 255–89, identifies the roots of the Welsh revolt in the latter years of Henry. J. Gillingham, 'The Context and Purposes of Geoffrey of Monmouth's *History of the Kings of Britain*', *Anglo-Norman Studies*, vol. 13 (1990), pp. 99–118, explores the impact of the Welsh revival upon the English.

7 In his introduction to the *Historia Novella*, King calls Stephen's action 'misplaced chivalry', p. liii. Cf. K.J. Stringer, *The Reign of Stephen* (1993), p. 21, who sees it as an attempt to localise opposition in the West Country and avoid a long siege of Arundel.

8 Wallingford was the lowest crossing point of the River Thames above the crossings guarded by the royal castle at Windsor, an important geographical factor which helps to explain twelfth-century strategy.

9 Contemporary chronicles blame her unfeminine haughtiness for her ejection by the Londoners, a mysogynist line which has been unthinkingly taken up by some modern historians, but it was a 'failure of policy rather than personality', as King points out in his introduction to the *Historia Novella*, ed. King, p. lviii.

10 The phrase is that of Davis, *King Stephen*, pp. 53, 58, and is widely used by

other historians, but it is an anachronistic one: see below, pp. 102–3.

11 In strategic terms the greatest blow to Stephen in 1141 was David King of Scots' seizure of great swathes of northern England: Northumbria and Durham; Cumbria; and parts of northern Lancashire and Yorkshire. Scottish rule was peaceful and endured for 16 years until dynastic accident delivered the territories back into the hands of Henry II: see Stringer, *The Reign of Stephen*, pp. 28–37.

12 The capture of Faringdon made a breach in the ring of Angevin-held fortresses which protected their lands in the south-west and represented a crucial strategic breakthrough.

13 Brown, 'Military Service', p. 27, points out that Henry's knights were like those who had accompanied William, duke of Normandy, in 1066, serving in expectation of reward, rather than 'professional' mercenaries. All such warriors serving for pay were in effect landless. This was true of mercenary garrisons too, and explains some of the devastation such troops might cause. It was not mercenaries *per se* that caused problems, but *unpaid* mercenaries, who had constantly to look for sources of income.

14 There had, of course, been earlier bouts of warfare towards the end of the reigns of Edward the Confessor and William I, and rebellions against Henry I, but these did not compare with the wars of 1138–53.

15 Although this last event did signal a period of royal supremacy, confirmed by the death of Robert of Gloucester in 1147, the arrival of Henry Plantagenet as a credible candidate for the throne forestalled Stephen establishing supremacy.

16 Not that I am suggesting that the use of mercenaries was a novel expedient in the medieval West; many had followed William the Conqueror for money in 1066. In the ninth century Charles the Bald took 'hired Saxon footsoldiers' on his 851 campaign against the Bretons. I owe this reference to Professor Janet Nelson; the quotation is from J. Nelson, *Charles the Bald* (1992), p. 165.

17 The paragraph that follows owes much to the *DNB*, vol. 21 (1909), pp. 356–58. See also Davis, *King Stephen*, p. 69, who provides a slightly different biography, accepting the claim of illegitimacy.

18 Although the war in Normandy is worthy of discussion (see Bradbury, *Stephen and Matilda*, esp. pp. 37–42 and 147–56), in the context of this collection of papers only English warfare is considered.

19 See Brown, 'Military Service', p. 35: 'Mercenaries were expendable, vassals were not. That was the price they paid for their mobility.'

20 Prestwich, 'The Military Household of the Norman Kings', p. 9.

21 A good comparative example is the role played by Hainaulters in Edward III's Scottish campaign of 1327. See R. Nicholson, *Edward III and the Scots* (Oxford, 1965), *sub verba*.

22 *The Historical Works of Gervase of Canterbury*, ed. W. Stubbs, 2 vols, Rolls Series (1879–80), vol. 2, p. 73, cited by E. Amt, *The Accession of Henry II in England, Royal Government Restored, 1149–1159* (Woodbridge, 1993), p. 87.

23 *Historia Novella*, ed. King, p. 62.

24 Ibid., p. 74. It is worth pointing out that William of Malmesbury's vituperative treatment of fitz Hubert includes a claim that the Fleming wanted to destroy his abbey and slaughter all the monks, so William's testimony is scarcely impartial: ibid., pp. 74–76.

25 Ibid., p. 104.

26 M. Strickland, *War and Chivalry: The Conduct and Perception of War in England and Normandy, 1066–1217* (Cambridge, 1996), p. 77, draws attention to this incident in an interesting discussion of the issue of sacrilege during Stephen's reign.

27 *The Anglo–Saxon Chronicle*, ed. D. Whitelock (1961), 'E' version, p.151. Following his arrest, punishment and release by Stephen, Geoffrey de Mandeville seized Ramsey abbey in 1143 and used it as a base for his depredations. The chroniclers are happy to ascribe his death at a siege soon afterwards to such abuse of religious buildings.

28 *Historia Novella*, ed. King, pp. 102–04.

29 *Historia Anglorum*, ed. Greenway, 'Introduction'.

30 For the following paragraph, see the discussion of the Anglo-Flemish community in Amt, *The Accession of Henry II*, pp. 83–84.

31 Bradbury, *Stephen and Matilda*, p. 173, makes the same contrast with William of Ypres, whom he regards having been made a scapegoat by Henry II's regime.

32 *Historia Anglorum*, ed. Greenway, p. 734 (translation slightly adapted).

33 See Gillingham, 'The Context and Purpose of the *History of the Kings of Britain*', pp. 99–118.

34 Crouch has no doubt that it was the latter. He is very critical of Stephen's Welsh policy in contrast to that of his predecessor: see Crouch, 'The March and the Welsh Kings', in *The Anarchy*, ed. King, passim. Cf. Stringer, *The Reign of Stephen*, pp. 9–10, who finds weaknesses in Henry I's dealings with Wales due to 'imperial overstretch'.

35 Crouch, 'The March and the Welsh Kings', p. 266.

36 Ibid., p. 268.

37 Cited by Crouch, ibid., pp. 276–77.

38 As the author was asked during questions at the Chester colloquium.

39 Madog ap Maredudd's patronage of Haughmond abbey, Shropshire, was intended to match that of his neighbours and rivals the fitzAlan Marcher lords. See *The Cartulary of Haughmond Abbey*, ed. U. Rees (Aberystwyth, 1986). I owe this reference to the kindness of Dr Charles Insley.

40 Famously described by William of Malmesbury as having had 'the rust of barbarity' polished off by this civilising influence.

41 Cited by Strickland, *War and Chivalry*, p. 293.

42 The *Constitutiones* of William I are an example of the constraints placed upon warfare by a chivalrous society. For the implications of this source, and of the Peace and Truce of God as a way of modifying the devastating impact of war, see M. Bennett, 'Violence in Eleventh-century Normandy: Feud, Warfare and Politics', in *Violence and Society in the Early Medieval West*, ed. G. Halsall (Woodbridge, 1998), pp.126–40, and also Halsall's introduction to the book, pp. 1–45.

43 Strickland, *War and Chivalry*, pp. 266–67, quoting from John of Hexham, Book VIII. For parallel descriptions in mid-twelfth century vernacular literature see M. Bennett, 'Wace and Warfare', *Anglo-Norman Studies*, vol. 11 (1988), pp. 37–57, esp. p. 40.

44 J. Gillingham, 'Conquering the Barbarians: War and Chivalry in Twelfth-Century Britain', *Haskins Society Journal*, vol. 4 (1992), pp. 67–84, explains the context of the criticisms voiced by self-consciously 'civilised' authors, such as John of Hexham, of their economically and culturally backward neighbours.

45 Strickland, *War and Chivalry*, p. 317

46 See, for example, Strickland, *War and Chivalry*, p. 81, n. 131, citing Henry of Huntingdon, *Historia Novella*, ed. King, p. 17: 'a class of men full of greed and violence who cared nothing for breaking into churchyards or robbing churches; moreover they not only rode down members of religious orders, but even dragged them off into captivity'. While there is no doubt that such incidents did happen, I would argue that they were the product of warfare in general rather than the activities of mercenaries in particular.

47 The conquest of the north by the Scots in 1135 and 1141 was almost bloodless in comparison to 'deep raids' of 1138; cf. Stringer, *The Reign of Stephen*, pp. 34–35.

48 Gillingham, 'Conquering the Barbarians', pp. 67–68.

Sir John Fastolf, John Lord Talbot and the Dispute over Patay: Ambition and Chivalry in the Fifteenth Century

Hugh Collins

Few reputations have suffered more at the hands of a playwright than that of Sir John Fastolf. In the first part of William Shakespeare's dramatic trilogy *Henry VI* we see Fastolf transformed from an able and experienced soldier, a veteran of 40 years continual warfare in France, into a cowardly braggart, a faithless knight whose desperate flight from the field at Patay left the heroic John, Lord Talbot, isolated and alone to face capture and imprisonment by the French. In vivid detail Shakespeare recalls the scene in Paris as Fastolf, entering the presence of Henry VI, is met by a hail of accusations, led by the newly ransomed Talbot: 'I vow'd base knight, when I did meet thee next, / To tear the Garter from thy craven's leg'. And so indeed is Fastolf degraded from the order of the Garter for his cowardice and banished from the presence of the king.[1]

In common with all the most effective pieces of historical theatre, however, fact and fiction are blended in almost equal measure. Fastolf – the real Sir John, that is – did indeed depart the field of Patay in 1429 and was as a consequence degraded or, more accurately, suspended from the Garter fraternity for his alleged misdeeds. Equally, Fastolf's harshest critic in the aftermath of the battle was certainly Lord Talbot, his bitterness sharpened by four years of imprisonment and the exaction of a particularly heavy ransom. At this point, however, the dramatic narrative fails us: it omits to mention either that Fastolf's suspension from the Garter was short-lived, since Bedford reinstated him to the order after an inquiry into the circumstances of the battle, or that the quarrel between the two veteran knights was to persist for another 13 acrimonious years, until finally settled in Fastolf's favour in 1442 by a tribunal of Garter knights.

These latter events are what principally concern us in this paper, and in particular the nature of the dispute and the reasons for its continuation into the 1430s and 1440s. Both Fastolf and Talbot were war-hardened professional soldiers, well used to the vicissitudes of warfare. Why then should the engagement at Patay have left such a bitter legacy? What moved Talbot to pursue the quarrel with his former companion-in-arms, and how well founded were his allegations of cowardice? And what of Fastolf? When there were no obvious material benefits to be gained, why did this shrewdest of medieval business-men take such careful steps to defend himself in what had become a purely honorific matter? The answers to these questions and to others will allow us an insight into the value system of English chivalric classes in the fifteenth century: not only in terms of how they perceived themselves and wished to be viewed by others, but also of how far personal ambition and concepts of honour and status were interwoven in the fabric of their beliefs. Let us begin, however, by tracing briefly the careers of these two knights in the period up to 1427, the point at which their lives became interconnected and where the origins of the quarrel are arguably to be found.

Born into a minor gentry family from East Anglia, Sir John Fastolf spent the early part of his career as a page and then esquire serving in the households of the dukes of Norfolk and Clarence. Though lacking by birth the advantages of wealth and status, Fastolf was able to achieve steady if unremarkable advancement through his competence as a soldier and an administrator, initially in Ireland and later in Gascony. This experience ensured Sir John's active employment in France following the re-opening of the conflict in 1415, and his martial services were to be rewarded by Henry V, not only with knighthood but also with receipt of a series of increasingly important military commands. It was Fastolf's astute decision, however, to enter the service of John, duke of Bedford, in the early 1420s that gave him the patronage so crucial to his eventual success. As grand master of the Regent's household and one of his most trusted councillors, Sir John's indispensable services at Verneuil in 1424 and in the subsequent suppression of Maine were recognised not only with promotion to the rank of banneret and the award of a series of grants of lands and titles in France, but also with the governorship of Anjou and Maine. It was through the direct intercession of his influential patron in April 1426 that Fastolf received his ultimate martial accolade, election to the elite ranks of the Garter fraternity.[2]

For John Talbot, the path to martial distinction in France was less direct than it was for his East Anglian counterpart. Despite an early debut in arms in 1404 serving against Glyn Dŵr in the Marches of Wales, and campaigning from 1414 onwards as the king's lieutenant in Ireland, it was not until the spring of 1420 that Henry V summoned the Marcher lord to France. Once on the continent, however, Talbot's martial skills were rapidly put to use, at the reduction of Meung in May of that year, and in 1421 at the sieges of Meaux and Melun. Although leading one of the contingents that invaded Anjou and Maine from Normandy in 1424, it is unlikely that Talbot was actually present at Bedford's victory at Verneuil. This, however, did not mean that his other valuable services were overlooked; earlier in the same year he had been installed as a Garter companion following participation in the relief of Le Crotoy. On his return from a brief sojourn in England in the spring of 1427, Talbot was to begin a period of almost continual residence in France lasting 18 years.[3]

Whilst already of some note as a soldier, John Talbot had only two years of experience fighting on the continent at the time of his return to France. Indeed he was, as A.J. Pollard suggests, 'virtually unknown to his French enemies as a military commander',[4] certainly less familiar than Fastolf, who had then been serving in France for almost 15 years. Despite this, Talbot was rapidly to supersede the East Anglian knight in terms of military authority, having preceded him into the ranks of the Garter fraternity by two years. Inevitably considerations of rank and social status influenced Talbot's superior advancement; inheriting the baronial titles of Strange of Blackmere and Talbot of Goodrich through his father, and the title of Lord Furnivall by right of his first wife, Maud Neville, Talbot enjoyed social connections reaching to the highest levels of magnate society.[5] Despite this obvious disparity in rank, there were nevertheless a number of parallels in the early careers of the two knights. Certainly both Fastolf and Talbot had served their martial apprenticeships in the Celtic peripheries, the traditional training grounds for the medieval English man-at-arms; and the experience gained, whether in Ireland or in Wales, had allowed each to establish his credentials as a soldier, thus providing for his future employment in France. Ultimately, however, it was Talbot's personality that lay at the heart of his rise to martial prominence: incautious, aggressive and daring, his skilled use of lightning raids and surprise assaults led to his emergence almost overnight as a leading commander in France. Ironically, it was these very same characteristics which were eventually to bring him into conflict with Sir John Fastolf.

To suggest that Fastolf's star waned on account of the waxing of that of Lord Talbot would be misleading. Nevertheless, the arrival in France of this charismatic and forceful personality, enjoying Bedford's particular favour and at a time when Fastolf's own military fortunes were suffering a downturn, was significant, not least in relations between the two men. The year 1427 had not gone well for the English forces in France, and for Sir John in particular. On 5 September, the same day that the French broke the siege of Montargis, a force under Fastolf's command was surprised near Ambrières in northern Maine. The resultant instability, evidenced in wide-scale uprisings in the county, saw La Ferté-Bernard, Nogent-le-Retrou and Nogent-le-Roi all return to French adherence. For Fastolf, as governor of Anjou and Maine, the situation reflected badly on both his military competence and his ability to hold such an elevated command. Noted more for his administrative skills than his gifts as a military leader, Sir John had striven hard during the early 1420s to establish his reputation as a field commander; diligent service punctuated with bouts of individual bravery, such as at Verneuil, had allowed him to rise high in the favour of the Regent. However, the defeat at Ambrières and the deterioration of English control in Maine must have signalled to Bedford that his lieutenant had reached the limit of his abilities. As a result, Fastolf was replaced as governor by Lord Talbot, who was then still enjoying the success of the capture of Pontorson with the earl of Warwick earlier in the year.[7]

In most chronicles of the period, Bedford's appointment of Talbot was motivated by the desire to strengthen the English command during the recovery of Maine. The question of Fastolf's competence, however, was to be given a renewed emphasis by the Tudor chronicler Edward Hall, who, drawing from a little-known contemporary source,[8] suggested that it was Sir John's failure to secure the siege lines around La Gravelle and thus ensure its surrender that finally prompted his replacement. According to Hall's account, the besieged French garrison had agreed to yield if not succoured within 12 days, exchanging pledges and hostages to that effect. Despite the reluctance of Dauphinist forces in the area to engage Bedford's waiting army, the garrison refused to adhere to the terms of surrender, having in the meantime been reinforced by a small but significant body of French troops. The situation was to cause great embarrassment to the English and in particular to Bedford, whose outrage at this example of French bad faith was demonstrated in his prompt execution of the hostages. It is not improbable that Bedford's anger was subsequently directed at Fastolf, whose poor handling of the siege had allowed the reinforcements to slip through the encircling English forces. Certainly there was little delay in the Regent's decision to appoint Talbot to the governorship, assigning Fastolf, in Hall's words, 'to another place'.[9]

If the seeds of the hostility and bitter rivalry that dogged relations between the two captains were sown in the incident at La Gravelle, they were not to flower for at least another year or so. Fastolf and Talbot co-operated closely in the winter of 1427–28 as they prepared a force at Alençon for the spring counter-offensive against the remaining Dauphinist pockets in Maine. Talbot's subsequent successes during the campaign, including the capture of Laval in March and Le Mans and La Ferté-Bernard in the following months,[10] returned the county once again to Lancastrian control, and in so doing served to confirm Talbot's ascendancy in the English field command. For John Fastolf, this precipitous rise must have been truly galling; although still enjoying the favour and support of the Regent, his rather more cautious, prosaic approach to military command was unlikely to generate the same enthusiasm or produce the same remarkable results as that of his rival. Equally, however, it was less likely to put at risk the hard-won gains of the war – a fact that only became fully apparent in the closing stages of the Orléans campaign.

The story of the siege of Orléans requires only the briefest of summaries. Following the recovery of Maine early in 1428, Bedford decided on an ambitious plan to extend English conquests southwards by attacking the city of Orléans in the winter of 1428–29. Despite the early successes of the campaign, capturing the bridgeheads of Beaugency, Meung and Jargeau along the line of the Loire, the overstretched English forces were soon to encounter severe difficulties in maintaining the siege – a situation only worsened by the departure of the Burgundian contingent and the loss of the charismatic leadership of the earl of Salisbury. With the arrival of fresh reinforcements and supplies under Joan of Arc in the spring of 1429, the French were able to counter-attack, forcing the English commanders to raise the siege and retire to their respective strongholds on the Loire.[11]

John Fastolf, unlike his baronial counterpart, had not been involved directly in the siege but had remained on the staff of the Regent in Paris, occasionally operating in a support capacity for the army at Orléans. Somewhat surprisingly, however, given the nature of these operations, Fastolf was to win one of the major engagements of his life during this period, defeating a Franco-Scottish force under the command of Sir John Stewart and the *comte* de Clermont at Rouvray-Saint-Denis on 12 February.[12] Known as the battle of the Herrings on account of the supplies of fish that were being escorted to Orléans for Lent, the dramatic success of the engagement, which saw the innovative use of a defensive *laager* to rout a numerically superior force, must have done much to enhance Sir John's martial reputation. Thus when news of the collapse of the siege of Orléans reached Paris, it was with some confidence that Bedford despatched his lieutenant south with a hastily assembled force of 3,000 men. And indeed, such was his reputation in the aftermath of the remarkable victory at Rouvray, that the duke of Alençon, who was then besieging Jargeau with a sizeable army, considered calling off the attack on hearing rumours of Fastolf's approach.[13]

Though not enjoying the same level of authority as Lord Talbot, who – since the death of Salisbury and the immobilisation of the earl of Suffolk at Jargeau – had become the leading field commander in the campaign, Fastolf was nevertheless a key figure in what remained of the English army. Had he enjoyed less authority, then conceivably the dispute with Talbot would not have risen to such a pitch. However, the combination of greater military experience and a naturally cautious, more considered personality on one side, and on the other, charismatic leadership underpinned by an intuitive and aggressive spirit, was unlikely to allow strategic differences of opinion to go uncontested. The fault lines between Fastolf and Talbot, perhaps already established as early as 1427, were to develop into open fissures during the remaining days of the campaign.

The first major dispute between the two captains arose at Janville on 16 June. Arriving in the town with a small force in the morning, Talbot was joined for dinner in his lodgings by Fastolf and the other English captains, including Sir Thomas Rempston, and Sir Walter Hungerford. As the conversation turned to discussing the planned campaign, it soon became apparent that opinion was sharply divided over the next course of action. Aware of the strength of French morale at the time, and equally of the concurrent depth of English spirits, Fastolf argued strongly that Beaugency should be left to secure the best terms of surrender available whilst the English army withdrew to its various strongholds in the Île de France in order to regroup and await the reinforcements promised by Bedford. This plan was clearly an anathema to Lord Talbot who, carrying the other captains with him, declared that, in the words of the chronicler, Waurin, 'if he had only his own men and those who were willing to follow him, he would go and fight the enemy with the help of God and St. George'. With his hand thus forced, Fastolf had little option but to consent to Talbot's planned march to the relief of the beleaguered English stronghold.[14]

So convinced was he, however, of the dangers in risking the last remaining field army available to the English in France in such an ill-considered advance that, even on the following morning, as the army assembled before the walls of Janville, Fastolf summoned one remaining council of war. Once again he restated his opposition to such a risky policy: in addition to reservations about the numerical superiority of the French and the devastating consequences for 'la France anglaise' should the gambit fail, Fastolf was anxious about the fighting quality of his own contingent which, despite Waurin's confident assertion that his company was 'as well chosen as any I have seen in France',[15] was composed largely of poorly trained garrison troops and unreliable French *milice*, serving under the Anglo-Burgundian banner.[16] Once again his arguments, however rational, were to receive a hostile reception from Talbot and the other captains present, forcing Fastolf to acquiesce.[17]

In fact it was only when news of the fall of Beaugency reached the advancing English army that it was finally decided to retire northwards to Paris and thereby attempt to save the precious army. By 18 June the English force had managed to retreat as far as the village of Patay, 18 miles to the north. It was here, in the hastily summoned council of war, that the last major dispute between Fastolf and Talbot occurred. Rather than a question of strategy, however, the difference of opinion centred more upon tactics.[18] With news of the rapid approach of the French advance guard, the decision was taken, most probably on the advice of Talbot, to halt and set an ambush for the pursuing forces, and thereby attempt to reverse the pattern of defeats that had followed the failure at Orléans. Again probably with some reluctance, Fastolf complied, adopting a defensive position with the main body of the army along the ridge south-east of the village whilst Talbot, with the pick of the troops including 200 elite archers from Fastolf's own company, held a covering position nearby. The French advance guard, however, alerted to the position of the English by the noise from Talbot's troops and spurred on by the exhortations of Joan of Arc and their own recent successes, poured down upon the enemy, taking by surprise the 400 archers, who were then still preparing their defensive line of stakes. Then, followed closely by the main body of the army, they swept over the ridge onto Fastolf's position, overwhelming his forces within a short space of time. In the rout that ensued, all the English captains who were on foot with Talbot in the rear-guard, including Thomas, Lord Scales, Sir Thomas Rempston and Sir Walter Hungerford, were taken prisoner. Sir John Fastolf, who had remained mounted in the vanguard, was more fortunate: with the remnants of the main body he managed to escape the field, evading the pursuit of the duke of Alençon, to reach Corbeil, from where he returned to Paris.[19]

The details of Fastolf's actions are, like the battle itself, somewhat obscure and certainly contradictory. The majority of French chronicles, when describing the closing stages of the battle, refer in rather bland terms either to Fastolf 'fleeing' – as seen in the accounts of Philippe Cochon, Gilles Le Bouvier, Guillaume Cousinot and Thomas Basin – or otherwise simply 'leaving' the field, as recorded in the chronicle of Jean Le Févre.[20] Jean Chartier takes a rather more neutral line, referring only to the fact that Fastolf 'and those other Englishmen who could escape' retired to Corbeil.[21] The most condemnatory account by far is that of Enguerrand de Monstrelet, who elaborates on the other sources, stating not only that Fastolf left the field of battle, but that he did so 'sans coup férir' – without striking a blow.[22] Regardless of the differing levels of criticism, the sheer number of negative references to Fastolf's actions at Patay suggests that, in the eyes of many contemporaries, his departure from the battle was, if not actually an act of cowardice, certainly, as will become apparent, one unbecoming of a Garter knight. However, in view of the textual similarities evident in a number of these chronicles, not least in phraseology, it is possible that most of the details of the engagement were taken from a single master copy. For this reason, we should perhaps focus on the earliest accounts, or at least on those derived from the evidence of witnesses, to gain a more accurate understanding of events.

Four key primary sources exist. The first, the *Chronique d'Arthur de Richemont*, was written by Guillaume Gruel on the basis of his experiences as a retainer of the duke of Brittany.[23] Although neither Gruel nor his master took an active part in the battle, he was nevertheless well placed to record detailed eye-witness accounts from those who did. Gruel's *Chronicle* represents the earliest negative reference to Fastolf's actions: he states simply that Talbot and the other English captains were taken prisoner, and that Fastolf fled, along with a number of others whose names the author does not know. The rather bland tone of Gruel's description is matched by the inconclusive nature of another important primary source, a letter written only five weeks after the battle by Jacques de Bourbon, *comte* de la Marche, to the bishop of Laon. Although generally detailed in its record of events, the letter not only fails, like most of the other contemporary French sources, to interpret Fastolf's flight in terms of the outcome of the engagement, it even suggests that he was captured along with Talbot, Rempston and Hungerford.[24]

Though damning to a degree, this evidence has to be set against the remaining primary sources, which present a less condemnatory picture. Not surprisingly the most comprehensive account is that of Jean de Waurin, who had served during the battle in the main body of the English army under Fastolf's command. Overall, Waurin's description of the conflict is rather confused, suggesting, in Alfred Burne's words, that the author may himself have had 'a confused notion of what really happened'.[25] Nevertheless, his proximity to Fastolf during the conflict makes the account both unique and – despite suggestions that, as a member of Fastolf's company, he might have had self-evident reasons for wishing to defend his captain's flight – arguably the most authoritative record of events. In it Waurin describes how Fastolf, seeing the collapse of the English line and the flight of the vanguard, was advised by a number of his companions to escape and save himself as the battle was clearly lost. Fastolf however refused declaring that he would rather die or be captured than abandon his men. In the end it was only through the intervention of Jean, bastard of Thiau, and a number of other captains in his company that Fastolf was dissuaded from returning to the fray. Instead he retired reluctantly from the field, displaying, as Waurin tells us, 'the greatest grief that I ever saw shown by a man'.[26]

This account is clearly the most detailed contemporary defence. Although one cannot discount entirely the author's own partisan feelings, it is more likely that Waurin was motivated by genuine sympathy for his captain's plight rather than a fear of association with his dishonour. Indeed, despite problems in reconciling the selflessness of Waurin's portrayal with the pragmatism and self-interest for which Fastolf was to become known in later life, the story has an overall ring of authenticity. This would certainly appear to be substantiated by the remaining 'eye-witness' accounts for the battle, most notably Jean de Bueil's *Jouvencel*.

As a source, the *Jouvencel* works on two levels, comprising both an allegorical romance and a detailed commentary setting actual chivalric deeds in a historical context.[27] Though written well after Patay, both the romance and its commentary have a particular validity, representing the perspective not merely of a former participant in the battle, but actually of someone who, like Waurin, was situated at the very heart of events. Jean de Bueil, lieutenant of Charles of Anjou and *comte de Maine*, was a veteran of the Orléans campaign and a leading supporter of Joan of Arc during her life; at Patay he had ridden with La Hire in the advance guard that had swept down upon Talbot's unprepared archers before then putting Fastolf's division to flight. De Bueil's memories of the war were scrupulously recorded by his esquire and literary collaborator, Guillaume Tringant, who later appended his commentary to the main text. This later prose account places a positive slant on Fastolf's conduct. Rather than castigating him for cowardice, Tringant, no doubt reflecting his master's views, commends the East Anglian knight for his soldierly behaviour in managing to escape the field, thus saving a company of men 'par sa bonne conduite'.[28] De Bueil's high regard for Fastolf is similarly evident in the pages of the *Jouvencel*, in particular in the tale of the meeting between Fastolf and the Jouvencel during a skirmish beneath the walls of Alençon in 1435. Seemingly oblivious to the accusations of cowardice that pursued Fastolf in his later life, the author portrays him in an orthodox chivalric fashion: indeed the tone of the meeting with Sir John – his name changed in accordance with the allegorical nature of the work to 'Msr Jehan Helphy', a 'noble knight, wise and wealthy' – is unquestionably one of mutual respect and regard.[29]

The same even-handedness is apparent in the last primary reference from the period, the *Mystère du Siège d'Orléans*, composed with the patronage of de Bueil's fellow Patay veteran, the notorious Gilles de Rais.[30] Written and performed within six years of the engagement, this chronicle play was intended by the inhabitants of Orléans as a celebration of Joan of Arc's liberation of the city. De Rais, who as Marshal of France had participated in the battle, took a leading role in the organisation of the massive project; in addition to underwriting it financially, it is also likely that he was involved in the composition of the piece and may perhaps even have acted in it. Although, in contrast with the *Jouvencel*, Fastolf is not celebrated as a chivalric exemplar, there is equally no reference made in the drama to his alleged flight at Patay. Rather, Sir John is portrayed in a similar light to the other English captains: confident, aggressive and, above all, a committed enemy of France. Had Fastolf fled, then surely such a perfect opportunity to ridicule the English through the cowardice of one of their leading commanders would not have been passed up.[31]

If not wholly conclusive, the evidence is nevertheless sufficient to cast doubt on the accusations against Fastolf at Patay, and at best to indicate that he behaved with nothing other than tactical good sense – a fact that would appear to be corroborated by Bedford's reaction in the aftermath of the battle. When news of the defeat reached Paris, the Regent initially responded angrily, blaming (or perhaps suspecting) Sir John for the defeat and degrading him, or so Waurin informs us, from the order of the Garter.[32] Monstrelet and Le Févre, though echoing Waurin's account, place a slightly different emphasis on his degradation, stating that the severity of the condemnation was due to Fastolf's status as a Garter knight: membership of the order clearly demanded a higher level of sacrifice than ordinary knighthood.[33] It would appear, however, that Bedford's anger was short-lived: following a formal inquiry into the affair held several weeks later, during the course of which Fastolf's successive arguments with Talbot over campaign strategy were recounted, as well as other 'apparent causes of good excuse by hym alledged', including no doubt his reluctance to quit the field, the insignia of the order was restored *par sentence de procès*.[34]

The Garter antiquarian John Anstis, writing in the eighteenth century, queried whether indeed Fastolf had been degraded in such a manner; he argued that as Bedford did not possess the authority either to invest or constitute Garter companions, it is unlikely that he would have been able to degrade a knight solely on the basis of one report, and without reference to the sovereign or any other companion-knights.[35] In strict statutory terms, Anstis' argument is correct: authority for such severe disciplinary action would ultimately have rested with the sovereign or, perhaps more pertinently, given the minority of Henry VI, with his appointed deputy.[36] Furthermore, he argued, had such an event occurred, surely some record would have been made of it in the annals of the order. Although compelling, Anstis' caution is not entirely convincing. Both Waurin and Monstrelet, whose respective accounts diverge so thoroughly on Fastolf's actions during the battle, are for once in total accord over his subsequent degradation; moreover, in the case of Waurin, he was particularly well placed to narrate these events, having accompanied Fastolf from Corbeil to Paris a week or so after the battle. As regards Bedford's

authority, whilst he may not have been able to degrade his chamberlain formally, it is not inconceivable – in view of both the exceptional
circumstances and his own position as the most senior Garter companion after the sovereign – that he felt able to suspend Fastolf pend-
ing an inquiry into his conduct. Constitutionally irregular certainly,
but, given the absence of any direct statutory regulations relating to
the punishment of cowardice or flight from battle, not necessarily in
contravention of the Garter's ordinances.[37]

None the less, it could not have been easy for Bedford to have disciplined Fastolf in such a fashion – even if we are to accept suspension
as more probable than degradation. The two men had been closely
associated since the early 1420s, serving together in the great victory
at Verneuil; it was Bedford who had intervened personally in the
Garter chapter two years later to secure the preferment of Sir John
over John Radcliffe, in honour, as the letter of certification states, 'of
his good, loyal, and honourable services'.[38] Not only was Fastolf grand
master of the Regent's household, a position of great trust and inti-
macy, he was also later nominated an executor of Bedford's will.[39]
Indeed, as a prominent figure both in the court and the council of the
Regent, his reputation was closely associated with the credibility of
the entire Lancastrian establishment in France. The findings of the
inquiry must therefore have come as some relief to Bedford, who was
then able to restore Fastolf to his previous honours, both as a Garter
companion and, with his reinstatement a few months later as lieutenant of Caen, as a field commander.[40]

Although references to the incident may have been consciously
expunged from the Garter's register following the results of the
inquiry, memories of Fastolf's dishonour did not fade easily amongst
his contemporaries. Talbot in particular cherished a grudge against his
former companion-in-arms, upon whose shoulders he felt blame for
the defeat must surely rest; indeed according to Hall, the restoration
of Sir John's Garter insignia had occurred much 'against the mind of
the lorde Talbot', who was then still imprisoned in France.[41] Following
his release in 1433, the quarrel between the two knights developed to
a new pitch. It is striking, however, that of the four English captains
who survived their captivity after Patay, only Talbot persisted in blaming Fastolf for the defeat. Certainly there is little evidence to suggest
that Sir Thomas Rempston bore him any particular ill-will, despite a
six-year spell in what his parliamentary petition described as 'harde
and streyte prison' – which was only ended in 1435 after the payment

of a considerable ransom of 18,000 écus.[42] As for Thomas, Lord Scales, he was known to have enjoyed a good relationship with Fastolf well into the 1440s, as evidenced by the tone of their correspondence; it was not until the latter retired permanently to England and the two former comrades found themselves in competition over the rights to Hickling manor that relations finally soured.[43]

Why then was Talbot so particularly outraged by Fastolf's conduct that chose to pursue the issue following his release from captivity? To understand this we must look back not only at the events leading up to the final battle, but also at what we know of Talbot's personality. Clearly his perception of the issue was coloured to a large extent by the earlier arguments with Fastolf over strategy. Fastolf's desire to pursue a more defensive policy had caused two heated exchanges: initially, at Janville, when the decision was taken to advance to the relief of Beaugency, and again on the following morning when the army stood mustered in marching order. Since on every occasion Talbot had overruled Sir John, carrying the other captains with him, his own culpability in the disaster would have become an issue. Although it would be too cynical to suggest that Talbot actively sought a scapegoat, his conviction that an aggressive policy could, and indeed should, have worked would inevitably have led him to single out reasons for its failure. The continual disputes over strategy, the reluctance to make a stand at Patay, perhaps even the tardiness with which the troops of Fastolf's main body were deployed, would only have suggested to the aggrieved lord that his former comrade had been at best half-hearted in his commitment to the battle – a suspicion clearly shared by a number of people on both sides of the conflict.

Talbot's anger at Fastolf's perceived failings would have only been worsened by the circumstances of his imprisonment and ransom. As the most active and vigorous of Bedford's lieutenants, Talbot's capture by the archers of Poton de Xaintrailles had been a remarkable coup for the Dauphinist forces; indeed the duke of Alençon, who had himself only recently been released from his capture at Verneuil, could not resist visiting the once feared Talbot on the following morning to crow over his imprisonment.[44] Little is in fact known of the period of captivity, either in terms of the ransom negotiations or even where Talbot was held. It would appear that the initial English response to his imprisonment was vigorous and determined, with strenuous efforts being made to raise what was considered an 'unresonable and importable raunceon'.[45] A petition to Parliament in 1429 was received favourably by the council, who requested that Bedford consider exchanging Talbot for the *sire* de Barbasan, captured in 1420.[46] Public donations were also made, municipal subscriptions being organised by the cities of Coventry and Canterbury.[47] In the end, however, with negotiations set back by the French rescue of Barbasan in January 1430, Talbot had to wait until the spring of 1433 for his release – and then only following an extended 18-month period in which an exchange involving the recently captured Poton de Xaintrailles was organised.[48] Despite the various donations from England, Talbot was forced to pay for the greater part of the ransom himself, liquidating assets such as the lordship of Douville in the process. By 1434, his finances were in such a parlous state that he was forced to seek assistance from the crown, which responded by granting him a sizeable sum of money to assist in his 'grande necessitee'.[49]

Defeat at Patay had been no more generous to Lord Talbot's fellow captives, not least Sir Walter Hungerford, who died in February 1435 just as his long and arduous imprisonment was coming to an end.[50] As for Sir Thomas Rempston, one of the foremost captains in France yet one of the poorest knights in Nottinghamshire with an assessed yearly income of only £60, the ransom demanded for his release, though commensurate with his military authority, placed an almost unbearable burden upon his finances.[51] In many respects, John Talbot was one of the more fortunate of the captives, having received a significant level of external assistance in the raising of his ransom. His character, however, was not the sort to allow injustices or failings to pass unnoticed or unpunished. Irascible, querulous and aggressive, his life had been punctuated by quarrels and bitter feuds pursued in what Talbot considered to be his just interests. Arguments with Reginald, Lord Grey of Ruthyn, over rights to the lordship of Wexford; clashes with James, Lord Berkeley, over the disputed Berkeley inheritance, and with the duke of Gloucester over his authority as marshal in Normandy; and of course, the long-standing and bitter feud with the earl of Ormond for political supremacy in Ireland:[52] these were but a few of many. Nor was he any more sympathetic in matters of military or chivalric conduct. In 1433 Talbot indicted the earl of Stafford for the loss of La Ferté-Bernard 'without assuault or engines';[53] whilst six years later, in September 1439, he was to imprison his lieutenant, William Chamberlain, whom he accused of treason for the surrender of the vital fortress of Meaux, with which he had been entrusted. Indeed only after a period of sober reflection on Talbot's part, and the realisation that the stronghold could not have withstood a determined artillery siege, was Chamberlain released.[54]

Although the quarrel over Patay was essentially a private one, the accusations of cowardice and unknightly behaviour made against Fastolf were nevertheless to reach a far wider audience. The extent of this can be guessed from the details of Fastolf's legal wrangle in the Parlement of Paris with his former receiver, Thomas Overton, during the early 1430s. The suit, which extended from 1432 until brought to a conclusion by a specially appointed committee in December 1435, centred around accusations of fraud and extortion made against Overton.[55] What made the case remarkable was the scurrilous tone with which each party sought to defame the character and reputation of the other: Fastolf portraying Overton as low-born, feckless and dishonest, whilst he in turn replied in a variety of ways, not least by abusing his former master as a 'chevalier fuitif' in reference to his actions at Patay.[56] If we are to believe Sir John's account, these slanders, which also included attacks upon Bedford and the whole Lancastrian establishment, were not restricted solely to verbal assaults in France but also extended to the distribution of libellous pamphlets in England. In defending his reputation, however, Sir John was emphatic: not only did he declare his nobility, indeed his descent from an ancient and noble line, he also stressed the longevity of his service to the crown in both peace and war and his valour, proven in numerous deeds of arms. He was, he claimed, considered at all times 'saige, vaillant et preux'. For Fastolf, the overriding concern in the case was the defence of honour, to rebut the many slanders that had been made; to clear his name of the accusations of treason, falsity, evil counsel, and disloyalty; and above all, to defy the charge of cowardice, which, as his statement asserts, 'est la plus grant charge qu'on puist dire d'un chevalier'.[57]

Despite the rumours that continued to circulate after Patay, Fastolf was nevertheless able, thanks largely to the keen support of Bedford, to continue his active role in the war. In 1431 he captured the duke of Bar at the siege of Vaudemont; in the following year, he assisted the duke of Brittany in his conflict with the duke of Alençon; and in 1434, in probably the last major military exploit of his career, he led a mobile column to the relief of the besieged English forces in Caen.[58] With Bedford's death a year later, however, Fastolf – no longer able to rely upon the support and influence of his powerful patron – became increasingly vulnerable to the attacks on his honour, attacks which made the task of securing a new source of patronage increasingly difficult. Indeed, as a man who 'felt strongly against any personal slight or disadvantage that might detract from his own possessions or reputation', the need to clear his name was imperative.[59]

It thus seems more likely, given this concern and the litigiousness for which Fastolf was renowned, that the move to bring the Patay case once again to trial was initiated not by Talbot but by Fastolf himself. As in so much concerning Patay, the details of the case and its settlement are obscure. The main evidence comes from a belated claim dated to 1460 for expenses incurred by Fastolf's secretary, William Worcester, for his 'great and diligent labours working day and night' to compile evidence for his master's defence in the 'magnum litigium et guerra' with Lord Talbot which had been ongoing for 13 years.[60] Although no details of the trial are given, it is probable, as McFarlane has suggested, that the main charge brought against Fastolf was that of conduct unbecoming a Garter knight. This would appear to be supported by the composition of the tribunal, which, as Worcester informs us, included the king, Cardinal Beaufort, then the prelate of the order, the duke of Gloucester, Lords Fanhope and Hungerford 'et aliorum militum de la Gartier'. Thomas Bekyngton, Bishop of Bath and Wells, and Stephen Wilton, both doctors of law, were included to give the proceedings a legal weight. According to Worcester's account, the tribunal was held in the twentieth year of Henry VI's reign, most probably at Windsor or Westminster. McFarlane's calculations, based upon the movements of Bekyngton and Wilton, restrict the dates of the case either to a period before 5 November 1441, or between 2 April and 5 June 1442.[61] As we know that Talbot returned briefly to England in February 1442 to raise reinforcements for the war,[62] and assuming that he gave evidence personally in the case, then it is probable that the trial was held sometime in the spring of that year.

Sadly, the specifics of Fastolf's defence can only be surmised. According to William Worcester, he had been employed by his master to collect letters of testament under Bedford's seal from Thomas, Lord Scales, Sir Thomas Beaumont, and 'others of good name who were at Patay with the earl of Shrewsbury'.[63] If the mainstay of the defence was based largely upon the collation of these eye-witness accounts, it also presumably placed considerable emphasis on Fastolf's general record of service in arms. This would certainly explain the extensive lists of honours that seem to litter William Worcester's later literary works, the legacy perhaps of his research for the 1442 tribunal. Not only do we find a comprehensive record of offices detailed in the *Itineraries*,[64] we also see Fastolf's honours listed in much the same fashion in the prologue to the English translation of *Tullius of Olde Age*. In fact the tone and structure of these chivalric liturgies echo distinctly Fastolf's earlier defence in the Overton case of the 1430s: baron of France, grandmaster of the Regent's household, governor of Anjou and Maine, captain of innumerable towns and cities. The list goes on and always with the same emphasis on length of service, 'exercysing the warrys in the Royaume of Fraunce and other countrees'.[65]

Of equal importance no doubt were the individual chivalric exploits and deeds of arms. As in the litigation against Thomas Overton, Fastolf stressed the capture of Soubise in 1413 and his prominent role in the English landing of 1415,[66] so he is likely to have reminded the council in 1442 of his various and distinguished services at Verneuil, at Rouvray-Saint-Denis, and indeed at Caen. Surely it is not coincidental that in the *Boke of Noblesse* these three engagements are added to a list of famous French defeats, including Agincourt and Cravant, with Fastolf's name listed in Worcester's own hand amongst the major participants;[67] equally it would explain why the diligent secretary chose in the *Itineraries* to list in detail the names of those involved in the relief of Caen, arguably one of the most spirited actions of his master's martial career.[68]

In the end, Fastolf's attempts to vindicate himself and to erase the stain of dishonour that had besmirched his reputation since 1429 proved successful. After considering the letters of testament provided by the defendant, Henry VI and the lords of the council ruled in his favour, dropping the charges of misconduct, much to the increase, as we are told, of Fastolf's honour.[69] In all the tribunal had been an expensive and risky affair, even if Worcester had not actually been paid for his services, as his account would suggest. Fastolf had gambled not with any worldly fortunes but rather with his reputation and status – as a knight and, more specifically, as a companion of the order of the Garter. In its ideal form the Garter fraternity embodied the highest aspirations of the English chivalric classes. With its socially exclusive membership and elaborate ceremonial life, the order celebrated the traditional qualities of the knightly vocation – honour, loyalty, diligence in arms and, above all, valour. Since its foundation in 1348, the society had enjoyed a pre-eminent position in English noble society and a reputation for knightly prowess that extended throughout Christendom. For those honoured with investiture, the Garter insignia gave visible recognition to their dignity and to their nobility. In the medieval scheme of values, it was a prize truly to be coveted.

For Sir John, the value of membership was incalculable. Election to the order's exclusive ranks represented all that he had fought so hard to achieve during his life: chivalric renown, social prestige and even political influence. We should remember that, despite the ancient lineage of the Fastolf family, their place in political society was far from elevated. Like his father, a former esquire to Edward III, Sir John had spent much of his career in the service of great princes; as McFarlane reminds us, he was still only an esquire to Thomas, duke of Clarence, at the age of 35;[70] his big career break, his appointment as grandmaster of the Regent's household in 1422, came fairly late in life. Despite the rapid acquisition of material wealth, Sir John, like all *nouveaux arrivés*, prized above all else confirmation of this new-found status. Though he undoubtedly acquired a number of aristocratic tastes during the years spent in princely households, not least his love of books and predisposition for literary patronage, Fastolf's extravagance, his obsessive investment in land (as Peter Lewis puts it, 'for prestige purposes'),[71] the lavishness of his spending, and even the enthusiasm for chivalric distinctions – whether it was the Garter or Bedford's own personal order of the Root – all grew out of a desire on Sir John's part to project his prestige and status, and thereby consolidate his position in the ranks of the noble estate.[72]

Looking back to the suit against Thomas Overton, it is very marked the extent to which Fastolf emphasised his membership of the Garter, not simply to signify his knightly worth, but more specifically to give evidence of his proven courage in arms.[73] Even after the tribunal of 1442 and the vindication of his honour, there is little to suggest a lessening in Fastolf's sensitivity to the accusations and rumours that had threatened his position as a Garter companion. In William Worcester's *Boke Of Noblesse*, written during the 1450s most probably at the behest of his master, we see the same conscious promotion of the fraternity, a reflection both of Fastolf's commitment to the institution and the degree to which his position within noble society was tied into his status as a companion-knight. The 'vaillant chosen knights of the noble and worship-fulle ordre of the Garter', we are told, were elected 'for gret prowesse and here manlynesse in armes'; always at the forefront of the conflict, they fought 'in example of good corage, to opteyne the overhande of here entreprise'. Above all, the text reassures us, they would never void the field, 'but abide the fortune that God

lust sende'.[74] As explicit and forthright as this statement is, it is reiterated by Worcester with a defensiveness bordering on the obsessive: of
the Garter company, he argues, 'none suche were never sene with-
drawers or fleers frome batailes or dedis of worship, but rather vigor-
ouslie foryeting theymsilfe'.[75] Undoubtedly the most illuminating
section of the *Boke*, however, relates not to the denial of cowardice but
rather to the relative qualities of courage. Worcester recalls, in a note
added to the margin of the main text, how he once heard his master
declare to an attendant company of young knights and nobles that
there existed two types of courageous men: the first the 'manly' man
who acted with caution and good sense, to the 'ovyr hande of hyse
adversarye' and the safety of his men; and the other the 'hardy man',
rash and foolhardy by temperament, who though courageous 'bethout
dicrecion of gode avysement', often to the detriment of his company.[76]
Waurin himself could not have drawn a better analogy for Patay.

The prominent place of the Garter in Fastolf's public and private
persona was also mirrored in the iconographic legacy of his life:
whether in the Garter insignia proudly encircling his arms in the
stained-glass windows in Pulham Mary church in Norfolk, or in the
ostentatious Garter design carved into the relief over the oriel window
in his castle at Caister, Fastolf was at all times keen to proclaim to contemporary society and to posterity alike his honour and pride as a
companion-knight.[77] Even in death, he chose to remember his association with the order, bequeathing money to the chapel of St George for
the provision of masses for his soul in the will of 1459.[78]

Though unquestionably one of the more prominent companions
of his age, Fastolf was far from unique amongst his generation for
wishing to be permanently commemorated in this form. Certainly in
the four decades following Bolingbroke's usurpation of the throne
there was a marked increase in the use of Garter iconography on
funeral monuments: William Phelipp, Lord Bardolph, Walter, Lord
Hungerford, and Sir John Beaufort, duke of Somerset, prominent
adherents of the house of Lancaster with established records of service
in France, all chose to be celebrated on their sepulchral effigies wear-
ing the Garter device, as indeed did Thomas, Lord Camoys, the first
knight elected by Henry V, whose memorial brass depicts him similarly attired.[79] In the case of Louis Robessart, Lord Bourchier (el.
1421), whose decision to fight and die a heroic death at Conty in 1430
was motivated – at least according to the Burgundian chroniclers
Lannoy and le Févre – by his membership of the order, his tomb was

decorated with a series of shields of arms encircled by garters;[80] a usage copied in the stained-glass windows commemorating the life of John Cornwall, Lord Fanhope, one of the key lords in the 1442 tribunal.[81]

This trend towards iconographic association was paralleled by a concurrent rise during the same period in the number of bequests made in the wills of former companion-knights to the college and chapel of St George. Of the limited number of examples that are known, the majority originate from the early Lancastrian period, and in particular from those companions elected before 1422. Thomas Beaufort, duke of Exeter, Ralph Neville, earl of Westmorland, and Sir Robert Umfraville were all elevated to the ranks of the order during the reign of Henry IV;[82] Thomas Montagu, earl of Salisbury, whose death at the siege of Orléans precipitated the collapse of the Loire campaign and the eventual defeat at Patay, was nominated by Henry V;[83] whilst Fastolf, of course, was installed in the fourth year of the reign of Henry VI. The largest single benefaction from a Garter knight to the college of St George, though not made in the form of a testament, was the duke of Bedford's gift in 1421 of the alien priory of Ogbourne St George in Wiltshire.[84] This, however, was the exception, the majority of bequests taking the form of donations to the Garter chapel to provide masses for the souls of former brethren, underlining clearly the fraternal commitments of the order.

That such developments should have occurred during the first half of the fifteenth century is not surprising. The Garter's sense of unity and corporate endeavour as an institution was never more pronounced than during the early years of the Lancastrian dynasty. Largely as a result of Bolingbroke's re-ordering of the fraternity in the aftermath of his usurpation, with dynastic loyalty featuring prominently in the criteria for election, the order evolved into a far more cohesive body, a true *corps d'élite* of tried and trusted soldiers committed to the interests of their sovereign. With the reopening of the war in France under Henry V, the Garter assumed a leading role in monarchical attempts to galvanise the military support of the magnate classes. To Englishmen and foreigners alike it came to symbolise both the majesty of Lancastrian kingship and the achievements of English chivalry. For those companions who survived Henry's death in 1422, their shared commitment to the ideals and aspirations of their former sovereign made them the natural guardians of his legacy: not only of the Lancastrian claim to the French crown, but also of the chivalric spirit that had provided much of the underpinning for the renewed involvement of the English nobility in France.

Fastolf and Talbot, the duke of Bedford, and for that matter Lord Scales, all belonged to that generation of Garter knights whose careers in arms had been forged successively under Henry IV and Henry V, and for whom the Garter held a particular significance in their lives.[85] Although John Talbot was not amongst those companions who made provisions in their wills for the chapel or brethren of the fraternity, he was nevertheless sufficiently concerned with the spiritual role of the order that he donated to the church of the Sepulchre in Rouen an ornate set of altar decorations adorned with Garter insignia, specifically for use in celebrating the annual feast day of St George.[86] If not in his will, in almost every other respect Talbot epitomised the type of companion-knight elected in the early Lancastrian age, in his commitment to the institution and to the dynasty which it served. Perhaps the most explicit expression of this is found in the beautiful volume of romances and poems in French, commissioned by Talbot as earl of Shrewsbury, to be presented to Margaret of Anjou in 1445 on the occasion of her marriage to Henry VI.[87] In the illuminated frontispiece, depicting Talbot in Garter robes presenting the volume to Queen Margaret, the order's livery is used to project not only the chivalric stature of the donor, but also his loyal adherence to the ruling house.[88] These same dynastic associations are reiterated in another plate in the book detailing the lineage of the royal family, with the Talbot arms shown encircled by the Garter insignia.[89] In common with his East Anglian counterpart, Talbot very consciously sought to promote his associations with the Garter, during his life and in death; judging by John Piggot's eulogistic verse written in 1451 – 'for by his knighthode and his chivalrye, a Knight of the Garter first he was made'[90] – and by the tomb erected in 1493 by Talbot's grandson, Gilbert, depicting him in full Garter livery,[91] he was largely successful.

It is in this last point that we perhaps come closest to understanding the real nature of the dispute over Patay. Although on the surface Fastolf and Talbot were very similar in their level of personal attachment to the Garter society, it was their sharply diverging interpretations of membership and the obligations implicit in election that brought them into such bitter conflict after the battle. In saying that, it is important not to deny the contribution of a personality clash between the two men dating back at least to the arguments in the closing days of the Orléans campaign, if not even earlier to La Gravelle and Fastolf's replacement by Talbot as governor of Anjou and Maine. The successive disputes over strategy, and the atmosphere of rivalry, mistrust, and mutual hostility that they created, can only have served to raise the intensity of the Patay feud, largely by compounding Talbot's sense of injustice. This clash of personalities, however, though significant, is not sufficient in its own right to explain the issues at stake in the quarrel, or the reasons for its continuation into the 1440s.

Clearly Sir John Fastolf was not a coward; his exploits at Verneuil, Rouvray and Caen bear ample testament to his bravery, his martial experience and his diligence in arms. Indeed it is inconceivable that Fastolf would have risen through military service from the minor gentry to become a baron of France and grandmaster of the Regent's household had he been no more than a competent soldier. The key to the matter lies in Sir John's interpretation of chivalry. Although it would be unfair to suggest that the motives behind his devotion to the Garter were entirely disingenuous, he was nevertheless an unscrupulous, acquisitive and deeply pragmatic man whose involvement in the war in France was not a little touched by self-interest. His promotion of the fraternity, whether in the *Boke of Noblesse*, the window-head at Caister, or indeed in his will of 1459, was founded as much upon the desire to consolidate his social position through the acquisition of visible symbols of honour and status as it was upon a deep-seated commitment to the Lancastrian cause. Equally it was Fastolf's fear of losing the dignity imparted by these hard-won honours that lay behind the tribunal of 1442.

For Talbot, the Garter held a different significance in his view of the world. In stark contrast to Fastolf, who retired – astutely some might say – from France in 1439, Talbot never forsook the cause to which he had dedicated his life, preferring instead to continue fighting against increasingly hopeless odds until his death at Castillon in 1453. His commitment to the house of Lancaster was an integral part of his devotion to the code of chivalry: not the aggressively individualistic conception of Froissart, where the pursuit of martial glory was an end in its own right, but rather the more functional interpretation of the fifteenth century in which renown could only be achieved through the service of the prince. In Talbot's eyes, the Garter society, as the most elevated expression of this 'proto-nationalist dimension',[92] was a conduit through which the disparate energies of the noble estate could be effectively channelled for the service of the ruling house. Thus Talbot's anger with Fastolf, though undoubtedly coloured by the privations, financial and otherwise, suffered during his imprisonment in France, was motivated primarily by a sense of betrayal, not only of himself and the other captains at Patay, but also in more general terms as a betrayal of the duty that Fastolf as a knight of the Garter was honour bound to fulfil. To a modern eye, if not also to a number of Fastolf's contemporaries, the decision to retire from the field of Patay was an eminently sensible one, particularly given the obvious hopelessness of the situation. Yet to Talbot, a greater sacrifice was demanded, particularly from a companion of the Garter; in his didactic interpretation of the obligations of membership, there was no room for expediency, only a total devotion to the service of the sovereign and a preparedness, if needs be, to die for it – as Robessart did at Conty and as he was later to do at Castillon.[93]

NOTES

1 W. Shakespeare, *Henry VI: Part I*, Act IV, Scene I, lines 13–29.

2 *DNB*, vol. 6, pp. 1099–1104: J. Anstis, *The Register of the Most Noble Order of the Garter*, 2 vols (1724), vol. 1, pp. 136–37: A.R. Smith, *Aspects of the Career of Sir John Fastolf* (unpublished PhD thesis, Oxford University, 1982), pp. vii, 2–4; K.B. McFarlane, 'The Investment of Sir John Fastolf's Profits of War', *TRHS*, 5th ser., vol. 7 (1957), pp. 91–116; *English Suits Before the Parlement of Paris, 1420–1436*, eds C.T. Allmand and C.A.J. Armstrong, Camden Society, 4th ser. (1982) vol. 26, pp. 292–93.

3 A.J. Pollard, *The Family of Talbot, Lords Talbot and Earls of Shrewsbury in the Fifteenth Century* (unpublished PhD thesis, Bristol University, 1968), 1, pp. 139–145; R. Brill, *An English Captain of the Later Hundred Years War: John, Lord Talbot, c. 1388–1444* (unpublished PhD thesis, Princeton University, 1966) pp. 2–71; J. Hunter, *Hallamshire: The History and Topography of the Parish of Sheffield* (1819), pp. 44–46; *DNB*, vol. 19, pp. 319–320.

4 A.J. Pollard, *John Talbot, Earl of Shrewsbury, and the War in France, 1427–1453* (1983), p. 13.

5 John Fastolf's career similarly benefited from an advantageous alliance when he married Millicent Scrope in 1408. As the daughter of Robert, Lord Tiptoft, and widow of Sir Stephen Scrope, Millicent belonged to an established baronial family enjoying five times the landed wealth of her second husband: see McFarlane, 'Investment of Sir John Fastolf's Profits of War', p. 104.

6 *Chronique de la Pucelle d'Orléans, ou Chronique de Cousinot*, ed. M. Vallet de Viriville (Paris, 1859), p. 248; J. Chartier, *Histoire de Charles VII, Roy de France*, ed. D. Godefroy (Paris, 1661), p. 14; J.H. Ramsay, *Lancaster and York*, 2 vols (Oxford, 1892), vol. 1, p. 375.

7 Chartier, *Histoire de Charles VII*, pp. 15–16.

8 Edward Hall used a number of Burgundian chroniclers for his work, in particular Enguerrand de Monstrelet. However, for the account of the conflict in western France during the period 1422–29, it appears that Hall relied on previously unused material compiled by Peter Basset and Christopher Hanson, two veterans of the French war who had served with John Fastolf: see B.J.H. Rowe, 'A Contemporary Account of the Hundred Years' War from 1415 to 1429', *EHR*, vol. 41 (1926), pp. 504–13; C.L. Kingsford, *English Historical Literature in the Fifteenth Century* (Oxford, 1913), pp. 68–69, 262.

9 E. Hall, *The Union of the Two Noble Families of Lancaster and York* (Menston, 1970), p. xx.

10 Ramsay, *Lancaster and York*, vol. 1, p. 381; Chartier, *Histoire de Charles VII*, p. 15.

11 Ramsay, *Lancaster and York*, vol. 1, pp. 382–96.

12 *Chronique de Cousinot*, ed. Vallet de Viriville, pp. 266–69; *Chronicles of London*, ed. C.L. Kingsford (Oxford, 1905), p. 132; *Journal d'un Bourgeois de Paris, 1405–1449*, ed. A. Tuetey (Paris, 1881), pp. 230–33.

13 E. Carleton Williams, *My Lord of Bedford, 1389–1435* (1963), p. 170.

14 J. de Waurin, *Recueil des Croniques et Anchiennes Istories de la Grant Bretaigne*, ed. W. Hardy, Rolls Series (1879), vol. 3, pp. 288–90.

15 Ibid., p. 284.

16 A.H. Burne, *The Agincourt War* (1991), p. 253.

17 Waurin, *Croniques et Anchiennes Istoires*, 3, pp. 290–92.

18 Burne, *Agincourt War*, p. 258.

19 Waurin, *Croniques et Anciennes Istoires*, 3, pp. 302–4; *La Chronique d'Enguerran de Monstrelet*, ed. L. Douët-D'Arcq, 6 vols, Société de l'Histoire de France (SHF) (Paris, 1857–62), vol. 4 (1860), pp. 329–32; G. Gruel, *Chronique d'Arthur de Richemont*, ed. A. le Vavasseur, SHF (Paris, 1890), pp. 73–74.

20 *Chronique de Cousinot*, ed. Vallet de Viriville (1859), pp. 308, 456; G. Le Bouvier, *Les Chroniques du Roi Charles VII*, eds H. Courteault and L. Celier, SHF (Paris, 1979), p. 138; T. Basin, *Histoire des Règnes de Charles VII et de Louis XI*, ed. J.E.J. Quicherat, 4 vols, SHF (Paris, 1855), vol. 1, p. 74; *Chronique de Jean Le Févre*, ed. F. Morand, SHF (Paris, 1881), vol. 2, p. 145.

21 Chartier, *Histoire de Charles VII*, p. 27.

22 *La Chronique d'Enguerran de Monstrelet*, ed. Douët-D'Arcq, vol. 4, p. 332.

23 Gruel, *Chronique d'Arthur de Richemont*, pp. 72–74.

24 *Journal du Siège d'Orléans, 1428–1429*, eds P. Charpentier and C. Cuissard (Orléans, 1896), pp. 137–40. This confusion is echoed in *Le Mistère du Siège d'Orléans* when Joan of Arc similarly reports Fastolf among the captured, before being corrected by the duke of Alençon: see *Le Mistère du Siège d'Orléans*, eds F. Guessard and E. de Certain, SHF (Paris, 1862), p. 773.

25 Burne, *Agincourt War*, p. 267.

26 Waurin, *Croniques et Anchiennes Istoires*, vol. 3, pp. 302–4.

27 J. de Bueil, *Le Jouvencel*, eds. C. Favre and L. Lecestre, SHF (Paris, 1887–89).

28 Ibid., vol. 2, pp. 279–80.

29 Ibid., vol. 1, pp. lxix–lxx; 2, pp. 236–41.

30 *Saint Joan of Orléans; Scenes from the Fifteenth Century Mystère du Siège d'Orléans*,

eds J. Evans and P. Studer (Oxford, 1926), pp. vii–xvi; H.H. Moshowitz, 'Historical Veracity in the Gilles de Rais File', in *Fifteenth Century Studies I*, eds G.R. Mermier and E.E. Dubruck (Michigan, 1978), p. 267.

31 *Le Mistère du Siège d'Orléans*, eds Guessard and de Certain, pp. 767–75.

32 Waurin, *Chroniques et Anchiennes Istoires*, vol. 3, p. 306.

33 *La Chronique d'Enguerran de Monstrelet*, ed. Douët-D'Arcq, vol. 4, p. 332; *Chronique de Jean de Le Févre*, ed. Morand, vol. 2, p. 145.

34 Hall, *Lancaster and York*, p. xxvi ; Waurin, *Croniques et Anchiennes Istoires*, vol. 3, p. 306.

35 Anstis, *Register*, vol. 1, pp. 139–40.

36 Article 9 of the statutes of the Garter stipulated that, in the absence of the sovereign, the next most senior companion-knight present should be appointed as a deputy to officiate at the Garter festivities. Although not allowed to make new observances or ordinances, the deputy was able to 'correct and settle' with those who transgressed the order's statutes. As no specific article existed during the period for the censure of cowardice, this facility is unlikely to have extended to formal expulsion from the society. Moreover, with regard to Bedford's position, he had not been appointed deputy in 1429 and as such it is doubtful whether he would have had sufficient authority to take such radical action unilaterally.

37 In contrast with the order of the Golden Fleece, the statutes of the Garter fraternity contained no ordinances that prescribed punishments for cowardice during the medieval period. In fact it was not until 1522 that the grounds for 'reproach' and dismissal from the fraternity were formally defined by Henry VIII along lines very similar to those of the Burgundian order: see M.G.A. Vale, *War and Chivalry: Warfare and Aristocratic Culture in England, France, and Burgundy at the End of the Middle Ages* (1981), p. 43.

38 Anstis, *Register*, vol. 1, p. 132; E. Ashmole, *The Institutions, Laws, and Ceremonies of the Most Noble Order of the Garter* (1672), Appendix, n. xxi, xxii.

39 Rouen, [A]rchives [D]épartementales de la [S]eine–[M]aritime, G3573, cited in J. Stratford, *The Bedford Inventories* (1993), pp. 393–98.

40 *DNB*, vol. 6, p. 1100.

41 Hall, *Lancaster and York*, p. xxvi.

42 M.K. Jones, 'Ransom Brokerage in the Fifteenth Century', *Guerre et société en France, en Angleterre et en Bourgogne XIVe–XVe siècle*, eds P. Contamine, C. Giry-Deloison and M.H. Keen (Lille, 1990), p. 224.

43 Smith, *Career of Sir John Fastolf*, p. 195 and n. 95.

44 Brill, *English Captain*, p. 195.

45 Pollard, *John Talbot and the War in France*, p. 17; *Rotuli Parliamentorum* (RP), ed. J. Strachey (1783–1832), vol. 4, p. 338.

46 Ibid.

47 Brill, *English Captain*, p. 203; Hunter, *Hallamshire*, p. 45.

48 *Reports of the Deputy Keeper of the Public Records*, vol. 48 (1887), pp. 286, 290.

49 *Proceedings and Ordinances of the Privy Council of England* (PPC), ed. N.H. Nicolas (1835), vol. 4, pp. xxxiv, 202.

50 J.S. Roskell, *Parliament and Politics in Late Medieval England*, 3 vols (1981–83), vol. 2 (1981), p. 119; *RP*, vol. 4, p. 338; *PPC*, vol. 4, p. 149.

51 Jones, 'Ransom Brokerage', pp. 223–24.

52 M.C. Griffith, 'The Talbot-Ormond Struggle for control of the Anglo-Irish Government, 1441–47', *Irish Historical Society*, vol. 2 (1940–41), pp. 376–97; Brill, *English Captain*, p. 41; *DNB*, 19, pp. 319–23; Pollard, *Family of Talbot*, 1, pp. 42–43, 141, 144.

53 Paris, Archives Nationales (AN), X1 à 4797, fo. 106vo., cited in M.H. Keen, *The Laws of War in the Late Middle Ages* (1965), p. 124.

54 Keen, *Laws of War*, p. 125.

55 *English Suits*, eds Allmand and Armstrong, pp. 230–68.

56 Ibid., pp. 244–45, 263–64.

57 Ibid., p. 264.

58 *DNB*, vol. 6, pp. 1100–1101; *Chronicles of London*, ed. Kingsford, p. 137; Anstis, *Register*, vol. 1, p. 140.

59 J. Crosland, *Sir John Fastolfe* (1970), pp. 59–60.

60 Magdalen College, Oxford, Fastolf Paper (FP) 72, m. 8.

61 K.B. McFarlane, 'William Worcester: a preliminary survey', *Studies Presented to Sir Hilary Jenkinson*, ed. J. Conway Davies (1957), p. 200, n. 5.

62 Pollard, *Talbot and the War in France*, p. 58; Brill, *English Captain*, p. 446. Talbot, who returned to England on 18 February, also used the visit to pursue his claim to the Berkeley inheritance.

63 FP 72, m. 8.

64 William Worcestre, *Itineraries*, ed. J.H. Harvey (Oxford, 1969), pp. 352–55.

65 *The Prologues and Epilogues of William Caxton*, ed. W.J.B. Crotch, Early English Text Society, original ser., no. 176 (1928), pp. 41–42.

66 Allmand, *English Suits*, pp. 263–64.

67 *The Boke of Noblesse*, ed. J.G. Nicholls, Roxburghe Club (1860), p. 28.

68 Worcestre, *Itineraries*, pp. 352–55.

69 FP 72, m. 8.

70 McFarlane, 'Investment', p. 104.

71 P.S. Lewis, 'Sir John Fastolf's Lawsuit over Titchwell, 1448–55', *Historical Journal*, vol. 1 (1958), p. 1.

72 FP 79 and 91; Stratford, *Bedford Inventories*, p. 103. Included in the inventories created after Fastolf's death was a full set of Garter livery, held in the wardrobe at Caister castle, and a gold 'ouche' of a root, one inch across and enriched with a sapphire, which probably came from the collar that Sir John wore as a member of Bedford's personal order of the Root.

73 Allmand, *English Suits*, p. 235. One document states of Fastolf 'et pour sa vaillance lui a esté baillee la Jertiere ...'

74 *Boke of Noblesse*, ed. Nicholls, p. 46.

75 Ibid.

76 Ibid., pp. 64–65.

77 A.D.K. Hawkyard, *Some Late Fortified Manor Houses; A Study of the Building Works of Sir John Fastolf, Ralph, Lord Cromwell, and Edward Stafford, Third Duke of Buckingham* (unpublished MA thesis, Keele University, 1969) p. 32; Anstis, *Register*, 1, pp. 141–42.

78 *The Paston Letters*, ed. J. Gairdner (Gloucester, 1986), vol. 3, p. 154; C.F. Richmond, *The Paston Family in the Fifteenth Century: Falstoff's Will* (Cambridge, 1996), p. 192 n. 105.

79 A. Gardner, *Alabaster Tombs of the Pre-Reformation Period in England* (Cambridge, 1940), pp. 91, 99, plate 81; E.S. Prior and A. Gardner, *An Account of Medieval Figure Sculpture in England* (Cambridge, 1912), p. 703; M. Clayton, *Catalogue of Rubbings of Brasses and Incised Slabs* (1968), p. 38, plate 15. The effigies of William Phelipp, Walter, Lord Hungerford, and John Beaufort are situated respectively in the parish church at Dennington (Suffolk), Salisbury cathedral and Wimborne church (Dorset). The brass of Thomas, Lord Camoys is located in the church at Trotton (Sussex).

80 W.H. St John Hope, *Heraldry for Craftsmen and Designers* (1913), p. 223. The tomb is situated in Westminster abbey.

81 R. Marks, 'Some Early Representations of the Garter in Stained Glass', *Report of the Society of the Friends of St George's and Descendants of the Knights of the Garter*, vol. 5, no. 4 (1973), pp. 155–56.

82 The wills of these Garter companions are printed respectively in: (Exeter) *Register of Henry Chichele, Archbishop of Canterbury, 1414–1443*, ed. E.F. Jacob (Oxford, 1938) vol. 2, pp. 357–58; *The Inventories of St George's Chapel, Windsor Castle, 1387–1667*, ed. M.F. Bond (Windsor, 1947), pp. 288, 138, 170; (Westmorland) *CPR, 1436–41*, p. 134; (Umfraville) *CPR, 1422–29*, p. 454; *CPR, 1436–41*, p. 53; *CCR, 1429–35*, p. 27.

83 *Chichele Register*, vol. 2, pp. 392, 398.

84 A.K.B. Roberts, *St. George's Chapel, Windsor Castle, 1348–1446* (Windsor, 1947), p. 26, n. 8.

85 All three knights were admitted to the Garter fraternity within a year of each other: Talbot in 1424, Scales in 1425 and Fastolf in 1426.

86 Rouen, ADSM, sérié G, 9336, cited in Pollard, *Talbot and the War in France*, p. 124.

87 BL, Royal MS 15 E. VI.

88 BL, Royal MS 15 E. VI, f. 2b. This can be viewed in *British Museum Reproductions from Illuminated Manuscripts*, ed. G.F. Warner, ser. ii (1908), plate xxix and R.A. Griffiths, *The Reign of King Henry VI* (1981), plate 21.

89 BL, Royal MS 15 E. VI, f. 3a.

90 Hunter, *Hallamshire*, p. 46; Kingsford, *English Historical Literature*, pp. 166, 369, 371–72.

91 H. Talbot, *The English Achilles: An Account of the Life and Campaigns of John Talbot, 1st Earl of Shrewsbury (1383–1453)*, (1981), pp. 174–75.

92 Pollard, *Talbot and the War in France*, p. 128.

93 For a discussion of the motives behind, and contemporary perceptions of, Louis Robessart's decision to fight to the death at Conty in November 1430, see D. Morgan, 'From a Death to a View: Louis Robessart, Johan Huizinga, and the Political Significance of Chivalry', *Chivalry in the Renaissance*, ed. S. Anglo (Woodbridge, 1990), pp. 93–106.

The Queen at War: The Role of Margaret of Anjou in the Wars of the Roses

Diana Dunn

MARGARET'S REPUTATION AS THE 'WARLIKE QUEEN'

Of all Shakespeare's female characters, Margaret of Anjou stands out as one of the most evil and sadistic, capable of committing any heinous crime in order to achieve her ends. She is the 'warlike Queen', the leader of the Lancastrian army in contrast to her feeble-spirited husband, Henry VI, who prefers peace to war. Seated on a molehill, King Henry reflects that the queen and Lord Clifford fare better without him on the battlefield as the Lancastrian army prepares to face the enemy at Towton.[1] Clarence calls her 'Captain Margaret', York speaks of 'the army of the Queen' and, as she makes preparations to return to England from France to face King Edward, Margaret advises his messenger:

> Tell him my mourning weeds are laid aside,
> And I am ready to put armour on.[2]

The climax of her unwomanly militant behaviour comes in the scene when Richard, duke of York, is brought before her at the battle of Wakefield and she taunts him in the cruellest manner, thrusting a napkin soaked in the blood of his dead son into his face. York curses her thus:

> She-wolf of France, but worse than wolves of France,
> Whose tongue more poisons than the adder's tooth!
> How ill-beseeming is it in thy sex
> To triumph like an Amazonian trull
> Upon their woes whom Fortune captivates![3]

Margaret's response is to urge Clifford to join her in stabbing York to death, ordering his head to be cut off and set upon the gate of the city bearing his name.

Shakespeare's image is so powerful that it has coloured most subsequent views of Margaret of Anjou. His influence can clearly be seen in the nineteenth-century biography of Margaret in Agnes Strickland's *Lives of the Queens of England*. Strickland presents Margaret as the victim of circumstance and a heroine who, from the mid-1450s, had to fight to defend herself, her husband and her son against the duke of York. Having witnessed the 'disastrous defeat' of Lord Audley's army at Blore Heath,

> far from being dismayed or regarding it as the death-blow to the hopes of Lancaster, it appears to have had the effect of rousing a dormant faculty within her soul, – the courage and enterprise of a military leader. Hitherto she had fought her enemies from the cabinet; now she had caught the fierce excitement of her combative nobles, and kindled with the desire of asserting the rights of her husband and her son in battle-fields[4]

Strickland picks up directly on Shakespeare's version of the events of the battle of Wakefield, derived from Edward Hall's *Chronicle*, claiming that Margaret

> advanced to Wakefield, and appearing under the walls of Sandal castle, defied the duke to meet her in the field day after day, and used so many provoking taunts on 'his want of courage in suffering himself to be tamely braved by a woman', that York, who certainly had had little reason to form a very lofty idea of Margaret's skill as a military leader, determined to come forth and do battle with her.[5]

While most historians today would agree that Shakespeare's and Strickland's versions of medieval history need to be treated with extreme caution, their influence endures and militant descriptors deriving from these sources are still regularly applied to Margaret's name.[6] Central to any reassessment of the queen must be a consideration of her political and military role in the Wars of the Roses. What part did she play in the preparations for civil war and the military campaigns themselves? How accurate is it to describe her as leader of the Lancastrian army? What circumstances provoked a queen into taking the lead in time of war and how far did such militant behaviour colour subsequent judgements of her actions? These questions may profitably be considered in comparison with the experiences of other medieval queens, and with reference to contemporary attitudes to women and warfare.

THE ROLE OF QUEENS IN
THE LATE MEDIEVAL PERIOD

Queens had clearly defined roles in late medieval government and society, closely linked to society's general expectations of womanly behaviour.[7] Contemporary literature presents us with many examples of the ideal woman: she should be gentle, submissive, obedient, virtuous and pious, modelled on the perfect woman, the Virgin Mary. The essential duty of a queen was to produce a male heir as quickly as possible to ensure the continuity of the dynasty and to be a companion and support to her husband. Her maternal role included the moral and spiritual guidance of her children, both male and female, until they came of age. Additionally queens were expected to provide leadership in a number of areas of life – spiritual, educational, charitable and cultural – but to remain outside politics.[8]

Recent scholarship has demonstrated that there were opportunities for queens to play more active roles depending on their individual personalities and, most importantly, the circumstances of their queenship. If the king was particularly feeble-minded and physically weak, like Henry VI, there was much greater potential for the queen to exercise power and to influence decision-making. It is generally recognised that a queen was in a strong political position because of her closeness to the king, which gave her power because she could control access to the source of authority. Potentially she could help maintain peace and stability or, alternatively, create division and cause tension. Contemporaries, and later commentators, have often judged the success or failure of a queen on her ability to influence events in such a way as to sustain harmony, regarding the role of peacemaker and intercessor, whether in the context of the household, the court or the wider diplomatic stage, as being particularly appropriate for a queen.[9] Many royal marriages were arranged specifically for the purpose of sealing treaties after a long period of negotiation, those of Edward II and Isabella of France, Henry V and Katherine of Valois, and Henry VI and Margaret of Anjou, being obvious examples.[10] After marriage, a queen was expected to counsel and aid her husband, but the line between counsel and domination was a fine one and difficult to judge. A queen perceived to be too dominant was criticised and condemned as grasping, greedy for power and interfering. Margaret of Anjou was accused of all these.

The changing ceremonial of the coronation of the queen in

England between the tenth and the fourteenth centuries offers the historian a commentary on the changing role of a medieval queen. By the tenth century the practice of queenly anointing had been adopted from the continent: the anointing with holy oil rendered a queen fertile and blessed by God, emphasising her primary function as the bearer of heirs to the throne.[11] The act of consecration gave little formal power to a queen, being designed rather to link her with the dynasty into which she was married than to confer any independent authority. She was a sharer in royal power, *regalis imperii participem*.[12] The medieval coronation ceremony offered, as a model for English queens, the Biblical figure of Esther, who used her exalted position to influence King Ahasuerus to intercede on behalf of the oppressed people.[13] At her coronation at Westminster abbey on 20 January 1236, Eleanor of Provence made a petition to the king (Henry III) for the pardon of William de Panchehall, imprisoned for an offence against the forest law. Margaret Howell describes this act as 'a set piece' emphasising the queen's role as intercessor.[14] A useful source of contemporary views of queenship is the fourteenth-century *Coronation Book of Charles V of France*, which contains a series of miniatures showing the coronation of Queen Jeanne de Bourbon in 1364.[15] These images confirm the queen's lack of independent political power whilst suggesting that she had other functions, especially spiritual, as protector of the church and fighter against heresy, as well as charitable responsibilites associated particularly with regular almsgiving and offering protection to the poor and needy in society, very much in line with Christine de Pisan's views.[16] Her duties are also made clear in the lengthy prayers which form an essential part of the section of the book on the queen's coronation.[17]

Here then is the ideal to which queens might aspire. In practice, however, different circumstances and personalities produced a variety of responses from women whose common concern was their own survival and the continuity of the dynasty. It was often necessary and prudent for queens to behave in a way far removed from the ideal which society held up to them, but, in consequence, they risked condemnation or harsh criticism for not conforming to their expected role. Throughout the medieval period we find examples of queens whose behaviour attracted adverse comment for a variety of reasons, but most commonly because they were regarded as too powerful and strident, even warlike, earning themselves the derogatory title *virago*. Attitudes to women who behaved in this way seem to have hardened over time.[18] There is a difference in the way powerful women of the Anglo-Saxon period are perceived by their contemporaries compared with later commentators: Aethelflaed, daughter of King Alfred and 'Lady of the Mercians', who was a highly successful ruler in her own right, is presented in Old English sources as a woman accorded great respect, but, by the twelfth century, writers such as Henry of Huntingdon and William of Malmesbury regarded her behaviour as unfeminine.[19] Aethelflaed may have modelled herself on Judith from the Old Testament, who, along with Esther, fought in battles and ruled kingdoms, thus saving her people from being overrun by their enemies.[20] By the late twelfth century the position of queens in England and France had changed and it was no longer regarded as acceptable for them to exercise independent power.[21] Those who did not conform might expect unpopularity with their contemporaries and to receive criticism.

This hardening of attitude is evident in the way the Empress Matilda, 'Lady of the English', was censured for her unwomanly actions when she took over political and military leadership following the capture of Stephen in 1141. She is censured by the author of the *Gesta Stephani* for being arrogant and haughty, arbitrary and headstrong, greedy and grasping for power, because she seeks to make herself queen.[22] And yet, according to her recent biographer, there is little evidence to indicate that she took an active lead in military campaigns, rather using her position to secure support and act as a focal point for resistance to Stephen.[23] This is in contrast to Stephen's queen, Matilda, who personally defended the kingdom by raising an army and leading it against the enemy: she 'brought a magnificent body of troops across in front of London from the other side of the river and gave orders that they should rage most furiously around the city with plunder and arson, violence and the sword, in sight of the countess and her men.' It is surprising to find the author of the *Gesta Stephani* expressing admiration for her unconventional behaviour: 'forgetting the weakness of her sex and a woman's softness she bore herself with the valour of a man.'[24] In contrast, it is her feminine qualities, in particular her skills as a mediator, that are praised by Richard of Hexham.[25]

This then was the dilemma faced by medieval queens. What could a queen do in the event of a power vacuum and failure of effective leadership from the expected source of authority? Were there any circumstances in which it could be acceptable for a queen to involve herself in politics and military affairs, and what effect might such actions have on her reputation? Probably the best-known example of a medieval queen wielding independent power was Eleanor of Aquitaine, who dominated her first husband, Louis VII, in the early years of their marriage, and acted as regent during the long absences on the continent of her second husband, Henry II. It has been said of her that she was interested in things military more than things domestic.[26] She was active in recruiting her Poitevin vassals for the purpose of a crusade and actually accompanied Louis VII on crusade in 1146, an unusual step for a woman to take.[27] After Henry's death in 1189, Eleanor, aged 67, became more directly involved in politics and governed in the name of her son, Richard, until he came to England, and again after his capture by Duke Leopold of Austria in December 1192. She was active in raising money for his ransom and securing his release in 1194. After his death in 1199 she took over control of his mercenaries and used them to back her son John against her grandson Arthur of Brittany, a rival claimant to the throne.[28]

How was Eleanor viewed by contemporaries and how did her unconventional behaviour affect her reputation? Although she attracted great interest from contemporary commentators because of her unconventional behaviour, she was never the subject of a serious biography. Churchmen regarded her actions with deep suspicion and were especially critical of her relationship with her kinsman, Raymond of Antioch, while on crusade.[29] She was treated sympathetically by Richard of Devizes when she fulfilled her conventional queenly role of mediator in 1192, intervening with the bishop on behalf of the people of Ely whose dead relatives lay unburied.[30] Her colourful life made Eleanor the subject of literary romance and it is difficult for the historian to disentangle fact from fiction. There is no doubt that she sought power for herself and was determined to exercise control over her life and the lives of her children, with some considerable success. Although she did not conform to contemporary expectations of queenly behaviour, and despite her nationality, Eleanor has not been subject to the universally hostile press experienced by other French-born queens.

Another politically active queen, Eleanor of Provence, was regarded by some contemporary commentators as overstepping the mark and was blamed for the outbreak of civil war in Henry III's reign.[31] She possessed a strong temperament and an appetite for power, though she generally acted in support of her husband, who valued her abilities of organisation. She was unpopular because of her association with foreigners, imported to England for political and military reasons. In 1260 she was active in assembling a force of French and Flemish knights to assist the king against Simon de Montfort and the barons, distributing gifts of rings to the lords and ladies of Flanders via Isabella Fiennes, the wife of the Anglo-Flemish knight Ingram de Fiennes. The following year she received the count of St Pol and eight of his foreign companions at Winchester independently of the king, presenting them with gifts of rings. The strength of public feeling against the queen is evident in the shocking physical attack made on her person on 13 July 1263, when her barge was pelted with dirt, rotten eggs and stones from London Bridge as she journeyed from the Tower to Windsor. News of this humiliating incident quickly spread abroad and provoked outrage at the attack on the dignity of the queen from some contemporary writers. In the ensuing civil war Eleanor was active in assembling men and ships, directly appealing to Alphonse of Poitiers for assistance. The army which gathered at the Flemish port of Damme in the summer of 1264, made up of those with personal loyalties to the queen, was specifically said to be under her leadership. Although the queen's army failed to engage, the author of the St Albans *Flores* paid tribute to her part in dispersing the enemy. He praised her actions in support of her husband and son and described her as striving valiantly and vigorously like a heroine of old. She commanded respect from some contemporaries for her experience in diplomatic and military matters, being described in her own day as *virago*, meaning a politically and militarily active female possessing male strength and spirit.[32] Subsequent judgements have not been so favourable, and she has been condemned for being 'unthrifty', 'extravagant' and 'indomitable'.[33]

Isabella of France shares with Margaret of Anjou the unflattering description 'She-Wolf of France', bestowed upon her by the eighteenth-century poet Thomas Gray.[34] It is an indication of the hostility felt towards this queen, which endured long after her death. Comparisons with Margaret of Anjou are appropriate because Isabella also married a king who failed to fulfil the requirements of medieval kingship. It could be argued that the inadequacies of her marriage partner drove her to commit two of the most heinous crimes for a queen – involvement in politics (which included military action) and adultery. The marriage was part of the peace settlement between England and France reached in 1308, consequent upon a betrothal arranged as far back as 1299 under the terms of the treaty of Montreuil.[35] Some historians have expressed doubts about the success of the marriage from the very beginning, based on the concerns voiced by French visitors attending the coronation when the king's favourite, Piers Gaveston, appeared to receive more attention from Edward than the young queen herself.[36] It quickly became evident that Isabella's position at court was undermined by her husband's relationships with his favourites and she became the focus for those hostile to Edward's regime. Initially she played the traditional queenly role of mediator between the king and his barons in 1318 and 1321, facilitating a peace treaty with the Lancastrian faction.[37] In 1324 the pope appealed to her to mediate between Edward and her brother, Charles IV of France, to try to bring the war to an end, and in 1325 Isabella departed for France with her son and heir to the throne. She began to associate with the influential group of exiles on the continent, including Roger Mortimer, who became her lover, and to rally support for an expedition to England to remove the king's evil counsellors. Her behaviour turned contemporary opinion against her because her actions no longer conformed to conventional expectations of queenship.[38] In September 1326 Isabella returned to England at the head of an army of supporters who were dissatisfied with Edward's rule. It is difficult to assess her exact role in subsequent events which led to the deposition of her husband, but it is said that the queen's followers took their revenge on their enemies, the Despensers, by plundering their estates. Her suspected involvement in the king's murder was regarded as a demonstration of her vengeful, cruel and pitiless personality and she was condemned as the archetypical faithless woman, an image which has endured.[39]

These queens are notable because they did not conform to the accepted code of behaviour and, as a result, they were heavily censured by contemporary commentators. An interesting perspective is provided by the Dominican friar Jacobus de Cessolis in his treatise *The Solace of the Game of Chess* composed between 1275 and 1300.[40] The treatise contains a commentary on 'the forme and maners' of the queen, who should be chaste, wise, well-mannered and modest, paying great attention to the upbringing of her children. The queen's movements on the chess board were very restricted, as in real life; she is not a military person unless she accompanies the king to camp to enhance the likelihood of progeny:

And she hath not the nature of knights; And it is not fitting nor a covenable thing for a woman to go to battle for the fragility and feebleness of her; And therefore holdeth she not the way in her draught as the knights do; And when she is moved once out of her place she may not go but from one point to another and yet cornerly whether it be forward or backward taking or to be taken; And here may be asked why the queen goeth to battle with the king; certainly it is for the solace of him and ostencion of love; And also the people desire to have succession to the king; And therefore the tartars have their wives in to the field with them; yet it is not good that men have their wives with them but that they abide in the cities or within their own termes; For when they be out of their cities and limits they be not sure but holden suspect they should be shamefast and hold all men suspect.[41]

Here we have expressed a contemporary view of the role of women in time of war; essentially there is no place for a respectable woman on or near a battlefield except in exceptional circumstances, her role being strictly limited to that of companion and comforter to her husband.

MARGARET OF ANJOU'S ROLE IN THE WARS OF THE ROSES

In order to assess Margaret's political and military role in the Wars of the Roses, it is important to bear in mind the unique situation in which she found herself as queen consort to Henry VI by the end of 1453.[42] During the summer of that year the king suffered a complete physical and mental breakdown, identified by medical historians as acute catatonic schizophrenia, which lasted initially for about 18 months, but with enduring consequences.[43] In October 1453, Margaret gave birth to a long-awaited son and heir, Prince Edward. Although Henry resumed kingly duties early in 1455, there remained a question mark over his state of health, with evidence of a gradual deterioration in his physical and mental condition, so that the direction of government increasingly lay elsewhere. The extent to which the queen herself was involved in government is unclear because of the paucity of records. She made a bid for the regency in January 1454, but this was rejected by the lords in favour of a protectorate headed by Richard, duke of York. Many historians argue that during the later 1450s the queen was increasingly regarded as a potential source of power and authority and that she played a significant part in influencing the direction of government, motivated primarily by her desire to see her son succeed to the throne when he came of age. But the central problem of how to govern when the king is incapable remained. A recent study of Henry VI's reign has identified the key issue as one of a conflict over the source of authority which had the potential to escalate into civil war if left uncontrolled, as happened at St Albans in 1455.[44] Margaret is usually blamed for stirring up enmity and creating factions, ultimately being held reponsible for the renewal of civil war in 1459. Is this a fair assessment, or is it simply the view of her political opponents and detractors, who were looking for a scapegoat and exaggerated her political and military role?

The evidence seems to indicate that by 1456 Margaret was working towards the creation of a household faction focused especially on the household and council of the prince of Wales. The withdrawal of the court from Westminster to Kenilworth castle, the heart of Margaret's west Midlands dower estates, in the summer of 1456, symbolised the shift in the focus of power. This was also reflected in the change of government personnel in October 1456, when the queen's chancellor, Laurence Booth, was appointed keeper of the privy seal and John Talbot, earl of Shrewsbury, treasurer. Historians have interpreted these actions as a deliberate attempt to create a coherent Lancastrian affinity as an effective power base which might be drawn upon not just for political support but also as a military resource.[45] The value of the duchy of Lancaster as a source of manpower for military retinues had been recognised by John of Gaunt in the 1380s and 1390s, and recent studies have emphasised the crucial role played by leading officials of the duchy in the organisation and financing of Gaunt's military expeditions.[46] Under both Henry IV and Henry V the Lancastrian affinity retained both its administrative and military functions, now harnessed to royal authority. But the long minority of Henry VI, the survival of Henry V's widow until 1437 and the provision made under Henry V's will to pay off massive debts by granting away duchy lands to feoffees diminished the potential value of the duchy to the crown.[47] Helen Castor sees the duchy during Henry VI's reign as essentially a source of revenue rather than of political power, with the abandonment of the use of the duchy estates to support an extensive regional affinity around the king's lordship.[48] However, as Margaret of Anjou's dower settlement included lands worth £2,000 from the duchy, with a further £1,000 annuity paid from duchy revenues, the potential existed for the queen to revive a regional power base in the traditional duchy heartland.

It is difficult to know how effective Margaret's actions were

because of the paucity of records for the administration of the du
of Lancaster for the later 1450s.[49] We know that the queen toured her
Midland estates with the young prince in 1456, visiting Tutbury castle
and Chester during the summer.[50] The financial administration of her
dower estates, as well as of the principality of Wales, was tightened up
by closer supervision and personal intervention. Control over the
region, extending into north and south Wales, was also enhanced by
the promotion to high office of prominent noblemen who held estates
adjoining the duchy, including the duke of Buckingham, the earls of
Shrewsbury and Wiltshire and Viscount Beaumont, as well as Lord
Dudley, Lord Sudeley and Thomas, Lord Stanley.[51] But did this pay
off? Could these magnates be relied upon to provide support in a time
of political crisis?

The test came in 1459 at the battle of Blore Heath when Richard,
duke of York and his noble supporters, the earls of Salisbury and Warwick, having failed to negotiate themselves into a position of power,
had been driven to take up arms against an increasingly hostile
monarch. By early summer 1459 the Lancastrians were making preparations for an armed confrontation with their Yorkist rivals, who were
indicted for treason at a meeting of the great council held at Coventry
in late June. Letters were sent to the shires summoning military aid to
come to Leicester and 3,000 bows were ordered from the royal
armoury.[52] The queen toured her Cheshire estates with her son, distributing liveries of the swan and ostrich feathers to the gentlemen of
the county.[53]

On 23 September 1459 a Yorkist force led by Richard Neville, earl
of Salisbury, was intercepted at Blore Heath on the road between New-
castle-under-Lyme and Market Drayton as it was marching south-
west towards Ludlow to join the main Yorkist army. This was the first
so-called 'battle' of the Wars of the Roses when contemporary writers
indicate the queen's direct involvement as the source of authority
behind the Lancastrian army led by John Tuchet, Lord Audley. The
army is described in Gregory's *Chronicle* as made up of the 'Quenys
galentys' and in Benet's *Chronicle* as composed of 'octo millia
hominum bellatorum de Galantibus regine'.[54] The exact composition
of 'the queen's army', made up of men from her duchy of Lancaster
estates and the principality of Wales, has been the subject of much
debate, especially the part played by the Cheshire gentry, who are
popularly believed to have suffered heavy casualties.[55] A recent
examination of the composition of Lord Audley's army has led to a

reassessment of the numbers of Cheshiremen fighting at Blore Heath as well as the fatalities amongst them. It has been pointed out that Audley's retainers would have been drawn not just from Cheshire but from his estates across Shropshire, Staffordshire and Derbyshire, and that their identities are largely unknown. Many Cheshire families may have had divided loyalties when it came to the test. Even so, it would appear that men from the region, particularly Cheshire, played a significant part in 1459, the only time during the Wars of the Roses until 1483, and that Margaret's efforts to raise military aid from her duchy estates bore results.[56] However, one of the most prominent local noblemen, Thomas, Lord Stanley, failed to engage his men on the queen's behalf. In the parliament that met at Coventry in November 1459, Lord Stanley was accused of failing to heed a summons to the royal host and of impeding the tenants of the prince of Wales in the Cheshire hundreds of Wirral and Macclesfield from joining Lord Audley's force.[57] His brother, William Stanley, whose estates lay mainly in Lancashire, fought with the Yorkist earl of Salisbury. The battle was a disaster for the Lancastrians, who suffered an estimated 2,000 casualties, including Lord Audley himself. As for the king and queen, neither were present on the battlefield but, according to local tradition, Margaret watched the fighting from Mucklestone church tower, and seeing the defeat of the Lancastrian army, took flight, reversing the shoes of her carriage horses, in order to evade pursuit.[58]

Politically the battle of Blore Heath was crucial because it provided the queen and her supporters with the reason to indict the Yorkist lords with treason. The acts of attainder passed against them in the Coventry parliament of November 1459 forced Richard, duke of York, his sons and the earls of Salisbury and Warwick into exile. They remained overseas, in Ireland and Calais, until they considered the time propitious to stage a political comeback, in the following year. It made the continuation of civil war inevitable as the queen increasingly showed her determination to destroy the power of her political rivals. Her position was considerably weakened by the capture of the king's person by the earl of Warwick at the battle of Northampton, fought on 10 July 1460, but Margaret continued to get the support of most of the lords whose loyalty to the anointed king remained steadfast, with a corresponding coolness in their reaction to Richard, duke of York's claim to the throne expressed in October 1460. The disinheritance of her son, agreed by Henry VI under pressure from York, was wholly unacceptable to the queen and provided her main incentive to continue the fight.[59] Margaret's and her son's refuge after the La____ trian defeat at Northampton was Scotland, where she got a sympathetic hearing from the recently widowed queen, Mary of Guelders, who was acting as regent for her young son James III. Contrary to widely accepted accounts,[60] this is where Margaret was residing at the time of the battle of Wakefield, fought on 30 December 1460. The dramatic scenes presented by Shakespeare and repeated, time and again, in what can only be described as fictitious reconstructions of events, have no historical accuracy whatever.

Margaret once again came to the forefront of national political and military events in the early weeks of 1461, when she was active in rallying a Lancastrian army to march on London to regain possession of the king and resume control of government.[61] This campaign, involving the movement of a large number of northern men southwards over several weeks, did more than anything else to damage the queen's reputation at a time of acute political tension and uncertainty. The Lancastrian army, numbering perhaps as many as 25,000 men,[62] was made up of a combination of Scottish and French mercenaries provided by Mary of Guelders; northerners led by Henry Percy, earl of Northumberland; other northern Lords including Neville, Clifford and Dacre; and contingents provided by Henry Beaufort, duke of Somerset, Henry Holland, duke of Exeter, and John Talbot, earl of Shrewsbury. A number of contemporary sources describe this army as a rabble from the north, John Whethamstede, abbot of St Albans, comparing it to Attila's Huns.[63] The prior of Crowland in Lincolnshire, near whose abbey the army passed on its route south, reflected the state of panic felt by people experiencing the movement of an army across their land, comparing it to 'a plague of locusts covering the whole surface of the earth'.[64] However, the abbey remained free from attack and the prior's description is highly suspect because of its vagueness and its evident tendency towards exaggeration.[65] These accounts highlight some of the problems of the reliability of the limited evidence available for the study of the military aspects of the Wars of the Roses.[66] It has often been said that accounts of the second battle of St Albans reflect a southern bias against northerners, since they are presented as undisciplined thugs bent on the wholesale plunder and systematic destruction of property, as well as pro-Yorkist in sympathy. Despite a Lancastrian victory at St Albans, the reputation of the Lancastrian army had been so damaged that the Londoners refused to admit it into the city. During lengthy discussions with the city authorities in the aftermath of the battle, a deputation of ladies, the dowager duchess of Buckingham and the dowager duchess of Bedford, was sent to negotiate with the queen, but they failed to reach an agreement and the Lancastrians were forced to withdraw and retreat northwards.[67]

These events were crucial to the eventual loss of the throne by Henry VI and the establishment of Edward, earl of March, as king in March 1461. Not only had a significant section of the country, notably the Londoners and many in the south-east, lost faith in the Lancastrian king, but they had also become alienated from the Lancastrian cause itself as represented by the queen and her son. An alternative king had now become acceptable to many people of influence and standing in the country.[68] A question still remains as to whether Margaret of Anjou was the cause of this situation, as her enemies maintained, or whether she was rather the victim of her circumstances. When it came to actual physical fighting, as a woman she was in a weak position, and she was no match for the challenge posed by the young, dynamic soldier, Edward, earl of March, whose success at Towton on 29 March 1461 clinched the Yorkist victory. Margaret, with her husband and her son, awaited news of the outcome of the battle from the safety of the city of York and, on hearing of the Lancastrian defeat, fled north over the border to Scotland.

After 1461 Margaret continued to play an active role as the rallying point of opposition to the new Yorkist king, Edward IV and she worked hard to obtain foreign support for the recovery of the throne for either her husband or her son. Determined to get the backing of the French king for her cause, she made expeditions to France in 1462 and 1463, settling permanently at St Mihiel in the duchy of Bar in 1464.[69]

Her final attempt to place her son on the throne was made in 1471, by which time he was aged 17 and, according to some contemporary commentators, inclined to war.[70] In July 1470 the unlikely alliance between Queen Margaret and her former enemy Richard Neville, earl of Warwick, was sealed with the marriage of Prince Edward to Warwick's daughter Anne, at Angers cathedral. Warwick, who had taken refuge in France in 1470, returned to England ahead of the royal family to secure London, where the deposed king, Henry VI, was held captive in the Tower. Margaret was not prepared to risk her son's life until convinced that there was adequate Lancastrian support in the south of the country. Despite Warwick's initial success in gaining control of the capital and bringing about the readeption of Henry VI, by the time

Margaret and Prince Edward landed at Weymouth on 14 April 1471 Warwick was dead, having been defeated by King Edward at the battle of Barnet fought on that very day. Nonetheless Margaret had considerable success in raising an army under the military command of Henry Beaufort, duke of Somerset, and John Courtenay, earl of Devon. It made its way north-eastwards through Dorset, Devon, Wiltshire and Somerset, reaching Bristol on 1 May, where it was given a friendly reception and supplied with provisions, additional men, artillery and cash. This was not repeated on 3 May at Gloucester, where the gates remained firmly shut, Edward having sent strict instructions to Richard Beauchamp, the constable of the castle, to keep them out.[71]

Despite the survival of an eyewitness account of the battle of Tewkesbury, fought on 4 May, we have no reliable figures for the relative size of the armies. It is thought that the two sides were fairly evenly matched, perhaps numbering as many as 10,000 on each side.[72] During the battle Margaret took shelter in a neighbouring religious house with her daughter-in-law, Anne Neville, the countess of Devon and her lady-in-waiting, Katherine Vaux. Here she heard the news of the final humiliating defeat of the Lancastrian army and the death of her son at the hands of the Yorkists. Three days later she was found with her female companions, now all widowed, and was taken prisoner by Edward IV. The death of her husband in the Tower of London under mysterious circumstances during the night of 21 May put an end to Margaret's political career, and the remainder of her life was spent in relative obscurity and comparative poverty, as a semi-captive in England until 1475, and in France until her death in 1482.

Contemporaries and later writers have regarded Margaret as providing political and military leadership of the Lancastrian party in place of the increasingly ineffective king, and in the interests of her under-age son. But what did this actually mean? It is difficult to give a categorical answer to this question because of the paucity of documentary material: according to John Watts, 'in the later 1450s, the documentation of governmental activity in all spheres, including justice and finance, all but broke down.'[73] The lack of records of estate administration for the duchy of Lancaster for this period has already been noted and this deficiency is not made good by the picture of events provided by contemporary chronicles and narrative accounts.[74] One of the major shortcomings of the evidence is the lack of first-hand accounts of battles, so that we have little information about who was actually present on the battlefield, let alone details of the course of events themselves. Rarely is there any mention of the queen's movements but generally it is fair to assume that she was not present on the battlefield, since this would have been totally inappropriate as well as far too dangerous. She was usually to be found a short distance away located safely within the walls of a castle, or at the top of a church tower, awaiting news of the outcome of the battle.

The factual vagueness of so many contemporary chronicles does not inhibit their authors from holding strong opinions on the cause of events and objects of blame. As the Lancastrian position deteriorated a scapegoat was sought, at a time when it was imprudent to find fault with the king himself. The obvious victim was his wife, who came to be regarded as the source of all Henry VI's troubles from the time of his marriage in 1445.[75] This process of the victimisation of queens for the faults of their husbands is common in the medieval period and tends to exaggerate the role of queens as controllers of events, especially when the political situation deteriorated to such an extent that civil war ensued, as it did during the reigns of Henry III, Edward II and Henry VI. The common factor in the experiences of Eleanor of Provence, Isabella of France and Margaret of Anjou is marriage to a king who failed to fulfil his duties effectively, thereby losing the support of his people. A weak king provided the opportunity for his queen to exercise power on his behalf but this was regarded with deep suspicion by contemporary observers, invariably resulting in condemnation and criticism of her actions.[76] Such judgements should therefore be seen as a reflection of contemporary attitudes and prejudices towards women in positions of power rather than any fair assessment of the abilities or shortcomings of the queens themselves.

NOTES

1 W. Shakespeare, *Henry VI, Part III*, Act ii, Scene v, lines 14–18.

2 *Henry VI: Part III*, Act iii, Scene iii, lines 229–30.

3 *Henry VI, Part III*, Act i, Scene iv, lines 111–15.

4 A. Strickland, *Lives of the Queens of England*, 8 vols (1851–52), vol. 2, p. 229.

5 E. Hall, *Chronicle of Lancaster and York 1399–1547*, ed. H. Ellis (1809), p. 250; Strickland, *Lives of the Queens*, p. 238.

6 See, for example, her biography by J.J. Bagley, *Margaret of Anjou Queen of England* (1948) and J. Gillingham, *The Wars of the Roses* (1981), ch. 7 entitled 'Margaret of

Anjou: The Warlike Queen, 1455–9'.

7 The most useful recent general studies of medieval queenship are: P. Stafford, *Queens, Concubines and Dowagers: The King's Wife in the Early Middle Ages* (1983); *Medieval Queenship*, ed. J.C. Parsons (Stroud, 1994); *Queens and Queenship in Medieval Europe*, ed. A. Duggan (Woodbridge, 1997).

8 See A. Crawford, 'The King's Burden?: the Consequences of Royal Marriage in Fifteenth-Century England' in *Patronage, the Crown and the Provinces in Later Medieval England*, ed. R.A. Griffiths (Gloucester, 1981) and the 'Introduction' to *Letters of the Queens of England 1100–1547*, ed. A. Crawford (Stroud, 1994).

9 The role of a queen as a mediator is particularly emphasised by the early fifteenth-century writer Christine de Pisan in her book of advice to women written in 1405, see Christine de Pisan, *The Treasure of the City of Ladies*, trans. S. Lawson (Harmondsworth, 1985), pp. 49–51. J.C. Parsons has written several papers on the role of the queen as intercessor: see 'Ritual and Symbol in the English Queenship to 1500', in *Women and Sovereignty*, ed. L.O. Fradenburg (Edinburgh, 1992), pp. 60–77, and 'The Queen's Intercession in Thirteenth-Century England', in *Power of the Weak: Studies on Medieval Women*, eds J. Carpenter and S.B. MacLean (Urbana, 1995), pp. 147–77.

10 On the marriage of Edward II and Isabella of France, see E.A. Brown, 'The Political Repercussions of Family Ties in the Early Fourteenth Century: The Marriage of Edward II of England and Isabella of France', Speculum, vol. 63 (1988), pp. 573–95; on the marriage of Henry V to Katharine of Valois, see C.T. Allmand, *Henry V* (1992), pp. 131–45; and on the marriage of Henry VI to Margaret of Anjou, see B.M. Cron, 'The Duke of Suffolk, the Angevin Marriage, and the Ceding of Maine, 1445', *Journal of Medieval History*, vol. 20 (1994), pp. 77–99.

11 Stafford, *Queens, Concubines and Dowagers*, pp. 127–34; Parsons, 'Ritual and Symbol', pp. 61–62.

12 P.E. Schramm, *A History of the English Coronation* (Oxford, 1937), pp. 29–30.

13 L. Huneycutt, 'Medieval Queenship', *History Today*, vol. 39 (1989), pp. 16–22, and L. Huneycutt, 'Intercession and the High–Medieval Queen: The Esther Topos', in Carpenter and MacLean, *Power of the Weak*, pp.126–45.

14 M. Howell, *Eleanor of Provence: Queenship in Thirteenth-Century England* (Oxford, 1998), p. 20.

15 The manuscript is BL, Cotton Tiberius B. VIII. For a discussion of the images see: C.R. Sherman, 'Taking a Second Look: Observations on the Iconography of a French Queen, Jeanne de Bourbon (1338–1378)', in *Feminism and Art History: Questioning the Litany*, eds N. Broude and M.D. Garrard (New York, 1982), pp. 101–17; C.R. Sherman, 'The Queen in Charles V's *Coronation Book*: Jeanne de Bourbon and the Ordo ad reginam benedicendam', Viator, vol. 8 (1977), pp. 255–97.

16 Pisan, *Treasure of the City of Ladies*, pp. 49–50.

17 Sherman, 'Taking a Second Look', p. 104.

18 See the discussion of changing attitudes to women's participation in war in M. McLaughlin, 'The Woman Warrior: Gender, Warfare and Society in Medieval Europe', *Women's Studies*, vol. 17 (1990), pp. 193–209.

19 P. Coss, *The Lady in Medieval England 1000–1500* (Stroud, 1998), p. 31; Stafford, *Queens, Concubines and Dowagers*, pp. 140–41.

20 Stafford, *Queens, Concubines and Dowagers*, p. 26.

21 Howell, *Eleanor of Provence*, p. 261.

22 *Gesta Stephani*, pp. 118–19, 122–23.

23 M. Chibnall, *The Empress Matilda* (Oxford, 1991), pp. 96–97.

24 *Gesta Stephani*, pp. 122–23, 126–27.

25 Richard of Hexham, *De Gestis Regis Stephani*, in *Chronicles of the Reigns of Stephen, Henry II and Richard I*, ed. R. Howlett, 4 vols, Rolls Series (1884–89), vol. 3, p. 176.

26 *Letters of the Queens*, ed. Crawford, p. 30.

27 See J.A. Brundage, *The Crusades, Holy War and Canon Law* (1992), ch. XV, in which he discusses the delicate problem of the position of the crusader's wife.

28 *Letters of the Queens*, ed. Crawford, pp. 31–34.

29 D.D.R. Owen, *Eleanor of Aquitaine* (Oxford, 1996), pp. 104–7.

30 Richard of Devizes, *Chronicle*, ed. J.T. Appleby (1963), pp. 59–60.

31 Howell, *Eleanor of Provence*, p. 152; the author of the *Chronicle of Melrose* in 1263 described her as the foremost of the king's evil counsellors, susceptible to the influence of foreigners and the cause of discord between the king and his barons.

32 Ibid., pp. 168, 182, 196–97, 221, 260.

33 See the preface to Howell, *Eleanor of Provence*.

34 Thomas Gray, 'The Bard', written in 1757, refers to Isabella of France as 'She-Wolf of France, with unrelenting fangs, / That tearest the bowels of thy mangled mate.' See H. Johnstone, 'Isabella, the She-Wolf of France', *History*, vol. 21 (1936), pp. 208–15.

35 *Letters of the Queens*, ed. Crawford, pp. 81–82; Brown, 'The Marriage of Edward II', pp. 573–74.

36 N. Fryde, *The Tyranny and Fall of Edward II 1321–1326* (Cambridge, 1979), p. 18; M. Prestwich, *The Three Edwards: War and State in England 1272–1377* (1980), p. 80.

37 Fryde, *Tyranny of Edward II*, p 50; S. Menache, 'Isabelle of France, Queen of England – A Reconsideration', *Journal of Medieval History*, vol. 10 (1984), p.108.

38 Fryde, *Tyranny of Edward II*, pp. 146–47; Prestwich, *Three Edwards*, pp. 96–97. See also the final section of P.C. Doherty, 'Isabella, Queen of England, 1296–1330' (unpublished DPhil thesis, Oxford University, 1977), which discusses different opinions of Isabella's personality. Doherty regards her as a successful mediator and manipulator of men and a competent politician, whose infatuation for Mortimer was her ultimate undoing.

39 Menache, 'Isabelle of France', pp. 110–24, contains a useful discussion of the shift in contemporary attitudes towards Isabella as a result of her actions in 1326.

40 R.N. Combridge, 'Ladies, Queens and Decorum', *Reading Medieval Studies*, vol. 1 (1975), pp. 71–83.

41 Jacopus de Cessolis, *The Game of Chess*, facsimile edition of Caxton's *Game and Playe of Chesse* of 1474 (1883), p. 170.

42 The relationship between Henry VI and his queen is discussed in R.A. Griffiths, *The Reign of King Henry VI: the Exercise of Royal Authority, 1422–1461* (1981); B.P. Wolffe, *Henry VI* (1981) and J. Watts, *Henry VI and the Politics of Kingship* (Cambridge, 1996). A recent discussion of the political role of Margaret of Anjou is contained in A. Gross, *The Dissolution of the Lancastrian Kingship* (Stamford, 1996), pp. 46–69.

43 The nature of Henry VI's illness is discussed by C. Rawcliffe in 'The Insanity of Henry VI', *The Historian*, no. 50 (1996), pp. 8–12.

44 'The Search for Authority' is the title of the final chapter of Watts, *Henry VI*.

45 Griffiths, *Reign of Henry VI*, pp. 778–808; D.A.L. Morgan, 'The House of Policy: The Political Role of the Late Plantagenet Household, 1422–1485', in *The English Court from the Wars of the Roses to the Civil War*, ed. D. Starkey (1987), pp. 50–53; D.J. Clayton, *The Administration of the County Palatine of Chester 1442–1485* (Manchester, 1990), p. 58; Watts, *Henry VI*, pp. 326–40. This view has recently been challenged by Michael Hicks, who plays down the political role of the queen and argues that during this period Henry VI was far more active in his efforts to make peace than historians have suggested: see M. Hicks, *Warwick the Kingmaker* (Oxford, 1998), pp.127–38.

46 A. Goodman, *John of Gaunt: The Exercise of Princely Power in Fourteenth-Century Europe* (1992), pp. 217–22; S. Walker, *The Lancastrian Affinity 1361–1399* (Oxford, 1990).

47 R. Somerville, *History of the Duchy of Lancaster*, 2 vols (1953), vol. 1, pp. 202–7.

48 H. Castor, 'The Duchy of Lancaster in the Lancastrian Polity, 1399–1461' (unpublished PhD thesis, Cambridge University, 1993), pp. 44–54.

49 Ibid., pp. 317–18. Christine Carpenter has questioned the effectiveness of Margaret's attempts to build up a power base in the west Midlands and actually sees her efforts as counter-productive, having the effect of alienating substantial sections of the gentry who were unwilling to commit themselves unreservedly to the Lancastrian cause: see C. Carpenter, *The Wars of the Roses: Politics and the Constitution in England, c. 1437–1509* (Cambridge, 1997), pp.142–44, 153–54.

50 *Paston Letters and Papers of the Fifteenth Century*, ed. N. Davis, 2 vols (1971–76), vol. 2, p. 148.

51 *CPR, 1452–1461*, p. 515. On 23 July 1459 the prince was directed 'to go to all such places in England and Wales and there stay as long and return as speedily as shall seem good for the increase of the revenues of the principality [of Wales], duchy [of Cornwall] and counties [of Chester and Flint]': see Griffiths, *Reign of Henry VI*, pp. 797–808.

52 Gillingham, *Wars of the Roses*, p. 102.

53 *An English Chronicle of the Reigns of Richard II, Henry IV, Henry V and Henry VI*, ed. J.S. Davies, Camden Society, old series, vol. 64 (1856), pp. 79–80. The Chronicle was written in *c.* 1461 and reflects strong Yorkist bias against the queen, whom the author seems to have particularly disliked.

54 *Three Fifteenth-Century Chronicles*, ed. J. Gairdner, Camden Society, 3rd series, vol. 28 (1880), p. 204; *John Benet's Chronicle for the years 1400 to 1462*, ed. G.L. Harriss, Camden Miscellany, vol. 24 (1972), p. 224.

55 The fullest and most useful discussions of the battle of Blore Heath are in Clayton, *County Palatine of Chester*, pp. 74–90, and J.L. Gillespie, 'Cheshiremen at Blore Heath: A Swan Dive' in *People, Politics and Community in the Later Middle Ages*, eds J. Rosenthal and C. Richmond (Gloucester, 1987), pp. 77–89.

56 Clayton, *County Palatine of Chester*, pp. 79–89; Gillespie, 'Cheshiremen at Blore Heath', pp. 78–79. The Rolls of Parliament, which describe the measures taken against the Yorkists in the parliament which met at Coventry in November 1459, contain the fullest contemporary account of the battle: see *Rotuli Parliamentorum*, ed. J. Strachey et al., 6 vols (1767–77), vol. 5, p. 348.

57 *Rot. Parl.*, vol. 5, p. 370.

58 Gillingham, *Wars of the Roses*, p. 103.

59 The events between the battles of Blore Heath and Wakefield are described fully in Griffiths, *Reign of Henry VI*, pp. 821–71, and Gillingham, *Wars of the Roses*, pp. 104–22.

60 See, for example, the account in *Gregory's Chronicle* in *The Historical Collections of a Citizen of London in the Fifteenth Century*, ed. J. Gairdner, Camden Society, new series, vol. 17 (1876), p. 210; Hall, *Chronicle of Lancaster and York*, p. 250.

61 B.M. Cron, 'Margaret of Anjou and the Lancastrian March on London, 1461', *The Ricardian*, vol. 11, no. 147 (Dec. 1999), pp. 590–615.

62 Estimates of numbers of men fighting in the battles of the Wars of the Roses are liable to be very variable because of the inadequacies of the sources: see the discussion in C.D. Ross, *The Wars of the Roses* (1976), pp.135–40. For an estimate of the size of the armies that fought at the battle of St Albans on 17 February 1461, see P.A. Haigh, *The Military Campaigns of the Wars of the Roses* (Stroud, 1995), pp. 46–48.

63 J. Whethamstede, *Registrum Abbatiae Johannis Whethamstede*, ed. H.T. Riley, Rolls Series, 2 vols (1872–73), vol. 1, p. 389.

64 *Chronicle of the Abbey of Crowland*, trans. H.T. Riley (1854), pp. 421–23.

65 Griffiths, *Reign of Henry VI*, p. 868; for a general discussion of perceptions of the north in the period, see A.J. Pollard, 'The Characteristics of the Fifteenth-Century North', in *Government, Religion and Society in Northen England 1000–1700*, eds J.C. Appleby and P. Dalton (Stroud, 1997), pp. 131–43.

66 Some of the problems of using the sources for a study of military aspects of the wars are dealt with by Ross, *Wars of the Roses*, pp. 109–50 and A. Goodman, *The Wars of the Roses: Military Activity and English Society, 1452–97* (1981), pp. 162–226.

67 Gillingham, *Wars of the Roses*, p. 130; newsletter written on 22 February by Carlo Gigli to Michele Arnolfini, *Calendar of State Papers, Milan, 1385–1618*, vol. I (1919), pp. 49–51.

68 William Gregory recorded the reaction of Londoners to Edward, earl of March, thus: 'Let us walk in a new vineyard, and let us make a gay garden in the month of March with this fair white rose and herb, the earl of March', *Gregory's Chronicle*, p. 215.

69 A reliable narrative account of the period 1461 to 1471 is C.L. Scofield, *The Life and Reign of Edward the Fourth*, vol. 1 (1923). See also A. Gross, 'Lancastrians Abroad, 1461–71', *History Today*, vol. 42 (1992), pp. 31–37.

70 Sir John Fortescue, chancellor of the Lancastrian court in exile, describes him as energetic, physically strong and learned in law, more resembling his grandfather than his father, in the opening section of his *De Laudibus Legum Anglie*, ed. S.B. Chrimes (Cambridge, 1942), pp. 2–3, 16–19. In 1467 the Milanese ambassador wrote: 'This boy, though only thirteen years of age, already talks of nothing but of cutting off heads or making war, as if he had everything in his hands or was the god of battle or the peaceful occupant of that throne.' *CSP, Milan*, vol. I, p. 117. According to one anonymous account, Prince Edward, urged on by his mother, ordered the execution of the Yorkist leaders after the second battle of St Albans in 1461: see *An English Chronicle*, ed. Davies, p. 108, and Jean de Waurin, *Recueil des Croniques*, ed. W. and E.L.C.P. Hardy, Rolls Series, 5 vols (1864–91), vol. 5, p. 330.

71 Gillingham, *Wars of the Roses*, pp. 203–4.

72 John Warkworth puts the number on each side at 4,000 men, whereas the author of *The Arrivall* says that King Edward had 3,000 footmen: *Warkworth's Chronicle*, ed. J.O. Halliwell, Camden Society (1839), p. 17 and the *Historie of the Arrivall of Edward IV in England* ..., ed. J. Bruce, Camden Society (1838), p. 28. For a discussion of the relative size of the armies fighting at Tewkesbury see: Ross, *Wars of the Roses*, p. 139, and P.W. Hammond, *The Battles of Barnet and Tewkesbury* (Gloucester, 1990), p. 95.

73 Watts, *Henry VI*, p. 331; Gross, *Dissolution of Lancastrian Kingship*, p. 47.

74 An overview of the source material for the study of the Wars of the Roses is provided in *The Wars of the Roses*, ed. A.J. Pollard (1995), ch. 1, and a detailed discussion of individual sources can be found in A. Gransden, *Historical Writing in England II, c. 1307 to the Early Sixteenth Century* (1982), pp. 249–307.

75 *The Brut*, ed. F.W.D. Brie, Early English Text Society, old series, vols 131 and 136 (1906–8), pp. 511–12. Margaret was blamed for the general deterioration of the political situation as early as 1447, when an indictment for seditious speech against the queen was brought before the court of King's Bench: PRO, KB9/256/12. For a discussion of her reputation, see P.A. Lee, 'Reflections of Power: Margaret of Anjou and the Dark Side of Queenship', *Renaissance Quarterly*, vol. 39 (1986), pp. 183–217, and D. Dunn, 'Margaret of Anjou, Queen Consort of Henry VI: A Reassessment of her Role, 1445–53', in *Crown, Government and People in the Fifteenth Century*, ed. R.E. Archer (Stroud, 1995), pp. 107–143.

76 It is interesting to compare the experiences of queens of England with those of France, for example, Isabeau of Bavaria, who was unfortunate enough to be married to an ineffective king (Charles VI) who went mad, resulting in civil war. See R. Gibbons, 'Isabeau of Bavaria, Queen of France (1385–1422): The Creation of an Historical Villainess', *TRHS*, 6th series, vol. 6 (1996), pp. 51–73.

Caricaturing Cymru:
Images of the Welsh
in the London Press 1642–46

Mark Stoyle

Some months before the outbreak of the civil war a propaganda campaign was launched in London: a campaign which was to be sustained,
in various guises, throughout the next five years, but one which –
despite its extraordinary virulence and longevity – has been virtually
ignored by historians. The initiators of this campaign were anonymous
pamphleteers, men (it may be presumed) who were sympathetic to the
parliament in its rapidly developing struggle with King Charles I and
who had been freed from the traditional constraints of censorship by
the collapse of the royal regime. Their targets were the people of Wales,
a people who had long been the butt of English humour,[1] and who had
now had the temerity to dissent from majority opinion in the capital by
hinting at an inclination to favour the royal cause. As parliamentarian
suspicions that Wales would side with the Crown turned to certainty
during summer 1642, so the outpouring of anti-Welsh literature
increased – and the arrival of thousands of Welsh troops in England to
join the king's armies during the following year stirred the Roundhead
satirists to still greater efforts.

Between January 1642 and May 1643 at least 17 pamphlets entirely
devoted to attacks upon the Welsh were published in London, a number of them accompanied by abusive woodcuts.[2] To put this figure into
perspective, it may be observed that, over the same period, fewer than
a dozen comparable satires were printed against all the other nations
of Europe combined.[3] When one considers that, in addition to these
occasional publications, many of the weekly diurnals which poured off
the parliamentary presses were likewise suffused with anti-Welsh
rhetoric,[4] the full scale of the propaganda offensive which had been
unleashed against the Principality's inhabitants becomes clear. No
other people came under such sustained assault in the London press
during the first year of the civil war. Even the Irish, who had attracted

a veritable fire-storm of obloquy in the aftermath of the October 1641 rebellion, were the subject of fewer condemnatory pamphlets than the Welsh during 1642.[5] Yet whereas the printed attacks made upon the Irish have been examined in great depth by historians,[6] those made upon the Welsh have attracted only rather cursory attention.[7] This paper sets out to redress the balance by exploring the ways in which Wales and the Welsh people were depicted by the parliamentary satirists.

I

Of the authors of the anti-Welsh satires practically nothing is known. The pamphlets were usually presented to their readers as the work of Welsh writers, and are often attributed on the title pages to individuals with mock-Welsh names, like 'Shinkin ap Morgan' and 'Shon ap Shones'.[8] Yet these were patent fictions, designed to conceal the identities of the true authors, who were almost certainly well-educated Englishmen. As Stephen Roberts has observed, the possibility that the pamphlets' authors were gentlemen 'should put us on our guard against too easy an acceptance that this was genuine popular culture'.[9] On the other hand, the anti-Welsh satires of the 1640s – cheaply produced; almost devoid of classical allusions; and resolutely down-market in tone – were clearly designed to *appeal* to a popular audience. And that they succeeded in this aim is strongly suggested by the sheer number of anti-Welsh pamphlets which eventually appeared: publishers would hardly have persisted in backing such works if they had failed to sell. The anti-Welsh pasquinades of the 1640s cannot convincingly be depicted as publications which were intended for an elite audience alone, therefore, still less as the unheeded rantings of a handful of isolated xenophobes. Instead they must be regarded as deliberate attempts to profit from – and, if possible, to swell – the poisonous stream of anti-Welsh prejudice which lay just beneath the surface of mid-seventeenth-century English society.[10]

Although there had been no armed conflict between the Welsh and the English since the fifteenth century, and although Wales had been formally incorporated within the kingdom of England since the 1530s, popular opinion – on both side of Offa's Dyke – continued to take it for granted that the Welsh were set apart, distinct. Outright hostility between the two peoples certainly declined during the peaceful years which followed Henry VII's accession, but many in England remained unwilling to accept the Welsh as equals. It was this latent prejudice which the pamphleteers of the 1640s set out to exploit – and they did so firstly by evoking scorn for the physical landscape of Wales itself. To the seventeenth-century satirists, just as to English medieval writers, that landscape could be best summed up in a single word – 'mountainous' – and references to the 'barren', 'craggy' and 'stony' nature of the Principality's terrain were frequent in the pamphlet literature of the civil war.[11] The overwhelmingly rural nature of Welsh society was constantly stressed, and the satirists characterised the typical Welshman as a poverty-stricken hill-farmer, cut off from the rest of the world by the mountainous terrain and bad roads which together accounted for the notoriously intractable nature of the 'Welsh miles'.[12] It was frequently asserted that the Welsh lived in hovels – 'cabins' or 'poor cottages', as they were termed – and one scornful writer averred that most Welsh parishes consisted of nothing more than 'a few pighouses, out of which a little smoak doth break forth at the top of chimneys'.[13]

If Welsh houses were depicted as beggarly, then those who dwelt in them were depicted as veritable beggars. To the London journalists, the archetypal Welshman was barefoot, verminous and dressed in rags from head to toe.[14] What tattered remnants of clothing he *did* possess had clearly ceased to be à la mode some decades, if not centuries, before, while his weapons were similarly antiquated. Typical items in the armoury of the mock-Welshmen who featured as the anti-heroes of the parliamentary tracts included the 'Welsh-Bill', a long blade attached to a wooden handle, the 'Welsh-Hook', another variant on the same theme, and the double-edged sword, or 'Back-sword' – all weapons which would have been regarded as hopelessly archaic in England by this time.[15] Of musketry, it was claimed, the Welsh knew little, while their attitude towards 'great guns' or heavy ordnance was typically represented as a mixture of baffled incomprehension and fear (rather like that of the 'Red Indians' in a 1950s western). Pamphleteers averred that the mere sound of cannon-fire sparked off superstitious dread in the Welshmen's hearts – not to mention a distressing 'looseness' in their bowels.[16]

It was not only by his ragged dress and antiquated weaponry that the mock-Welshman was known, for the pamphleteers provided him with a wide array of other props as well, all of them held to be emblematic of Welshness. Thus his favourite drink was alleged to be the spiced variety of mead known as metheglin and his favourite food cheese, preferably toasted.[17] When cheese failed to tempt, the mock-Welshman was said to partake instead of the leeks which he customarily wore in his hat to celebrate St David's day, and when both of these staples ran short, it was claimed, he was not above dining on horse-meat.[18] Such culinary emergencies aside, horses rarely featured in the mock-Welshman's day-to-day round: the pamphleteers clearly preferred to give the impression that, in contrast to prosperous Englishmen, Welsh 'beggars' did not ride. Instead, the creatures most commonly associated with the mock-Welshman were the 'stolen' sheep and cattle which grazed in his fields; the goats who shared the rocky crags of his homeland with him; and the lice which were alleged to live in more intimate proximity still.[19] Should the mock-Welshman feel amorously inclined – an all too frequent occurrence according to the pamphleteers – it was claimed that he would not find his female neighbours over-scrupulous, while for mental recreation he had his Welsh harp, his family pedigrees, and the old 'tales & stories' of his people.[20]

The composite image of Wales and the Welsh outlined above was a deeply traditional one: a stock collection of stereotypes which would have been as familiar to English men and women of the Tudor period as it was to their Stuart descendants.[21] Yet it is important to stress that the propagandists of the 1640s added a novel politico-religious element to this basic template in order to emphasise Welsh hostility to the puritan-parliamentarian cause. Great play was made of the Welsh attachment to the traditional 'festive culture', for example, while the religious conservatism of ordinary Welsh people was constantly underlined.[22] Thus one mock-Welshman was shown declaring his affection for the Book of Common Prayer, while another was made to observe that he could 'never apide ... Puritants in awle ... [his] life'.[23] The political conservatism of the Welsh was stressed more strongly still; indeed, it was averred that they were an innately Royalist race. In 1643 a fictitious Welshman named 'Shinkin' (i.e. Jenkin) was made to boast that 'Shinkin [is] no Roundhead, nor ever any came out of Wales was ever any Roundhead'.[24] And behind these new charges of anti-parliamentarianism there lurked other, much more sinister allegations, which had been resurrected from the medieval past.

Throughout the civil war, parliamentary pamphleteers repeatedly made it clear that – while they took it for granted that Wales was an appanage of the English state – they did not regard it as a part of England proper. 'Before we return to England, we will touch upon Wales' one diurnalist remarked in passing to his readers as he conducted

them on a 'virtual tour' of the British Isles in 1644, and similar comments were made by many other writers.[25] Wales was routinely
depicted as a quasi-foreign country, then, and this opened the way for
the most damning charge of all to be levelled against the Principality's
inhabitants: that they were irredeemably 'alien', 'other' and 'un-
English'. It is hard to doubt that the overriding aim of the anti-Welsh
satirists of the 1640s was to ram this simple message home to their
English readers. Almost all of the alleged 'characteristics' of the Welsh
which have been touched upon so far – poverty, raggedness, ignorance,
sexual immorality and religious and technological backwardness –
were clearly designed to convey the idea of 'otherness' to contemporary English men and women, as well as of straightforward primi-
tivism and contemptibility.[26] Nor were the satirists content to let
matters rest there, for they adopted a whole range of other devices in
order to 'alienise' the Welsh still further.

Most notable of all, perhaps, was the use which they made of the
linguistic division which existed between England and Wales. By
making frequent allusions to the Welsh tongue – and by occasionally
even incorporating brief snatches of Welsh within their texts[27] – the
pamphleteers were able to underline repeatedly the fact that the Welsh
were culturally distinct from the English. But more effective still was
the tactic which they habitually employed of adopting the persona of
a bilingual Welshman, and then spewing forth a violent stream of criticisms of Wales and the Welsh in a mock-Welsh accent. Not only did
this have the effect of making the Welsh look thoroughly ridiculous, it
also constantly reminded the reader that the Welsh were unable to
speak English properly and were thus, by definition, *un*-English. It
was a simple device, but an immensely effective one, and this surely
helps to explain why the satirists remained wedded to it throughout
the entire course of the war.

An alternative tactic was to refer to the Welsh in the same breath
as other demonstrably non-English peoples. In 1643, for example, a
pamphleteer reported that Prince Rupert had many soldiers in his
army 'not onely of this Nation, but fetcht from Ireland, Wales and
Denmark'.[28] And, significantly, the 'foreigners' with whom the Welsh
were most commonly equated were not the inhabitants of continental
Europe – grudgingly accepted by contemporary Englishmen as at least
semi-civilised – but the 'backward' peoples of the Celtic fringe: the
Cornish, the Irish and the Scottish Highlanders.[29] As early as December 1642 it was alleged that there were many 'Irish and Welsh' soldiers

and their 'trulls' in the royalist army, and that the King's English soldiers were greatly afraid of 'this cruell and murderous people'.[30] Thereafter, it became commonplace for the Welsh and 'Irish' forces in the
king's service to be conflated, and for Welsh soldiers to be depicted
using the stock Irish lamentation of 'O Hone, O Hone!'[31]

By deliberately confusing the Welsh with the Irish – a people who
had long been regarded in England as virtual savages[32] – the pamphleteers were not only seeking to 'alienise' the inhabitants of Wales but to
go one step further and to 'barbarise' them as well. The constant links
which were drawn between the two peoples in the parliamentary press
tarred the Welsh with the brush of Irish 'barbarism' and implied that
they, like the Irish, were morally and culturally inferior to the English.
This assumption was reinforced by references to the Welsh as 'hea-
thens', as 'pagans' and as 'inhumane barberous commoners'.[33] There
was a more subtle way, too, in which the message that the Welsh were
barbarians was continually underlined. As we have seen, the single
word which English folk invariably associated with Wales at this time
was 'mountainous' – and 'mountainous' was a contemporary synonym
for 'barbarous'. So when the satirists twitted the Welsh for their
'Mountainous Language', and claimed that they were as 'wilde as the
Mountaines on which they marche', it was this dual meaning which
they were attempting to exploit.[34] The extent to which the physical
landscape of Wales helped to shape English views of Welsh 'national
character' is again made very clear.

II

The primary objective of the Roundhead satirists was obviously to
inspire their English readers with a feeling of utter contempt for the
Welsh: contempt for them as paupers, as rustics, as cowards, as religious ignorants, as unthinking royalists, as 'foreigners' and as 'barbarians'. Yet this was by no means the limit of the pamphleteers'
ambition. Contempt alone is seldom sufficient to stir men and women
into violent action against the objects of their disdain. For full-scale
racial hatred to be unleashed, a sense of fear must also be aroused. And
if previous historians have only dimly appreciated the extent to which
the anti-Welsh pasquinades of the 1640s encouraged English people to
despise the Welsh as aliens, what has escaped them altogether is the
sly, insinuating way in which the pamphleteers sought to persuade

their readers that the Welsh, in their turn, hated the English as foreign oppressors, chafed at their subordinate position within the English state and planned to recover their former independence under the cloak of military support for the Crown. It is to this wholly neglected subject that the remainder of the present paper will be devoted.

Hints that the Welsh despised the English were evident in the pamphlet literature from the very first. The chronology of the anti-Welsh tracts has never been examined in depth, but the earliest of them would appear to be a single-sheet broadside printed by William Oly of London in late 1641 or early 1642.[35] Entitled *The Welch Man's Inventory*, this brief libel does not initially strike the twentieth-century reader as in any way remarkable. Phrased throughout in 'Wenglish' – that parody of Welsh-accented English speech in which the terms 'her' and 'she' are used as all-purpose pronouns[36] – it purports to be an inventory of the household goods of one William Morgan of Glamorgan, 'Shentleman'. As one might expect, bearing contemporary English assumptions about the Welsh in mind, most of these goods are portrayed as being of little or no value. Morgan's barn is said to contain just half a goblet of oats, seven peas and two beans, for example, while his garden is described as overrun with worms.[37] On a superficial reading, it would be easy to dismiss this broadside as just one more example of the long-standing English contempt for the supposed poverty and rusticity of their Welsh neighbours. Yet, on closer examination, it becomes evident that the document was altogether more innovative – and altogether more subversive of Anglo-Welsh relations – than it at first appears.

The feature which most obviously distinguished *The Welch Man's Inventory* from any previous printed satire on the Welsh was the fact that it was illustrated by a woodcut of a sinister-looking Welshman: an image which had been specifically designed to accompany the text. For what appears to have been the first time in history, in other words, visual and verbal attacks on the Welsh had been brought together in a single publication.[38] Broadside ballads were the cheapest form of contemporary printed literature,[39] and it is hard to doubt that the *Inventory*'s combination of relative affordability with visual allure would have enabled its anonymous author's message to reach an unusually wide audience. Yet what was that message intended to be? It seems highly unlikely that the satire's sole purpose was to confirm English readers in the belief that the Welsh were poverty-stricken rustics: there would have been little point in commissioning an expensive new wood-

Han Infentory of the Couds of *William Morgan*, ap Re-nald, ap *Hugh*, ap *Richard*, ap *Thomas*, ap *Evan*, ap *Rice*, in the County of *Clamorgan*, Shentleman.

Imprimis, IN the *Pantry of Poultry* (for hur own eating) One creat Pig four Week old, one Coose, one Cock-gelding, two Black-puddings, three Cot-loois.

Item, In the *Pantry of Plate,* one Crid-iron, one Fripan, one Tripin, three Wooden Ladle, three Carn.

Item, In the *Napery*, two Towel, two Table-cloath, four Napkin, one for hur felf, one for her Wife Shone, two for Cufen Shon ap Powell and Thomas ap Hugh, when was come to hur Houfe.

Item, In the *Wardrope,* one Irifh Rugg, one Frize Shirkin, one Sheep-skin Tublet, two Irifh Stocking, two Shoor, fix Leather Point.

Item, In the *Tury,* one toafting Sheet, three Oaten-cake, three Pint of Cow-milk, one Pound Cow-putter.

Item, In the *Kitchen,* one Pan with white Curd, two white Pot, two lead Herring, nine Sprat.

Item, In the *Cellar,* one Firkin of Wiggan, two Gallon lower Sider, one Pint of Perry, one little Pottle of Garmarden Sock, alias, Metheglin.

Item, In the *Armory of Weapon,* to kill her Enemy, One Pack-fword two Edge, wo Welfh-hook, three long Cloo, one Cunn, one Moule-trap.

Item, In the *Garden,* One Ped Carlike, nine Onion, twelve Leek, twelve Worm, fix Frog.

Item, In the *Leas-may,* Two Tun Cow, one Mountain Calf.

Item, In the *Comman-field,* Two Welch Nag, twelve long-leg'd Sheep, foorteen and twenty Coat.

Item, In the *Preom-clofe,* Three Robin Run-hole, four Hare; hur own Coods, if hur can catch hur.

Item, In the *Parn,* one half Heblet of Oate, feven Pea, two Pean.

Item, In the *Study* [py Cot hur was almaft forgot hur,] One Welch Pible, two Almanack, one Erra-Pater, one Seven Champions, for St. Taffy fake, twelve Pallat, one Pedigree.

Item, In the *Clofet,* Two Straw-hat, one Houfe.

Item, In the *Ped,* Two naked Pody, one Shirt, one Flannel-fmock at hur Ped's Head.

Item, More Cattle about the Houfe, Two Tog, three Cat, twelve Moufe, fox or hur, was eat hur tost Cheefe, one White Flea with black Pack.

Item, More Lumber about the Houfe, One Wife, two Shild, one call hur Plack Shonk, and t'other Little Morgan.

Item, In the *Yard* under the Wall, One Wheel, two Packet, one Ladder, two Rope.

This Inventory taken Note in the prefence of hur own Ofien Rowland Meridieth ap Howel *and* Lowen in Morgan ap William, *in Anno, 1849, opon the Ten and Thirtieth of Shun.*

The above named William Morgan did when hur wat for four and twenty years, tuirteent Months, a Week, and feven Days.

A NOTE *of fome* LEGACY *of a creat deal of Cods bequeathed to hur Wife and hur two Shild, and all hur Cufens, and Friends, and Kindred, in manner as followeth:*

Imprimas, WAS give hur teer Wife, Shone Morgan; owl hur Coods in the Ped, over the Ped, and under the Ped.

Item, Was give to hur eldeft Son Plack Shonk, 40 and 12 Card to play at Whippet Shinny, 4 Ty to fheat hur Cufen; befides owl hur Land to the full Value of 20 and 10 Shillings 3 Groats per Annum.

Item, Was give to hur fecond Son, Little Morgan ap Morgan, hur fhort Ladder under the Wall in the Yard, and two Rope.

Item, Was give to hur Cufen Rowland Meridieth ap Howell, and Lowell in Morgan, whom was made her Executor, full Pow'r to pay owl hur Tet, when hur can get Money.

Seal'd and deliver'd in the Prefence of Evan ap Richard, ap Shinkin ap Shone, hur twn Cufen, the Cap and Bear about written.

Licens'd and Enter'd.

London, Printed by and for W. O. and fold by the Bookfellers.

cut simply in order to illustrate what was already an established truism. Rather, both image and text appear to have been designed to re-awaken ancient English suspicions of the Welsh as potential enemies, under the cover of more 'traditional' forms of mockery and abuse.

The first hint that 'Morgan' is not just a harmless poltroon, but that he has the potential to transform himself into something more sinister, emerges at that point in the text where he refers to his possession of an 'Armory of Weapon, to kill her Enemy'. The contents of the Welshman's personal arms-store are then listed in full, including one gun, one back-sword, two Welsh-hooks, 'three long Club[s]' and, rather puzzlingly, 'one Mouse-trap'. The detailed enumeration of this motley collection of weapons was clearly intended to provoke the scorn of the broadside's English readers. Yet it may also have been designed to play upon their subconscious fears by suggesting that the Welsh retained a latent capacity for violence. Certainly, the fact that the most prominent of the three background images which are placed around the figure of the Welshman at the head of the text is a cupboard filled with dangerous-looking edged weapons – a cupboard specifically labelled 'Hur Armory' – implies that the connection between Welshmen and weapons was a point which the author of the satire was particularly keen to impress upon his audience.[40]

Nor was this all. As we have seen, Morgan is specifically made to state that his weapons are intended to be used against his 'Enemy'. This casual-seeming remark at once prompts the reader to speculate as to who that enemy might be – and a possible answer emerges shortly afterwards, when Morgan breaks off from listing his goods in order to curse the mice who infest his land. 'Pox on … [them]', he cries, '[they] eat hur tost[ed] cheese!'.[41] As the mice are the only characters whom Morgan attacks in this way it is tempting to assume that it is they who should be regarded as his 'Enemy[s]'. And this assumption is strongly reinforced by the – otherwise inexplicable – presence of a 'Mouse-trap' in Morgan's armoury: a mousetrap which is not only alluded to in the text but depicted in the accompanying illustration as well. Yet why should the *Inventory*'s author have gone to such lengths to suggest that this stereotypical Welshman was both inclined and equipped to wage war on a tribe of mice? At the most basic level, of course, he was simply trying to make the Welsh look ridiculous. Yet he was also presenting his readers with a deeply sinister political allegory – for during the 1640s the mouse was associated, rather surprisingly, with the English nation.[42]

Once this point has been recognised, it becomes possible to appreciate *The Welch Man's Inventory* in its true colours: as nothing less than a coded warning to the people of England that they faced a potential military challenge from Wales. It was a warning charged with explosive significance, for – by presenting the English and the Welsh as potential adversaries, rather than as the ever-loving partners of official state rhetoric[43] – it threatened the stability of the entire kingdom. And it was a warning which formed part of a wider upsurge in English attacks upon the Welsh. In February 1642 an unprecedented petition was sent up to the House of Commons by the people of Wales.[44] In this document the petitioners alluded to the 'Epidemicall derision of us' which was currently sweeping across England, and complained that 'we are disrespected, and shamefully derided with ludibrious contempt, more than any Countrey whatsoever'. The petitioners' demand that the 'authors ... of the same' be punished suggests that they believed the satirists' jibes to have been partly responsible for stirring up popular hostility against them – and this view was clearly shared by the indignant Welsh writer who observed a few weeks later that the printed attacks upon his countrymen were 'in ... jeering manner cried up and down the streets'.[45]

Unfortunately for the people of Wales, their petition did nothing to stem the flow of anti-Welsh propaganda. If anything, indeed, it may be said to have had precisely the opposite effect, for it provoked the composition of the most ambitious satire to appear so far: an eight-page pamphlet entitled *The Welchmans last Petition and Protestation*.[46] Published in London towards the end of February 1642, this tract featured as its centrepiece a garbled petition allegedly composed by a mock-Welshman named 'Shinkin ap Morgan'. A long, rambling complaint against all sorts of petty and ridiculous grievances, this document not only derided the Welsh people in general, but also poured scorn on their recent petition to parliament. And like *The Welch Man's Inventory* – of which it was, in many ways, a more sophisticated elaboration – *The Welchmans last Petition* contained a coded warning that England was in mortal danger from Wales.

The main thrust of the *The Welchmans last Petition* is a bitter complaint against the mice who are alleged to infest the 'Countyes' of Wales, and who 'doe seeke to destroy her commodities and Trafficks, and eate up her bread and cheese out of her ... childrens mouths, and to devour all her other provisions'. These words parody a complaint made in the recent Welsh petition to parliament: that Welsh estates were 'miserably wasted by heavy impositions'.[47] Yet, by referring to mice, they also imply that it was the English whom the Welsh blamed for the burdens which had been laid upon them. And confirmation that this was indeed the author's purpose is provided by the appearance of a character named 'Master Mouse' who replies to the Welshman's lament – in scornful English. After having mocked 'Jenkin' for the 'broken' orthology of his petition, and made a series of unpleasant jibes against the Welsh, 'Master Mouse' goes on to dismiss the substance of the mock-Welshman's complaint. 'Your ... accusations are lyes', he jeers, 'and show you to be a right Brittaine, that will make a mountain out of a molehill'. Elsewhere, the railing rodent elaborates on his charge that the Welsh are a nation of inveterate whingers by claiming that they blame the English for every minor misfortune which befalls them. 'When anything is found knawd [i.e. gnawed]' in Wales, he scoffs, the people complain 'that the Mouse hath been here'. Finally, 'Master Mouse' hints that the Welsh blame parliament, too, for their supposed injuries. 'It doth seeme by this petition, Good Man Jenkin', he remarks, 'that your Welch bloud is up ... for as soon as you are angry, you are presently a top of *the house*'.[48] This pun marks the first occasion on which the charge that the Welsh were intrinsically hostile to parliament was made in the pamphlet literature of the civil war.

Having roundly abused both the Welsh in general, and the mock-Welsh petition in particular, 'Master Mouse' retires sardonically from the fray. One might have expected him to have been given the last word in the debate. Yet instead 'Jenkin' reappears to reply to his adversary's 'answer'. Predictably enough, the mock-Welshman is depicted as spitting with rage as a result of the barrage of derision which he has been forced to endure. Yet, rather surprisingly, it is not the scabrous insults which have been heaped on Jenkin's head that have infuriated him so much as the fact that the (English) Mouse has presumed to refer to him as his 'countryman'. The mock-Welshman furiously denies that he is any such thing. 'God's Body!', he cries, 'Call her her Countryman? Oh base, Oh intollerable! ... Her had best bring the Frog, and such like Catterpillars, and say her is her Country-man as well as the ... Mouse'.[49] The inference is plain: while the English, represented by the Mouse, remain prepared to tolerate the Welsh as their fellow-countrymen – albeit fellow-countrymen of a markedly inferior kind – the Welsh, represented by Jenkin, refuse to accept any degree of fellowship with the English at all. Indeed, they regard the (English)

'Mouse' as no less of a 'foreigner' than the (French or Flemish) 'Frog'.[50]

This was the clearest attempt yet to brand the Welsh as the enemies of the English nation. But the author of *The Welchmans last Petition* did not stop there, for – following the pattern established in *The Welch Man's Inventory* – he went on to imply that, even now, the Welsh were preparing to levy war against their 'hated' English neighbours. During the course of his original petition, Jenkin had declared that he would procure 'good store of Mouse Traps' to defend 'the whole Country of Wales ... from her enemies'. This was surely a hint that the Welsh were gathering arms to repel any future English assault, while Jenkin's subsequent boast that he meant to fight with his rodent enemies 'and beate them out of her country' was probably a warning that attempts would soon be made to expel the English from Wales. Worse was still to come, moreover, for – following the derisive rejection of his petition – Jenkin became more belligerent still, swearing 'that if her Petitions bee not regarded ... her will fetche... [all her weapons] ... and all her Country-men will march out with her in Warlike proportions and kill her enemies'.[51] This hysterical outburst was surely meant to convey the message that England herself might soon face attack from Wales.

If *The Welch Man's Inventory* and *The Welchmans last Petition* encouraged the belief that the Welsh hated the English, it was a pamphlet published some months later, apparently in May 1642, which took the final step of insinuating that they sought to break away from English rule altogether. Entitled *Newes from Wales, or the British Parliament*, this tract purports to reproduce a letter from a mock-Welshman named Morgan Lloyd 'giv[ing] all the world notice of her purpose to call a Welch Parliament'.[52] Morgan's reasons for summoning this assembly are closely connected with the alleged Welsh 'grievances' discussed in the previous pamphlets, for he declares the British parliament to have three main purposes: to protect 'the Honour and Reputation of the country of Wales' (presumably from English taunts); to ensure 'the relief of her Pritish Commons' (presumably from English taxes); and to secure the territory of Wales itself from 'her Roundheaded, Long-tayled enemies' (presumably from the pestiferous English 'oppressors', who are here, for the first time, openly conflated with the parliamentarian, or Roundhead, faction).[53] By claiming that the Welsh were about to summon a representative body of their own – in clear opposition to the one that was already sitting at

Westminster – and by suggesting that they were hostile to 'Round-heads', the satirist was effectively serving notice on his readers that the Welsh had declared against the parliamentary cause.

Yet this was by no means all that he was seeking to do – as his depiction of the putative Welsh parliament makes clear. The assembly would be held, Morgan declared:

> 'on one of the Welch Mountaines, in manners and fashions (though a farre off) like unto a Parliament, and then her will amongst her owne countrymen ... find respects ... and have all her Bills and Petitions ... read to the end, and ... revenges, votes and shudgements past ... upon her Round-headed, Long-tayld Enemies'.[54]

On the face of it, this was simply a caricature of a standard, English, parliament – and doubtless this is how many of the pamphlet's readers would have understood it. Once again, though, the satirist was working at several different levels, for the meeting which he described, and labelled a 'Welsh parliament', was in fact a thinly veiled portrait of one of the traditional Welsh gatherings know as *Cymanfuedd*: gatherings described by R.R. Davies as 'alternative assemblies ... where the Welsh gathered, often on hilltops, to vent a mythology which was ... a challenge to all that English authority and governance stood for'.[55] By conjuring up images of the *Cymanfuedd*, then, the satirist was indirectly reminding his readers of the long tradition of Welsh opposition to English rule and insinuating that that same tradition lay at the root of current Welsh hostility to the parliamentarian cause. Indeed, these self-same messages may have been conveyed by the very mention of a Welsh parliament, for the last time such an assembly had been called in Wales had been during the great national revolt against the English led by Owain Glyn Dŵr.[56] To allege that a Welsh parliament was on the point of being summoned again, therefore, was not just to hint that the forces of insubordination and rebelliousness were again on the rise in the Principality; it was to hint that Wales was once more beginning to act as an independent political entity.

And over the following year – as the kingdom descended into open warfare, and the pamphleteers threw off the residual fears of official censure which had muted their earlier criticisms – hints that the Welsh meant to exploit the current crisis in England in order to reassert their own independence grew ever more explicit. Thus mock-Welshmen began to refer not only to 'her Country of Wales', but to 'her

Kingdom of Wales': a title which was surely intended to suggest that the Welsh dreamed of resurrecting their own autonomous state.[57] This suggestion was subtly reinforced by claims that the Welsh believed themselves to possess their own ruler – 'her owne Prince of Wales'; by allegations that they were seeking to establish their own representative assembly – the 'British Parliament'; and by hints that they meant to initiate formal diplomatic relations with England by sending a 'Welch Embassadour' to London.[58] Hand in hand with these insinuations that Wales was a state in embryo went insinuations that the Welsh were fighting for the king, not just because they supported the royalist cause, but because they believed that, by doing so, they were defending the laws, liberties and religion of Wales itself, long 'untermined pi her Adversaries'.[59] The pamphleteers left little room for doubt as to whom the Welsh believed these 'adversaries' to be, moreover, for it was made clear that they blamed their troubles on puritans, on parliamentarians and, more generally, on the people of England as a whole. Thus the Welsh admired Prince Rupert, the satirists assured their readers, because he was 't[h]e onely enemy to t[h]e English Nation'; the king's Welsh soldiers flocked in to serve him because they sought to make themselves 'rich with t[h]e spoiles of t[h]e English' and to seize 'fertile ... English soyle'; while the whole history of Welsh political and military support for Charles I should be regarded as nothing less than a series of 'treasonable plots and actions against ... t[h]e English people'.[60] In the eyes of the Roundhead pamphleteers, in other words, the civil war was not just a politico-religious quarrel between king and parliament, it was also a national conflict between England and Wales – and the systematic campaign of vilification against the Welsh which I have outlined here helps to illustrate a much wider argument which I hope to make in detail elsewhere: that anxieties about 'race' and nationhood lay at the very heart of the English civil war.

NOTES

1 For some examples of the anti-Welsh humour current in England during the 50 years which preceded the civil war, see *Thomas Nashe: The Unfortunate Traveller and Other Works*, ed. J.B. Steane (Harmondsworth, 1985), p. 157; *A Critical ... Edition of A*

Match at Midnight, ed. S.B. Young (New York, 1980), pp. 59–175; and Anon., *A Banquet of Jests: Or Change of Cheare, Being a Collection of Modern Jests* (1639), pp. 6, 92, 99, 107, 113. For the medieval roots of the tradition, see R.R. Davies, *The Revolt of Owain Glyn Dŵr* (Oxford, 1995), pp. 21–23, and H.T. Evans, *Wales and the Wars of the Roses* (Cambridge, 1915), p. 99. For general discussions of the 'Taffy genre' during the early modern period, see A.H. Dodd, *Studies in Stuart Wales* (Cardiff, 1952), p. 1; J.O. Bartley, *Teague, Shenkin and Sawney: Being an Historical Study of the Earliest Irish, Welsh and Scottish Characters in English Plays* (Cork, 1954), especially pp. 48–77; P. Williams, 'The Welsh Borderland under Queen Elizabeth', *Welsh History Review*, vol. I (1960), p. 33; M. Spufford, *Small Books and Pleasant Histories: Popular Fiction and its Readership in Seventeenth Century England* (1981), pp. 56, 182–84, 191–92; G. Williams, *Recovery, Reorientation and Reformation: Wales, 1415–1642* (Oxford, 1987), pp. 464–65; and P. Jenkins, 'Seventeenth Century Wales: Definition and Identity', in *British Consciousness and Identity: The Making of Britain, 1533–1707* eds B. Bradshaw and P. Roberts (Cambridge, 1998), p. 222.

2 BL, Thomason Tracts [hereafter: E.] 137 (16), *The Welchmans Protestation*, February 1642; E.136 (18), *The Welchmans last Petition and Protestation*, February 1642; E.147 (4), *Newes From Wales, Or The Prittish Parliament*, May 1642; E.149 (32), *The Welch-Mens Prave Resolution*, 7 June 1642; E.154 (1), *The Welch Mans Warning-Piece*, June 1642; E.129 (20), *The Welchmans Publike Recantation*, 9 December 1642; E.245 (15), *The Welsh-Mans new Almanack*, 21 January 1643; E.245 (34), *Wonders Foretold By her crete Prophet of Wales*, 3 February 1643; E.89 (10), *A Perfect Tiurnall, or Welch Post*, 4–11 February 1643; E.89 (3), *The Welsh-Mans Postures*, 10 February 1643; E.246 (18), *The Welch Doctor*, 16 February 1643; E.91 (16), *The Welch Plunderer*, 1 March 1643; E.91 (30), *The Welch-Mans Complements*, 4 March 1643; E.96 (16), *The Welch Embassadour*, 13 April 1643; E.100 (3), *The True Copy of a Welch Sermon*, 29 April 1643; E.101 (12), *The Welchmens Lamentation and Complaint*, 10 May 1643; E.118 (4), *The Welchmans Declaration* [dated 17 September 1642, but in fact published much later, probably in May 1643]. See also BL, 816.m, 19/31, *The Welch Man's Inventory*, 1641; and BL, E.669, f.4, no. 89, *The Welch-Mans Life, Teath and Periall*, 1641 – both tracts which may well have been printed during the period January–March 1642.

3 See G.K. Fortescue, *Catalogue of the Pamphlets … Collected by George Thomason, 1640–61*, 2 vols (1908), vol. I, pt 1, pp. 57–263.

4 See, for example, E.13 (12), *The True Informer*, 12–19 October 1644. A short-lived periodical entitled *The Welch Mercury*, or *Mercurius Cambro–Britannus*, also appeared between October 1643 and January 1644, but as it had a rather different purpose to the other publications it will not be considered here. See J. Raymond, *The Invention of the Newspaper: English Newsbooks, 1641–49* (Oxford, 1996), p. 35; E.73 (10), *The Welch Mercury*, no. 1, 28 October 1643; and E.76 (14), *Mercurius Cambro-Britannus: The British Mercury, or the Welch Diurnall*, no. 4, 11–20 November 1643.

5 Fortescue, *Catalogue of the Pamphlets … Collected by George Thomason*, pp. 35–215.

6 See, e.g., K.J. Lindley, 'The Impact of the 1641 Rebellion upon England and Wales, 1641–5', *Irish Historical Studies*, vol. 18, pt 70 (September 1972), pp. 143–76, especially pp. 144–47; and E.H. Shagan, 'Constructing Discord: Ideology, Propaganda and English Responses to the Irish Rebellion of 1641', *Journal of British Studies*, vol. 36, pt 1 (January 1997), pp. 4–34.

7 J.R. Phillips, *Memoirs of the Civil Wars in Wales and the Marches*, 2 vols (1874), vol. I, pp. 97–98 and vol. II, pp. 24, 36–37; P. Gaunt, *A Nation under Siege: The Civil War in Wales, 1642–48* (1991), pp. 29–30; *Making the News: An Anthology of the Newsbooks of Revolutionary England, 1641–60*, ed. J. Raymond (Moreton-in-Marsh, 1993), pp. 84, 102–3; M.J. Stoyle, *Loyalty and Locality: Popular Allegiance in Devon during the English Civil War* (Exeter, 1994), pp. 238–41; P. Lord, *Words with Pictures: Welsh Images and Images of Wales in the Popular Press, 1640–1860* (Aberystwyth, 1995), pp. 37–43; Raymond, *Invention of the Newspaper*, p. 156; S. Roberts, 'Religion, Politics and Welshness, 1649–1660', in *Into Another Mould: Aspects of the Interregnum*, ed. I. Roots (Exeter, 1998), pp. 31–32.

8 *The Welch-Mens Prave Resolution* and *The Welch Doctor*.

9 Roberts, 'Religion, Politics and Welshness', p. 32.

10 Spufford, *Small Books and Pleasant Histories*, pp. 182–84.

11 Davies, *Owain Glyn Dŵr*, p. 21; E.13 (15), *Mercurius Britanicus*, 14–21 October 1644; and *Newes From Wales*.

12 For 'Welsh (and Cornish) Miles', see E.310 (8), *Mercurius Civicus*, 20–27 November 1645.

13 *The Welchmans Protestation*, p. 5; and *Newes From Wales*.

14 E.119 (2), *Speciall Passages*, 20–27 September 1642; *The Welchmens Prave Resolution*, pp. 4–5; E.116 (35), *Quotidian Occurrences*, 5–12 September 1642.

15 *The Welchmens Prave Resolution*, p. 3.

16 *The Welshmans Postures*; *The Welchmans Publike Recantation*; and *Wonders Foretold By Her crete Prophet of Wales*.

17 *The Welch Man's Inventory*; E.292 (4), *A Diary, or an Exact Journall*, 26 June to 3 July 1645; *The Welchmans Protestation*, p. 6. Cf. Bartley, *Teague, Shenkin and Sawney*, pp. 64–66.

18 *The Welchmans Protestation*, p. 5; E.136 (16), *The Welchmens Jubilee To The Honour Of St David*, February 1642; and E.99 (19), *The Second Intelligence from Reading*, 24 April 1643.

19 E.31 (10), *The True Informer*, 27 January to 3 February 1644; *Newes From Wales*; and *The Welchmens Prave Resolution*, pp. 4–5.

20 *Newes From Wales*; *The Welch Man's Inventory*; and *The Welchmans last Petition*.

21 See note 1.

22 Stoyle, *Loyalty and Locality*, pp. 239–40.

23 *The Welchmens Prave Resolution*; *The Welchmans last Petition*. According to Bartley, 'there is no indication' that the stage-Welshmen of the pre-war period 'were supposed to have any religious bias'; see *Teague, Shenkin and Sawney*, p. 67.

24 *The Welch Plunderer*; see also *The Welchmens Prave Resolution*, p. 6.

25 E.20 (3) *The London Post*, 3 December 1644.

26 Cf. M.G.H. Pittock, *Inventing and Resisting Britain: Cultural Identities in Britain and Ireland 1685–1789* (Basingstoke, 1997), p. 24.

27 See, e.g., *The Welchmans Life, Teath and Periall*; and *The Welchmans Publike Recantation*.

28 E.89 (25), *An Answer to Prince Ruperts Declaration*, 16 February 1643.

29 E.14 (13), *Mercurius Britanicus*, 21–28 October 1644; E.69 (12), *The Parliament's Scout*, 22–29 September 1643; E.56 (7), *The Parliament Scout*, 20–27 June 1643.

30 E.128 (34), *A Declaration sent from … His Majesties Army*, 1 December 1642.

31 *The Welchmans Lamentation.*

32 J. Gillingham, 'Images of Ireland, 1170–1600: The Origins of English Imperialism', *History Today*, vol. 37 (2), February 1987, pp. 16–22.

33 E.30 (1), *Mercurius Aulicus*, 7–13 January 1644; E.33 (27), *The Spie*, 13–20 February 1644; E.12 (15), *Englands Troubles Anatomised*, 11 October 1644.

34 *The Welchmans Complements*; E.296 (17), *The Parliaments Post*, 5–12 August 1645.

35 *The Welch Man's Inventory*. The fact that *The Welchmans Life, Teath and Periall* – the only other anti-Welsh satire attributed to the year 1641 – is illustrated by what appears to be a cut-down version of the image which features in the *Inventory* makes it seem probable that the latter is the earlier of the two broadsides.

36 Lord, *Words with Pictures*, pp. 34, 38; Bartley, *Teague, Shenkin and Sawney*, pp. 53–55, 70–71, 73–74.

37 *The Welch Man's Inventory*.

38 This important point is noted in Lord, *Words with Pictures*, p. 37.

39 B. Capp, 'Popular Literature', in *Popular Culture in Seventeenth Century England*, ed. B. Reay (1988), pp. 198, 231.

40 *The Welch Man's Inventory*.

41 The notion of a mock-Welshman 'run mad because a rat [or mouse] eat up [hi]s cheese' was familiar from several earlier stage plays: see Bentley, *Teague, Shenkin and Sawney*, p. 66.

42 See E.129 (3), *I Marry Sir, Heere is Newes Indeed*, 5 December 1642, which refers to the 'English Mouse ... Flemmish Frog ... [and] Spanish Kite'.

43 P.R. Roberts, 'The Union with England and the Identity of "Anglican" Wales', *TRHS*, 5th ser., vol. 22 (1972), pp. 60, 67–68, 70; and P. Roberts, 'The English Crown, The Principality of Wales and the Council in the Marches, 1534–1641', in *The British Problem, 1534–1707: State Formation in the Atlantic Archipelago*, eds B. Bradshaw and J. Morrill (1996), pp. 123, 141, and 144–45.

44 National Library of Wales, Wb 7844, *The Humble Petition of many hundred thousands, inhabiting within the thirteen Shires of Wales*, 12 February 1642.

45 Ibid., p. 3; and E.137 (26), *The Welshmans Answer*, February 1642.

46 *The Welchmans last Petition.*

47 *The Humble Petition of ... the thirteene Shires of Wales*, p. 3.

48 *The Welchmans last Petition* [my italics].

49 Ibid.

50 See note 42.

51 *The Welchmans last Petition.*

52 *Newes From Wales*. The fact that the author of this particular pamphlet chose to adopt the plain-sounding pseudonym of 'Morgan Lloyd' – rather than one of the intentionally ludicrous names which were usually accorded to mock-Welshmen – is interesting, and raises the intriguing possibility that the tract may have been intended to satirise the scheme for decentralised government in Wales which had recently been put forward by the Royalist Richard Lloyd. On this abortive 'proposal for [Welsh] devolution', see Dodd, *Stuart Wales*, pp. 66–67; P. Williams, 'The Attack on the Council in the Marches, 1603–42', *Transactions of the Honourable Society of Cymmrodorion* (1961) pt I, pp. 19–22; and Roberts, 'Council in the Marches', pp. 145–46.

53 Though the *possibility* that the (English) Mouse might have 'a round head' had already been raised, and dismissed, in the much earlier *Welchmans last Petition*.

54 *Newes From Wales*.

55 Davies, *Owain Glyn Dŵr*, p. 34. See also Evans, *Wales and the Wars of the Roses*, p. 33.

56 Davies, *Owain Glyn Dŵr*, pp. 116–17, 163–66.

57 *The True Copy of a Welch Sermon*.

58 *The Welchmans last Petition*; *Newes From Wales*; and *The Welch Embassadour*.

59 *The Welchmens Declaration*, p. 6.

60 Ibid., pp. 2, 4; and *The Welchmans Lamentation*.

'One of the Goodliest and Strongest Places that I Ever Looked Upon': Montgomery and the Civil War

Peter Gaunt

The English civil war of the mid-seventeenth century is often associated, at least in the popular mind, with grand set-piece field engagements like Edgehill, Marston Moor and Naseby, in which huge national armies hurled themselves at each other in a bid to settle the outcome of the whole conflict. Important as they were, battles of this order were the exception, not the norm. After the failure of either side to score an overwhelming victory in autumn 1642, the civil war became a struggle to control and to acquire territory, a rather dour and protracted conflict of raiding and counter-raiding, as garrisons and local or regional armies sought to tie down the towns and countryside of England and Wales, to dominate key centres of population, production and marketing, to control trade routes, major roads, river crossings, ports and estuaries. In these ways the men, money and supplies which were the life-blood of the conflict could be secured. The course and outcome of the war were determined, in large part, by this incessant local and regional campaigning – most civil war casualties fell, not in the few major and well-documented battles, but in small engagements, raiding and skirmishing – and by the fluctuating success of each side in controlling territory and continuing to draw off the resources of war. No single engagement of the civil war can plausibly be presented as somehow 'typical' of the conflict as a whole, just as broad conclusions about the costs and consequences of the civil war cannot safely be drawn from the limited evidence of the impact of the war upon a single community. The military action and its context and consequences outlined here are certainly not being presented in this way. However, it is fair to say that the conflict which unfolded in and around the border town of Montgomery in the late summer of 1644, and the direct and indirect effects visited upon the townspeople and the community in its wake, are more representative of the true nature of the civil war than the set-piece battles of Edgehill, Marston Moor or Naseby, the long and formal sieges of unfortunate urban centres such as Chester, Newark or Plymouth, or the bloody sackings of Brentford, Bolton or Leicester.[1]

Montgomery lies in a strategically important area, for centuries a key frontier zone, fortified and contested from the Iron Age. Here, where the lowlands of England and the rolling hills of west Shropshire give way to the uplands and mountains of Wales, the valley of the upper Severn provides one of the few relatively easy routes into mid-Wales, an obvious highway for attack from Wales into England and vice versa. Moreover, at this point, just south or upstream of its junction with the lesser River Camlad, there is a natural fording point across the Severn, called Rhydwhyman. From the time of the earliest known human occupation of the area, this was recognised as a key location and was fortified. In the Iron Age, an earthwork hill fort was erected on top of the steep-sided Ffridd Faldwyn, the highest hill in the vicinity, which stands about one mile south-east of the ford. The Romans built a large, earthen auxiliary fort, Forden Gaer, on low ground by the east bank of the Severn, immediately north of the ford. Within a generation of the Norman Conquest, the Norman earl of Shrewsbury constructed an earthwork and timber motte-and-bailey castle, Hen Domen, at the north edge of a low ridge, around 500 yards south-east of the ford. The earthwork remains of all three fortifications are still clearly visible; those of Hen Domen have recently been the subject of intensive archaeological excavation and interpretation.[2] Lastly, in 1223, as part of a drive to recover and strengthen English control of the borderlands in response to continuing Welsh opposition, the new king, Henry III, built a large timber and masonry castle on a lower but steep-sided spur of the hill upon which the Iron Age fort stands. Although the ford was not within direct line of sight of this new castle, it did provide an uninterrupted view from north to south-east across the rolling plain below. At the same time, the English crown established a new town, Montgomery, on the lower ground immediately east of the castle, with earthworks, walls and gates providing further defence for the new settlement.[3] It was this town and castle, founded by the crown in the early thirteenth century as part of the conflict between the English and the Welsh, which saw action in the mid-seventeenth-century conflict between royalists and parliamentarians and which witnessed probably the largest and bloodiest battle to take place in Wales during the civil war.[4]

During the opening two years of the war, north and mid-Wales had been solidly royalist in allegiance, whilst much of the northern Marches had been divided. By summer 1644, with the capture of Oswestry, the parliamentarians felt secure enough in southern Cheshire and north-western Shropshire to contemplate pushing into Wales, looking to the Severn valley as the natural highway into the Principality. A combined parliamentary force under two local commanders, Thomas Mytton and Sir Thomas Myddleton, raided Welshpool in early August and Newtown in early September, in both cases taking prisoners and supplies. These actions were supported by a propaganda campaign, the parliamentarians promising to remove the corrupt and burdensome royalists and to restore the cloth and cattle trades upon which the Montgomeryshire economy depended. In the wake of the successful capture of a royalist powder convoy around Newtown, the parliamentarians turned their attention to Montgomery.[5]

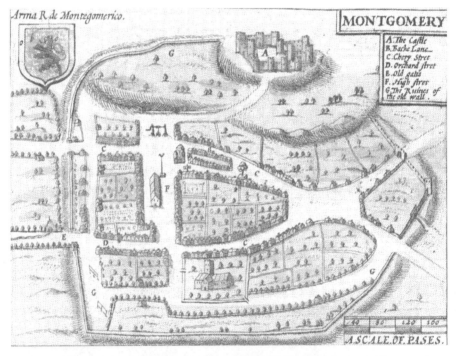

Figure 2 *Montgomery town and castle as they may have looked in 1644, from John Speed's* Theatre of Great Britain, *first published in 1611–12*

The parliamentarians seem to have entered the town unopposed on or around 4 September.[6] Indeed, with the Welsh threat long diminished, the town walls and gates had fallen ruinous and the town was largely undefended – Speed's plan of Montgomery (figure 2) shows that by the early seventeenth century the town walls were in 'ruines' and suggests that only one of the town's five medieval gates was still standing. In contrast, the castle on the hill overlooking the town seems to have been in good order – crude as it is, Speed's drawing of the castle, the only known illustration of the fortress as it stood before the civil war and its subsequent slighting, suggests a building in good repair. Although Edward I's conquest of Wales had effectively ended much of the castle's original purpose as a frontier zone stronghold, it had been kept in good order and was periodically refurbished, especially in the sixteenth century, when it became one of the seats of the crown's Council of the Marches. By the 1640s it was the residence of the aged Edward, Lord Herbert of Chirbury, who lived in state in a grand stone and brick mansion he had built 20 years before in the castle's middle ward.[7] However, the entire castle seems to have been in a reasonable state of repair and defensible at the time of the civil war, and it was described by one of the parliamentarian commanders, Sir John Meldrum, as 'one of the goodliest and strongest places that I ever looked upon'.[8] Yet the parliamentarians were able to capture the castle with remarkable ease.

Herbert had refused to allow the royalists to install a garrison[9] and instead the castle was held by a small personal retinue, nominally for the king but in reality almost as a neutral base. Although it was claimed that the 'tennants and neighbours of Edward, Lord Herbert' could supply a 'garrison' of up to 150 men, in practice only a much smaller retinue of household servants seems to have been in residence in early September and, disheartened by the failure of royalist troops immediately to rally to the defence of the town and castle in their hour of need, Herbert's tenants and neighbours 'came not up in sufficient numbers to defend the outworks' of the fortress.[10] Accordingly, when the parliamentarians approached the castle and demanded its surrender, Herbert had neither the stomach nor the means to offer much resistance and – to the horror of his much more warlike and royalist son – he swiftly opened negotiations. The parliamentarians offered as inducements both 'a large sum' of money and written assurances that Herbert's possessions, including all his 'household stuff, books, trunks and writings', would be undamaged and would be conveyed under guard to Herbert's London house if he so wished.[11] These carrots were backed up by a stick, for during the night of 5 September the parliamentarians fixed petards to the gates of the middle ward and demanded the castle's immediate surrender, though repeating their pledges that no harm would be done to anyone or anything within the castle if it was surrendered and that Herbert's books and other goods would not be damaged or taken – evidently he was particularly concerned about the fate of his library.[12] By 6 September Montgomery castle was in parliament's hands.[13]

The new parliamentary garrison, under Myddleton, was probably aware from the outset that the royalists would not allow parliament unhindered occupation of such a key stronghold and would attempt to recapture Montgomery at the earliest opportunity. Indeed, almost immediately royalist commanders in the region began preparing a counter-attack, gathering forces from Ludlow, Shrewsbury and other smaller garrisons which they held in Shropshire. This combined royalist army, numbering perhaps 2,500 men and commanded by Sir Michael Ernley, approached Montgomery on 8 September. They surprised and scattered a large part of the parliamentary garrison, which had ventured out on a foraging expedition. Mytton managed to get his 500 foot back into the castle, while Myddleton's horse escaped towards Welshpool. Ernley's royalists then set about taking the castle by formal siege, apparently digging siegeworks – earthwork banks and ditches – around the castle.[14]

It was now the turn of the parliamentarians to react, for they were unwilling to see their newly won and highly prized possession fall to the king. Myddleton was instrumental in persuading other parliamentarian commanders in the region to lend support, and by mid-September a combined force of around 3,000 troops, led by Myddleton, Sir William Fairfax, Sir William Brereton and Meldrum, who was in overall command, was en route to Montgomery to lift the siege of the castle. Meanwhile the royalists had been reinforced by further troops from North Wales and Cheshire, including remnants of the forces which had been brought over from Ireland the previous winter, only to be mauled and dispersed at Nantwich in January 1644. These reinforcements were led by John, Lord Byron, who took command of all the royalist forces at Montgomery, now numbering somewhere between 4,000 and 5,000 men.[15]

Like most of the lesser civil war engagements, the battle which was fought outside Montgomery on 18 September is quite poorly recorded.

As usual, no contemporary map or plan of the battle survives, and instead historians rely very heavily on the accounts given in the letters of some of the key commanders – in this case, the parliamentarians Brereton, Myddleton and Meldrum, and the royalists Ernley and Arthur Trevor – supplemented by the brief accounts which appeared in several of the weekly newspapers. Sadly, no account written by the royalist commander, Byron, has been found. From these surviving accounts, it is possible to reconstruct something of the course of events and the location of the battle.[16]

The combined parliamentary army would have approached Montgomery from the north and spent the night of 17–18 September 'in the field that was most advantageous to us',[17] probably the low, fairly flat ground flanking the River Camlad. In the process they secured an unnamed bridge, probably spanning that river. Royalist troops had made no attempt to hold that ground and had instead pulled back. Leaving a small force to man the siegeworks, Byron had deployed the bulk of his army 'upon the mountain above the castle, a place of great advantage for them',[18] almost certainly the hill immediately west of and overlooking the castle, crowned by the remains of the Iron Age hill fort. Battle began on 18 September when the royalists, noticing that roughly one third of the parliamentary cavalry had moved off to forage, swooped down and attacked their weakened enemies on the plain below. The parliamentary army was probably drawn up on the low, rolling ground north-north-east of the town. The remains of Offa's Dyke and the Camlad offered some protection to their left wing and rear. Their right wing was more exposed and vulnerable to out-flanking, which might perhaps enable the royalists to capture Salt Bridge, where the Welshpool road crossed the Camlad, so cutting off the parliamentarians' line of retreat (see figure 3). Indeed, several accounts refer to determined royalist attempts to capture a vital (though unnamed) bridge, Meldrum writing that the royalists attempted 'to break through our forces and make themselves masters of a bridge we had gained the night before, which would have cut off the passage of our retreat'.[19]

The initial parliamentary response to Byron's attack, a volley of shot, was delivered too soon, when the royalists were still 'at too much distance',[20] and fell short of the advancing enemy. Unhindered, the king's men closed on their enemies, firing their first volley at closer range and to greater effect. The royalist cavalry threw back their opposite numbers and then the royalist foot gained the upper hand over the

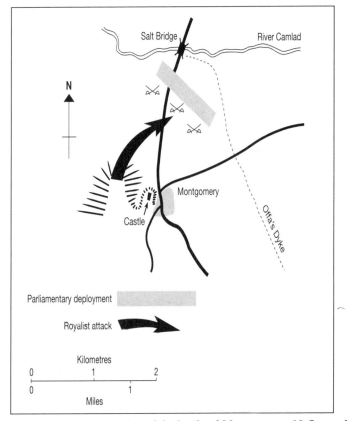

Figure 3 *A possible reconstruction of the battle of Montgomery, 18 September 1644*

parliamentary infantry in a close-quarter fight – 'it came to push of pike'.[21] But when victory seemed assured, the royalist advance was first halted and then reversed. The parliamentary commanders ascribed this change of fortune to the intervention of God and to the resolve of their men to hold their ground. According to Meldrum, the parliamentary foot 'carried themselves more like lions than men'.[22] Other newspaper accounts suggest that it was the parliamentarian cavalry regrouping and counter-attacking which turned the tide of battle.[23] A royalist account alleged that part of the royalist cavalry quite unnecessarily turned tail and galloped from the field through sheer cowardice, an action which understandably unhinged their colleagues.[24] Possibly the return of that part of the parliamentarian cavalry which was initially caught away foraging helped turn the course of the battle. Seeing their colleagues triumphant on the field below, Mytton's garrison emerged from the castle and overwhelmed the small royalist force left manning the trenches. The engagement ended in complete parliamentary victory and with surviving royalist troops in flight. The parliamentarians had lost about 40 dead, the royalists 500 dead and a further 1,500 captured. Like most civil war battles, it had been a brief affair – the engagement lasted barely an hour. Upon hearing news of the victory, on 23 September the Commons 'ordered that on Wednesday next ... being the Day of publick Humiliation, publick Thanks shall be given in all the Churches and Chapels within the Line of Communication to the giver of all victories, for the great victory it pleased Him to give the parliament forces over the king's forces at the raising of the siege of Montgomery Castle'.[25]

In some ways the battle of Montgomery was very significant, for it not only secured parliamentarian control of this key town and castle but also significantly weakened royalism in the area. Royalist regiments and garrisons had been greatly depleted to supply Byron's army and the crushing defeat, resulting in loss of men and supplies, weakened the royalist hold on Shrewsbury, Chester, Liverpool and other bases. For a time, Myddleton was left in command of the new garrison at Montgomery and he used it as a base for capturing Powis castle, outside Welshpool, in October, and Abbey Cwmhir in Radnorshire in December. By the end of the year, Myddleton had established a modest parliamentarian enclave in this part of eastern mid-Wales, centred on the castles of Montgomery and Powis, strengthened by a handful of other outposts and supported by some of the local gentry, who had abandoned their former royalist allegiances. On the other hand, the parliamentary high command in London did not accord the Welsh theatre a very high priority at this stage of the war, perhaps rightly judging that royalism in the Midlands and the south of England presented a greater threat. Accordingly, with only limited men and money available, Myddleton was not able to extend parliamentary control far into mid- or north Wales; Montgomery did not become the centre for grand operations or for an attempted invasion of royalist Wales. Indeed, neither the town nor the castle played a significant role in the closing stages of the war, though from autumn 1644 Montgomery maintained a substantial parliamentary garrison. Not until 1645–46 did royalist control over most of Wales falter and collapse, and then due as much to the exhaustion and disenchantment of the Welsh population as to the actions of parliamentary troops within Wales. Although the engagement of 18 September had resulted in a

clear and decisive parliamentary victory, the battle of Montgomery –
like most of the small and medium-sized engagements of the civil war
– did not immediately produce any fundamental or geographically
extensive consequences. Instead, it was but one of many local and
regional victories which cumulatively saw the tide of civil war change
during 1644 and which eventually led, almost two years later, to the
complete and national military victory for parliament.[26]

Montgomery's direct and active military involvement in the civil war
largely began and ended with the campaign of September 1644, which
culminated in the decisive and bloody battle. But how far did the war
impact upon local government and administration, upon local society,
the town and its people? At first sight, Montgomery seems neither to
have been drawn deeply into the conflicts of the mid-seventeenth century nor to have suffered heavily during or as a consequence of the
civil war.

By the mid-seventeenth century, Montgomery had a population of
around 500 or 600. Speed's plan shows it still contained within the cir-
cuit of then decayed medieval banks and walls, for no significant
extra-mural development is depicted. Post-Restoration Hearth Tax
records indicate that Montgomery was at that time one of the largest
settlements of the county, slightly larger than Machynlleth, Llanfyllin
and Newtown, but somewhat smaller than Llanidloes and less than
half the size of Welshpool, which was by some margin the biggest town
in the county. From the first royal charter of 1227 until 1885, when the
old corporation was replaced by an elected council, the town was in the
hands of hereditary burgesses; the burgesses elected two head or capital bailiffs annually at Michaelmas. They were assisted by two under
bailiffs or serjeants at mace, again elected annually, one or two coro-
ners and a town clerk. The royal charter, renewed and reissued periodically – at the time of the civil war, Montgomery was governed by
the 1562 charter of Elizabeth I – granted the town two extended fairs
annually, a four-day fair around St Bartholomew's day and an eight-
day fair around All Saints' day, plus a regular weekly fair or market on
Thursdays. In common with all the Montgomeryshire towns, the
county town relied economically upon agricultural produce and marketing, with pastoral farming dominant; trade in cattle, sheep, wool
and woollen cloth was its life blood.[27]

Montgomery was also a parliamentary borough, for the Henrician
Act of Union of 1536 had given one borough MP to Montgomeryshire,

to be chosen by the county town but with other boroughs contributing wages. An Act of 1543 had extended the franchise to the burgesses of the contributing boroughs. Montgomery and its burgesses were the focus of the borough constituency, and the two head bailiffs acted as returning officers, but the vote was also given to the burgesses of three out-boroughs, namely Welshpool, Llanidloes and Llanfyllin. Other medieval boroughs within the county, such as Newtown, Machynlleth and Caerwys, were not enfranchised. In practice, the Montgomery burgesses increasingly dominated the elections. This, in turn, ensured that the family which dominated the town for much of the early modern period, the Herberts of Montgomery castle, kinsmen of the Powis castle Herberts, had an influential voice in the (s)election of the MP. Thus Lord Herbert's son and heir, Richard, was returned for the Long Parliament in autumn 1640, though his pronounced royalism in 1642 led to him being 'disabled' or expelled from the Commons within a few weeks of the outbreak of war, effectively disenfranchising Montgomery for most of the civil war period.[28]

What was opinion in the town in the immediate pre-war years and how royalist was Montgomery in the opening phase of the war, down to the capture of town and castle for parliament in September 1644? It has to be admitted at the outset that the sources are meagre and that no full and clear answer can be given, for we lack for Montgomery the rich corpus of public and personal papers of the sort which has recently allowed David Underdown to reconstruct opinions and divisions in early Stuart Dorchester and Mark Stoyle to do the same for Exeter.[29] During the 1630s the town paid its share of the £833 Ship Money due from Montgomeryshire, apparently without resistance or visible opposition. The successive sheriffs of Montgomeryshire complained that the county was over-assessed, particularly in comparison to its near neighbours Denbighshire and Flintshire, noted that the ratings within the county rested upon outdated information and took no account of recent changes in the populations and wealth of hundreds and parishes, reported that an outbreak of the plague in the latter half of the 1630s, which particularly affected the towns of Llanidloes, Newtown and Machynlleth (no reference was made to Montgomery), was causing some delay in collecting in the money, and several times alluded to the relative poverty of the county – in 1637 Lloyd Pierce wrote that the county pays with 'all alacrity to their abilities, but being of itself generally poor, and depending much upon the sale of cattle, are not so ready paymasters as other counties, nor can they before their markets come in'.[30] These sorts of complaints and minor rating disputes are typical of the county response to Ship Money.[31] Yet, again typically, until the late 1630s they point to no principled opposition or clear resistance to Ship Money – in summer 1638 sheriff John Newton wrote that payment was 'indifferently well taken'[32] – and in the end all or almost all the county's quota was collected and paid over. There are hints in the letters of Richard Price, sheriff in 1639, that the mood was changing, with rumbling discontent caused by poverty and plague, perhaps given greater edge by the impressment of over 100 men from Montgomeryshire to join the newly raised English army which was gathering in the north to fight the Scots.[33] In 1640 the Deputy Lieutenants reported delays in raising the 200 men from Montgomeryshire required for the English army of that year, caused by rumours that the service would not, after all, be required and by the desertion or non-appearance of some men, though in the end all 200 were raised, equipped and dispatched.[34] Montgomery itself supplied 15 fighting men, which although not apparently a large number, still represented around 2.5–3 per cent of the town's population and a much larger proportion of its adult males.

It has recently been suggested that religion, far more than finance and secular politics, caused the deepest divisions within early Stuart urban and rural society and that religious aspirations and reactions to the state's religious policies in the pre-war years largely determined the response of a town, locality or county when the nation divided at the outbreak of the civil war.[35] The meagre surviving papers allow us a glimpse of religious divisions in Montgomery in 1637. In accordance with the high church or Arminian policies introduced in the 1630s by Charles I and his Archbishop of Canterbury, William Laud, sometime before Easter 1637 the east end of Montgomery church had been reorganised, converting the movable communion table into a permanent, east end altar, surrounded by an altar-rail. At the 1637 Easter Day service one of the local gentlemen, Richard Griffith, and his family made a show of defiance against the new arrangements. Griffith refused to receive communion at the new altar rails and instead took his 'usuall place in the Chancell, where ever before tymes it was given usually to the whole parish'. Ignored by the parson, Doctor Coote, Griffith called him over and requested that he be given communion in the customary way. Coote attempted to persuade Griffith and his family 'to come up to the Railes wherewith the Communion Table is Altarwise newly ingirt', but Griffith refused to do so unless Coote could justify the new arrangement. Coote went away to pray for Griffith, 'which he did and severall times with 18 low prostrate bows to the Altar'. Upon Griffith's continuing refusal to submit, Coote eventually administered communion to him 'in the ancient usuall place', asking 'all the Congregation to beare witnesse what he had done and desired them all to pray for his hardnesse of heart, pride and rebellion'. Griffith's stand against the newly introduced high church arrangement was apparently a lone gesture. There is no reference here of support for him from any of his fellow-parishioners and indeed it is stated that, Griffith and his family excepted, 'the whole Congregation was served' communion at the altar rails in the new way. Although he eventually relented and in a grudging fashion administered communion to Griffith while continuing to condemn him, Doctor Coote clearly accepted the new ecclesiastical arrangements and high church practices, complete with repeated 'prostrate bows' to the new altar.[36] Alas, this snapshot of church life and of a minor religious protest in the face of general compliance to the new order is almost all we know about religious sentiment in Montgomery before the civil war. In the absence of any surviving churchwardens' accounts, consistory court papers, quarter sessions papers, private diaries, journals, commonplace books and the like, no broad picture can safely be reconstructed.

The attitude of Edward, Lord Herbert, during the opening two years of the civil war may have been fairly typical of sentiments in Montgomery. Herbert showed mild royalist sympathies – he was briefly imprisoned for a speech favourable to the king's position made in the House of Lords shortly before war broke out, but was quickly released on making a fulsome apology – but he clearly attempted to keep his head down and to distance himself from the war. He played up his advanced age and declining health – perfectly genuine, it seems – to excuse himself from attending both the king and the royalist parliament in Oxford and Prince Rupert on his frequent visits to Shrewsbury. He repeatedly resisted offers by the king and Rupert to install a regular garrison within the castle.[37] In June 1643 he was in sombre mood, writing to his only surviving brother that although he had contemplated a trip to Spa, 'I doubt how I shall be able to go, my body beinge more infirme then to endure any labour ... I find myself grown older in this one yeare than in fifty-nine yeares before ... I shall pray for a good and speedy end to all those troubles'.[38]

There are signs of some resistance to the royalist cause in Montgomeryshire in the opening weeks of the war. The sheriff refused to publish the king's proclamations condemning parliament and the flexible Sir John Price, who was to change sides several times, opposed the king's commission of array and attempted to prevent the king's men securing the magazine at Newtown.[39] However, Herbert and the town of Montgomery – indeed, the county of Montgomeryshire as a whole – had little option but lukewarmly to embrace royalism during the opening years of the war, for they were surrounded by counties and regions which appear actively and enthusiastically to have supported the king's cause at this stage. Almost the whole of north and mid-Wales, much of Shropshire and parts of Herefordshire came out for the king in the opening weeks of the war and were secured and garrisoned by royalist troops. Lord Herbert's elder son and heir, Richard, was an enthusiastic royalist from the outset, and worked both to secure key strongholds within Montgomeryshire and to recruit a regiment in his home county. In the face of this, the town and county almost of necessity supported the royalist cause during the opening two years of the war, paying the various levies and contributions imposed by the king. Accused of being half-hearted in support of the royalist cause and of failing to pay all that was required, sometime during the winter of 1643–44 a petition was drafted by, or in the name of, the county pointing out that during 1643 the people of Montgomeryshire had paid almost £3,500 to the king's agents, had quartered and supplied a 300-strong royalist horse regiment under Sir Richard Willys for eight weeks, had quartered and supplied Captain Williams's foot regiment in and around Powis Castle for five weeks during the autumn and, during the closing weeks of the year, had supplied 500 pairs of shoes and stockings to Chester to equip royalist reinforcements being shipped back from Ireland. Doubtless the county town had shouldered its share of these burdens.[40]

It is a measure of the flexibility of the county's allegiances as well as of the changed political circumstances that at some point at the end of the war, probably in the late 1640s, a petition expressing in remarkably similar terms affection and support for the parliamentary cause was drawn up in the name of the 'gentry and inhabitants of the County of Montgomery'. It was signed by 20 Montgomeryshire gentlemen, at least one of them from Montgomery itself, though many more seem to have come from the Welshpool and Guilsfield area. Portraying the people of Montgomeryshire as truly and at heart parliamentarian rather than royalist in allegiance, the petition draws attention to 'the many and as wee think unparaleld suffering of this poore Countie of

Mountgomery' on behalf of parliament since autumn 1644, when it supported Sir Thomas Myddleton and the parliamentary cause against its then solidly royalist neighbours in north Wales, suffering repeated 'rapine and spoile' and plunder from the king's men in consequence. 'All which Stormes this poore countie patiently endured, hoping to see a glorious sun shine at length when all your enemies were dissipated'. A reduction in the taxes being levied upon the county by the now victorious parliament would, the petition suggested, help the sun shine on Montgomeryshire.[41]

There is no evidence that Montgomery itself was directly, physically involved in the civil war before the parliamentary occupation and resulting battle of September 1644. In the mid-1640s Lord Herbert, by that time expressing allegiance to and affection for parliament, claimed credit for keeping the royalists out of Montgomery during 1642–44 by refusing 'all attempts by the Adverse party to put a Garrison into the same'.[42] In the wake of the parliamentary occupation, town and castle were drawn more directly into the civil wars, not through further direct military action – there is little evidence that the royalists mounted any serious raids or attacks upon Montgomery after the defeat in battle in mid-September 1644, though the then governor of the castle, Sir John Price, flirted with royalism in spring 1645 before reaffirming his parliamentarianism in the wake of the king's defeat at Naseby in June – but because of the continuing parliamentary presence and garrisoning of Montgomery. This drew Montgomery into the civil war in several ways.

Firstly, and most obviously, the inhabitants had to quarter and/or supply the parliamentary soldiers. This was not free quarter, for in theory the townspeople were entitled to be paid for expenses incurred. However, as so often in the civil war, practice lagged some way behind theory, and the bills run up by the soldiers fell into arrears. In 1646 the inhabitants of Montgomery petitioned the parliamentary committee for North Wales, seeking settlement of £254 claimed as the arrears 'for quarteringe of souldiers in the sayde towne upon just accompt taken the 4th of November last'. They took the opportunity at the same time to seek a further £60, claimed to be the value of cattle and other provisions taken by the castle garrison during the siege of September 1644 'which is yett unsatisffyed'.[43]

Secondly, the county town was to some extent drawn into the intricate and, in the case of Montgomeryshire, very murky world of parliamentary local administration. In the wake of the parliamentary conquest of late summer 1644, many of the Montgomeryshire gentry quickly emerged to declare loyalty to parliament. On 26 September, barely a week after the battle, Myddleton wrote that 'yesterday we had a good appearance at Montgomery castle of the country people', and a month later he again reported that 'the Country comes in reasonably well'.[44] Some members of the local gentry were promptly appointed to the various financial and administrative committees which parliament established to run its newly won territory. As in many counties, the different individuals and committees sometimes clashed, though the dispute in Montgomeryshire was particularly bitter and well-documented. The story has been told in detail by A.H. Dodd and more briefly by several other historians and it does not, in the main, involve resident Montgomery gentlemen. In summer 1646 the parliamentary county treasurer, the former Ship Money sheriff Lloyd Pierce, was imprisoned in Montgomery castle on the orders of parliament's county committee for accounts for allegedly resisting the committee's investigation into his handling of county finances. However, the main parliamentary county committee, distancing itself from the accounts committee, supported Pierce and sought his release, offering to stand bail if necessary. Pierce's release was strongly resisted by the accounts committee, and particularly by its leading light, Edward Vaughan. The dispute proved long and bitter, involving both parliamentary national committees sitting in London and parliament itself, though eventually Pierce was released from close arrest in Montgomery castle and then eluded renewed attempts by the county's accounts committee to re-arrest him.[45]

Thirdly, as one of the principal seats of parliament's county administrators, Montgomery became an object of army discontent during 1647, a year of growing military discontent and mutiny nationally. In May 1647 a body of around 500 parliamentary horse and foot, apparently discontented because of lack of pay and supplies, swooped on Montgomery and occupied the town, taking free quarter, capturing and imprisoning a handful of parliamentary committeemen and threatening the rest, seizing the cattle and goods of committeemen, collecting money from the townspeople and committing 'other outrages'.[46] This may be the same event described in a letter written by Edward Allen, then governor of Montgomery castle, on 7 May, though Allen puts the number of hostile soldiers much lower, around 60, and claims that they marched on Montgomery from Pool, the Severn-side settlement north of Welshpool. According to Allen, the mutinous soldiers fired upon the castle, to little effect, though the governor would not allow his garrison to return fire for fear of imperilling the lives of the parliamentary committeemen held captive by them. Allen managed to gather some local reinforcements to safeguard his hold upon the castle, 'notwithstanding the threats of such desperate men as these soldiers are', and order was quickly restored, presumably through the intervention of other loyal and disciplined parliamentary troops, though this is poorly documented.[47]

Town government and administration apparently continued to operate fairly smoothly through the 1640s, largely, though not completely, unaffected by the war.[48] The Michaelmas election of a pair of head bailiffs occurred every year except 1644, when there seems to have been a short-lived hiatus in the immediate aftermath of the siege and battle; however, an election did take place, albeit rather late, for by spring 1645 a new pair of head bailiffs were in office.[49] The personnel of local government also indicates continuity, with no sign of a cohort of new figures gaining prominence during the apparently royalist period, 1642–44, nor of a dramatic change with the coming of parliamentary forces, leading to hitherto obscure men taking the reigns of power in 1644–46. For example, Richard Thompson served as head bailiff in 1637–38, 1642–43 and 1646–47, and Charles Broughton served terms both in 1643–44 and again in 1647–48.[50] The town's principal administrative and judicial bodies – the small town or borough court, which met regularly throughout the year, and the less frequent but larger and more formal gatherings of the Montgomery court leet – continued to function through the 1640s. The meetings – or at least the records thereof – become sparser in 1643–44, but there was no prolonged abeyance. The type of business, too, was little changed – the election of officers for the year, the admission of new burgesses, orders prohibiting strangers from trading in the town, the presentation of individuals for breaking the assizes of ale, beer or bread, orders for the maintenance of pounds and so forth.

Seventeenth-century Montgomery was also – typical of an early modern community – very litigious. The formal court records and supporting papers point to a steady stream of minor actions: cases between two townspeople for the recovery of small debts, generally less than £10, or on allegations of trespass and damage. The nature and quantity of such actions do not seem to have changed greatly in the mid-seventeenth century and nor do those actions of the war and immediate post-war years reveal clashes arising from divided civil war allegiances. Of course, some of the actions for debt, trespass and damage could be underlain by enmity between those who had found themselves on different sides in the civil war – one wonders, for example, what lay behind a 1652 action by Edward Allen, sometime governor of the castle, against Nathaniel Edwards, who had allegedly wandered around Montgomery telling everyone whom he met that Allen had robbed him of his horse, cloak and sword, refusing to be quietened by the head bailiffs but continuing to repeat his allegations at the top of his voice.[51] However, in only two cases do the surviving court records explicitly point to actions resulting from divided civil war allegiances.

In 1651 Richard Thompson, who had been town clerk and recorder of Montgomery throughout the war years, was accused of active royalism in the war, of aiding and assisting the enemies of parliament, of hiding arms from parliamentary commissioners and of holding back money collected in Montgomery to support the parliamentary cause; the jury found the allegations proved and he was dismissed, though his period of disgrace was short, for in 1658 he was elected one of the head bailiffs, his fourth term in that office.[52] And in March 1645, a few months after the parliamentary occupation, George Atkinson was prosecuted for attacking one of the head bailiffs, Phillemon Mason, taking him by the collar, throwing him down, striking and kicking him, threatening to pistol him and calling Mason 'a malignant rogue'.[53] Atkinson seems to have been one of the very few townspeople whose loyalty to the king was so pronounced that he openly and violently protested against the new parliamentary order and those officers who supported and acted on behalf of parliamentary control. Indeed, although a score or more of Montgomeryshire men were sequestered by parliament for active wartime royalism and subsequently compounded for their delinquency, the Herberts of the castle aside, Atkinson is the sole Montgomery resident to show up in the surviving papers of the London-based Committee for Compounding.[54]

If Montgomery does not come across as a hot-bed of royalism, it equally does not come across as having been greatly disturbed and dislocated by the experience of civil war, even though the largest civil war battle in Wales was fought on its doorstep. The townspeople did, of course, have to pay their share of the unprecedentedly heavy exactions imposed by king and parliament on the territories under their control. However, direct, physical sufferings seem, on the surface, to have been limited. The town had changed hands quickly in September 1644, apparently with little or no bloodshed occurring in the town itself or involving the townspeople; the castle had fallen by negotiated surrender and in an orderly fashion; and the subsequent battle had been fought not in the streets, but in the fields to the north-east. Yet on two grounds we need to reconsider this rather optimistic interpretation.

The first is the survival of a remarkable pair of documents amongst the Powis Castle archives, now at the National Library of Wales. Some time towards the end of the war, Lord Herbert drew up an account setting out his own losses as a direct consequence of the war. Herbert claimed that he had lost something approaching £5,000 through the actions of both royalists and parliamentarians in plundering his estates of livestock and timber and through non-payment of rents from his tenants, who had themselves been plundered and rendered unable to pay. More striking is a broadly similar paper drawn up by or in the name of the townspeople sometime late in 1644 or early in 1645, claiming losses totalling over £3,000. Seventy-five townspeople, from the bailiffs and rector down to shopkeepers and ordinary householders, alleged damage to their houses – three claimed destruction through burning – and losses of cash, personal and household goods, grain and cattle, perpetrated by both the royalist and parliamentarian armies in September 1644. Although doubtless exaggerated, the papers give an indication of the level of damage which could be inflicted in just a few days when rival armies fought for control of a town and its castle, even though the main clash had occurred outside the town itself.[55]

The second striking change to the physical and mental world of Montgomery occurred in summer 1649. In the wake of their capture of the castle in September 1644, parliament had maintained a garrison there. According to the terms of the surrender, Lord Herbert was permitted to remain in residence and indeed in 1646, after the first or main civil war was over, he was restored to a larger measure of control over his property, though sharing it with a governor and scaled-down garrison approved by parliament.[56] Herbert's death, however, in August 1648, brought this arrangement to an end, for parliament would never allow his arch-royalist elder son and heir Richard, now the second Lord Herbert, to take control over what remained an impressive fortress, especially at a time of renewed unrest and armed resistance to parliament. Steps were taken to deny the new owner access to the castle and in 1649 parliament ordered its degarrisoning and complete destruction. Richard, Lord Herbert, accepted the decision and kept a detailed account of the operation. The account reveals that it was no crude smash-and-flatten operation, but rather a careful selective demolition, in the course of which valuable and reusable materials were salvaged. Large-scale work took place between June and October 1649, employing at its height 150 general labourers as well as miners and craftsmen. Timber, tiles and glass were carefully removed and stored. The work cost £675. Although the account does not reveal how much was made from selling the salvaged materials, similar accounts of the demolition of Wallingford and Pontefract castles suggest that a healthy profit could be expected.[57]

The civil war had thus brought to an end the 450-year life of Montgomery castle. After generations, the town was no longer overlooked and to some extent dominated by a military, political, administrative and social strongpoint. Instead, post-Restoration Montgomery became a bustling market town, its prosperity still evident in the surviving Georgian buildings and attractive façades of its townscape.[58] At the same time, the Herberts' intimate link with Montgomery had been broken. It was briefly restored a generation later, for in the 1670s the Herberts returned in the person of the third Lord, building a new house not amongst the ruins or on the site of the castle, but on the rolling plain to the east of the town, the great estate at Lymore, complete with its rather incongruous and enormous black-and-white timbered house, described by Thomas Lloyd as the 'last great half timbered house in Britain'.[59] But just as Lymore, too, has now long gone, so the Montgomery branch of the Herberts soon faded and the direct male line became extinct early in the eighteenth century.

In the context of the civil war in Wales, Montgomery was unusual and unfortunate, for few other Welsh towns suffered a major field engagement fought within their vicinity. In many other ways, however, Montgomery's civil war appears more typical of the experience of many small and medium-sized towns throughout England and Wales: the patchy nature of the surviving source material; the reluctance of many townspeople to commit themselves too far to one side or the other until compelled to do so by an overwhelming military presence; a degree of normality and continuity in the life of the town and its community during the 1640s, but with undertones of discontent, enmity and division occasionally glimpsed in the surviving sources; evidence of a very heavy financial burden caused by the war and of more limited wartime physical destruction; and in the wake of the war, a very significant change in the landscape of the town resulting from the slighting of the medieval stronghold which had for many centuries overshadowed – in Montgomery's case, quite literally – the life of the town and its people. As in so many other urban centres, the civil war not only saw Montgomery's final flourishing as a military centre, the last echo of the role it had played in the conflicts of the Middle Ages, but also itself caused the destruction of the medieval physical means which had made such a role possible. The compass of a single human lifetime might witness Montgomery's change from Meldrum's military assessment of the civil war years – 'one of the goodliest and strongest places that I ever looked upon' – to the beginnings of the peaceful Georgian prosperity and elegance still so evident today in this 'small unspoilt Georgian town, the only one in Wales', 'a delightful place, and as quiet as could be'.[60]

NOTES

1 This focus on the (often bitter, bloody and disruptive) local, county or regional nature of the civil war, rather than upon national campaigns and the small number of major battles, has underlain much of the research and writing on the war of the last 20 years or more, but see especially the national studies by C. Carlton, *Going to the Wars: The Experience of the British Civil Wars*, 1638–1651 (1992), and M. Bennett, *The Civil Wars in Britain and Ireland, 1638–1651* (Oxford, 1997), and the outstanding regional study by P. Tennant, *Edgehill and Beyond: The People's War in the South Midlands, 1642–1645* (Stroud, 1992).

2 See the discussions in P. Barker and R. Higham, *Hen Domen, Montgomery: A Timber Castle on the English–Welsh Border* (1982) and P. Barker and R. Higham, *Hen Domen, Montgomery: A Timber Castle on the English-Welsh Border. Excavations 1960–1988: A Summary Report* (n.p., 1988), which examine the pre-Conquest importance and defence of the area as well as providing interim reports on the excavation of the Norman motte-and-bailey castle.

3 J.D.K. Lloyd and J.K. Knight, *Montgomery Castle* (2nd edn, Cardiff, 1981); J.K. Knight, 'Excavations at Montgomery Castle, Part I: Documentary Evidence, Structures and Excavated Features', *Archaeologia Cambrensis*, vol. 141 (1992), pp. 97–180; J.K. Knight, 'Excavations at Montgomery Castle, Part II: Metal Finds', *Archaeologia Cambrensis*, vol. 142 (1993), pp. 182–242.

4 That is, the largest and bloodiest battle of the principal civil war of 1642–46. It is probable that rather larger numbers fought and died around St Fagan's on 8 May 1648, when parliamentary troops crushed one of a series of anti–parliamentarian risings in England and Wales which, together with an attempted Scottish–royalist invasion, is sometimes labelled 'the second civil war'.

5 The general, regional context down to summer 1644 has been discussed by J.R. Phillips, *Memorials of the Civil War in Wales and the Marches*, 2 vols (1874), vol. I, chs

1–5; R. Hutton, *The Royalist War Effort, 1642–46* (Harlow, 1982), esp. chs 5 and 13; and P. Gaunt, *A Nation Under Siege: The Civil War in Wales, 1642–1648* (1991), chs 2–5. See also R.N. Dore, 'Sir Thomas Myddleton's Attempted Conquest of Powys', *Montgomeryshire Collections*, vol. 57 (1961–62), pp. 91–118.

6 'Sir Thomas Middleton, coming suddenly to Mountgomery upon Wednesday 4 September with about 800 foot and horse ...', National Library of Wales (NLW) Aberystwyth, Powis Castle Collection, Edward Herbert, 1st Baron Herbert of Chirbury, box 5, vol. 9, f. 3.

7 Knight, 'Excavations Part I', pp. 105–123 provides a concise 'tabulated' history of the castle drawn from surviving documentary evidence.

8 Reproduced in Phillips, *Memoirs of the Civil War in Wales*, II, p. 206.

9 In c. 1646–47 Herbert wrote an account of his actions, addressed to parliament, stressing that he had 'secured and defended my Castle for the space of about 2 yeares (to my no little Cost and Charges) against all Attempts by the Adverse party to put a Garrison into the same', NLW, Powis Castle Collection, Edward Herbert, 1st Baron Herbert of Chirbury, box 5, vol. 9, f. 15.

10 Paper relating 'By what means the Castle of Montgomery was delivered to Sir Thomas Middleton the 5th inst', reproduced in *Montgomeryshire Collections*, vol. 22 (1888), pp. 181–83.

11 NLW, Powis Castle Collection, Edward Herbert, 1st Baron Herbert of Chirbury, box 5, vol. 9, ff. 1–3.

12 Ibid.

13 Most of the important documents relating to the surrender of Montgomery castle and its aftermath which are to be found in NLW, Powis Castle Collection, Edward Herbert, 1st Baron Herbert of Chirbury, box 5, vol. 9, have been fully calendared in *Herbert Correspondence*, ed. W.J. Smith (Cardiff, 1968). Many of these, together with some other documents, were reproduced with a brief commentary in *Montgomeryshire Collections*, vol. 22 (1888).

14 Phillips, *Memoirs of the Civil War in Wales*, I, pp. 248–49, II, pp. 203, 208.

15 Ibid., II, pp. 201–9.

16 All the principal reports are printed in ibid., II, pp. 201–9; they are also printed, together with reports from the newspapers, in *Montgomeryshire Collections*, vol. 22 (1888), pp. 186–98. Comparison with the originals in the British Library, Thomason Tracts, confirm that these transcripts are accurate and together they provide a reasonably full picture of the action on 18 September. My reconstruction of events in the following paragraphs is based upon these documents, to which further reference will be made only on precise points of detail or where they have been quoted. There are a small number of modern, brief accounts of the battle: D.E. Evans, *Montgomery, 1644* (n.p., n.d. c. 1984–85); Gaunt, *A Nation Under Siege*, pp. 48–49; A. Abram, *The Battle of Montgomery, 1644* (Bristol, 1993); P. Gaunt, 'Cromwellian Britain X: Montgomery, Montgomeryshire', *Cromwelliana* (1997), pp. 50–59.

17 Phillips, *Memoirs of the Civil War in Wales*, II, p. 203.

18 Ibid.

19 Ibid., II, p. 205.

20 *Montgomeryshire Collections*, vol. 22 (1888), p. 193.

21 Phillips, *Memoirs of the Civil War in Wales*, II, p. 201.

22 Ibid., II, p. 205.

23 *Montgomeryshire Collections*, vol. 22 (1888), p. 194.

24 Phillips, *Memoirs of the Civil War in Wales*, II, p. 209.

25 *Journal of the House of Commons*, III (n.d.), p. 636.

26 See: Phillips, *Memorials of the Civil War in Wales* I, chs 5–7; Hutton, *The Royalist War Effort*, pts 5–6; Gaunt, *A Nation Under Siege*, chs 5–6; and Dore, 'Sir Thomas Myddleton's Attempted Conquest of Powys'.

27 *Montgomeryshire Collections*, passim, but see especially the 1561 town charter transcribed and translated in vol. 21 (1887), pp. 22–31; I. Soulsby, *The Towns of Medieval Wales* (Chichester, 1983); G. Williams, *Renewal and Reformation: Wales, c. 1415–1642* (Oxford, 1993); G.H. Jenkins, *The Foundations of Modern Wales, 1642–1780* (Oxford, 1993); J.G. Jones, *Early Modern Wales, c. 1525–1640* (Basingstoke, 1994); C.J. Arnold, *The Archaeology of Montgomeryshire* (Welshpool, 1990); J. Speed, *The Theatre of Great Britain: The Second Book Containing the Principality of Wales* (1676), p. 115, which noted the 'fruitfull … Soyle' of the county, especially the 'fruitfulnesse' of the eastern half, and which described Montgomery as 'the chiefest' of the six towns of the county, blessed with 'very wholesome … aire, and pleasant … situation, upon an easie ascent of an hill, and upon another farre higher mounted stands a faire and well-repaired Castle, from the East Rocke whereof the Towne hath beene walled, as by some part yet standing, and the tract and trench of the rest even unto the North-side of the said Castle, may evidently be seene'.

28 *The House of Commons, 1558–1603*, ed. P.W. Hasler, 3 vols (1981), vol. I, pp. 320–1; *The House of Commons, 1660–1690*, ed. B.D. Henning, 3 vols (1983), vol. I, pp. 516–18; P.D.G. Thomas, 'The Montgomery Borough Constituency, 1660–1728', *Bulletin of the Board of Celtic Studies*, vol. 20 (1962–64), pp. 293–304; D. Brunton and D.H. Pennington, *Members of the Long Parliament* (1954).

29 D. Underdown, *Fire From Heaven: Life in an English Town in the Seventeenth Century* (1992); M. Stoyle, *From Deliverance to Destruction: Rebellion and Civil War in an English City* (Exeter, 1996).

30 *Calendar of State Papers, Domestic Series, of the Reign of Charles I*, eds J. Bruce, W.D. Hamilton and S.C. Lomas, 23 vols (1858–97) ('*CSPD*'), *1635*, p. 555; *CSPD, 1635–36*, pp. 204, 216; *CSPD, 1636–37*, pp. 419, 448–49, 506–7; *CSPD, 1637*, pp. 64–65, 393; *CSPD, 1637–38*, pp. 92, 365, 490; *CSPD, 1638–39*, pp. 74, 401; *CSPD, 1639–40*, p. 430; *Herbert Correspondence*, ed. Smith, pp. 91–92.

31 See, for example, P. Lake, 'The Collection of Ship Money in Cheshire during the 1630s: A Case Study of the Relations between Central and Local Government', *Northern History*, vol. 17 (1981); C.A. Clifford, 'Ship Money in Hampshire: Collection and Collapse', *Southern History*, vol. 4 (1982); and K. Fincham, 'The Judges' Decision on Ship Money in February 1637: The Reaction in Kent', *BIHR*, vol. 57 (1984).

32 *CSPD, 1637–38*, p. 490.

33 *CSPD, 1638–39*, pp. 513–14; *CSPD, 1639*, pp. 103, 122, 525.

34 *CSPD, 1640*, pp. 205, 467–68.

35 See especially the work of Stoyle, *From Deliverance to Destruction* and *Loyalty and Locality: Popular Allegiance in Devon during the English Civil War* (Exeter, 1994). A. Duffin, *Faction and Faith: The Political Allegiance of the Cornish Gentry, 1600–42* (Exeter, 1996) also stresses the centrality of religion, as does D. Underdown, *Revel, Riot and Rebellion: Popular Politics and Culture in England, 1603–60* (Oxford, 1985), though Underdown links religion to broader cultural and socio–economic trends and patterns.

36 BL, Additional MS. 70002, f. 137. This document is noted and briefly discussed by J. Eales, 'Iconoclasm, Iconography and the Altar in the English Civil War', in *Studies in Church History*, vol. 28, *The Church and the Arts*, ed. D. Wood (Oxford, 1992), p. 325. See also Eales, *Puritans and Roundheads: The Harleys of Brampton Bryan and the Outbreak of the English Civil War* (Cambridge, 1990), p. 40.

37 *DNB*, vol. IX, pp. 624–32; *The Autobiography of Edward, Lord Herbert*, ed. S. Lee (1886); *The Life of Edward, First Lord Herbert of Cherbury Written by Himself*, ed. J.M. Shuttleworth (Oxford, 1976); *Montgomeryshire Collections*, vol. 16 (1883), pp. 106–7; ibid., vol. 22 (1888), pp. 182–83; NLW, Powis Castle Collection, Edward Herbert, 1st Baron Herbert of Chirbury, box 5, vol. 9, ff. 4, 13–15.

38 *Montgomeryshire Collections*, vol. 16 (1883), p. 107.

39 *CSPD, 1641–43*, p. 379; *Journal of the House of Commons, II* (n.d.), pp. 743, 762. For Price, see also *Montgomeryshire Collections*, vol. 31 (1899), pp. 65–114, 289–336, esp. p. 310, and Dore, 'Sir Thomas Myddleton's Attempted Conquest of Powys'.

40 BL, Additional MS. 42711, f. 66. Although undated, the petition relates a sequence of events and burdens down to December 1643 or January 1644, which might therefore be taken as the date when it was drawn up. The British Library catalogue suggests 'early 1644' as the probable date of the document.

41 BL, Egerton MS. 1048, f. 188. The document is reproduced and briefly discussed in *Montgomeryshire Collections*, vol. 16 (1883), pp. 388–94.

42 NLW, Powis Castle Collection, Edward Herbert, 1st Baron Herbert of Chirbury, box 5, vol. 9, f. 15; see also *Montgomeryshire Collections*, vol. 16 (1883), p. 107.

43 *Montgomeryshire Collections*, vol. 20 (1886), p. 25.

44 *CSPD, 1644*, pp. 534–35; *CSPD, 1644–45*, pp. 80–81.

45 A.H. Dodd, *Studies in Stuart Wales* (2nd edn, Cardiff, 1971), ch. 4; *CSPD, 1645–47*, pp. 441, 455, 458–59, 461, 491; *CSPD, Addenda 1625–49*, p. 706; PRO, SP 28/251, 256.

46 *Montgomeryshire Collections*, vol. 23 (1889), pp. 72–73.

47 *Historical Manuscripts Commission, 6th Report Appendix* (1877), p. 174.

48 Most of the surviving town records are now lodged at the Powys County Archives Office, Llandrindod Wells; the current Archives Office call numbers are noted here. For the early modern period, they principally comprise: a series of borough charters from 1486 to 1670 – 869 (33/8); a series of 'court books', relating to various leet courts and small courts, running from 1633 onwards, though with some overlaps and some gaps – 923–8 (34/2); a series of 'court files', unbound bundles of papers recording the declarations, pleadings and decisions of the small courts, running from 1647 onwards, though with some overlaps and some gaps – 917–22 and 934 (34/2); two bound volumes of transcripts of the various charters and customs of the town – 914 and 932 (34/2); and a bound volume of various original papers and later transcripts, spanning from the early sixteenth to the early nineteenth century, including some nineteenth-century transcripts from seventeenth century court books and files, the originals of which are no longer extant – 909 (34/1). This collection was discussed and listed by J.D.K. Lloyd, 'The Borough Records of Montgomery', *Montgomeryshire Collections*, vol. 45 (1937), pp. 19–43, though at that time it was held by the National Library of Wales and arranged somewhat differently. I am most grateful to the County Archivist, Gordon Reid, and his colleagues for their assistance in locating and making available much of this collection. The NLW, Powis Castle Collection, includes some further items relating to the administration of the town in the early modern period, especially several boxes containing bundles of loose, unbound papers relating to actions in the leet court – Powis Castle Collection, Manorial Records II, Borough of Montgomery (1525–1840). My comments in this and the next two paragraphs are drawn from these collections and documents, to which further reference will be made only on precise points of detail or where they have been quoted. Although the parish register covering the mid-seventeenth century does survive and is now held at Powys County Archives Office, it tells us little, for it was maintained very poorly during the civil war years; there are just a handful of entries for 1643, 1645 and 1646 and none at all for 1644.

49 As demonstrated by the relevant court books and court files, Powys County Archives Office, Montgomery Borough Council, 921, 923–4 (34/2). See also *Montgomeryshire Collections*, vol. 44 (1936), pp. 104–7.

50 Ibid.

51 Powys County Archives Office, Montgomery Borough Council, 921 (34/2), paper no. 64.

52 Powys County Archives Office, Montgomery Borough Council, 909 (34/1), p. 32; *Montgomeryshire Collections*, vol. 44 (1936), pp. 105–7.

53 NLW, Powis Castle Collection, Manorial Records II, Borough of Montgomery (1525–1840), unbound and unnumbered paper on the case in a bundle of papers relating to meetings of the leet court held during the 1640s; the paper is dated 2 March 1644 [1645].

54 *Calendar of the Committee for Compounding with Delinquents, 1643–60*, ed. M.A.E. Green, 5 vols (1882–92), pp. 2876, 3743. A small batch of papers relating to the activities of parliament's Montgomeryshire sequestration committee has recently come to light, but none appear to refer to property in, or residents of, Montgomery: NLW, Powis Castle Collection (1990 Deposit), loose and unnumbered bundle of papers; I am most grateful to Dr Stephen Roberts, of the History of Parliament Trust, for drawing these papers to my attention, and to Tudor Barnes, the archivist at the National Library of Wales, who is working on the 1990 Deposit, for allowing me access to them while they are still in the process of being sorted and catalogued.

55 NLW, Powis Castle Collection, Edward Herbert, 1st Baron Herbert of Chirbury, box 5, vol. 9, f. 42. It is also noticeable that the town's church needed quite extensive repairs in the mid-1650s, for which a local rate was imposed: *Montgomeryshire Collections*, vol. 20 (1886), pp. 35–38.

56 *Montgomeryshire Collections*, vol. 20 (1886), pp. 24–25; *Montgomeryshire Collections*, 23 (1889), pp. 74–77; NLW, Powis Castle Collection, Edward Herbert, 1st Baron Herbert of Chirbury, box 5, vol. 9, ff. 15–20, 37.

57 *CSPD, 1648–49*, p. 232; *CSPD, 1649–50*, pp. 53, 78, 167, 171; NLW, Powis Castle Collection, Edward Herbert, 1st Baron Herbert of Chirbury, box 5, vol. 9, ff. 21–31, 36, 38; the account book for the demolition has been transcribed and reproduced by M.W. Thompson, *The Decline of the Castle* (Cambridge, 1987), appendix 4, pp. 186–93.

58 R. Haslam, *The Buildings of Wales: Powys* (Harmondsworth, 1979), pp. 163–71.

59 T. Lloyd, *The Lost Houses of Wales* (2nd edn, 1989), p. 41.

60 D. Verey, *A Shell Guide to Mid Wales* (1960), p. 74; Haslam, *Buildings of Wales: Powys*, p. 164.

Index

Note: 'n.' after a page reference indicates the number of a note on that page.